THE POTENTIAL OF
FANTASY AND IMAGINATION

The Potential of
Fantasy and Imagination

Edited by

Anees A. Sheikh
Marquette University
Milwaukee, Wisconsin

John T. Shaffer
The Well-Being Center
Jacksonville, Illinois

Brandon House, Inc., New York

Library of Congress Catalog Card Number: 79-88092
ISBN: 0-913-412-31-7

For orders write to P.O. Box 240
Bronx, New York 10471

Printed in the United States of America

With sincere appreciation to
KATHARINA SCHWITAN
for her valuable assistance in the
preparation of this volume

Contributors

Akhter Ahsen · Eidetic Analysis Institute, 22 Edgecliff Terrace, Yonkers, New York 10705.

Rudolf Arnheim · Department of Art History, University of Michigan, Ann Arbor, Michigan 48109

Theodore X. Barber · Proseminar Institute, Research Division, Cushing Hospital, Framingham, Massachusetts 01701

Barbara L. Forisha · Department of Psychology, University of Michigan-Dearborn, Dearborn, Michigan 48128

Charles S. Jordan · Department of Psychiatry and Behavioral Sciences, Medical University of South Carolina, Charleston, South Carolina 29401

Robert G. Ley · Department of Psychology, University of Waterloo, Waterloo, Ontario, Canada

Peter McKellar · Department of Psychology, University of Otago, Dunedin, New Zealand

L. Martin Moleski · Marin General Hospital, Greenbrae, California 94902

James K. Morrison · Private Practice, 678 Troy - Schnectady Road, Latham, New York 12110

Alexander Pickens · University of Hawaii, Honolulu, Hawaii 96822

Phyllis Richardson · Eastside Community Mental Health Center, 2253 140th Avenue NE, Bellevue, Washington 98005

John T. Shaffer · The Well-Being Center Inc., 349 West Morgan, Jacksonville, Illinois 62650

Peter W. Sheehan · Department of Psychology, University of Queensland, St. Lucia, Australia 4067

Anees A. Sheikh · Department of Psychology, Marquette University, Milwaukee, Wisconsin 53233

Jerome L. Singer · Department of Psychology, Yale University, New Haven, Connecticut 06520

Gisela E. Speidel · The Kamehameha Schools, 1850 Makuakane Street, Honolulu, Hawaii 96817

Dwight Turner · The Retreat Hospital, 2205 Beltline Road, S.W., Decature, Alabama 35603

George E. Twente · The Retreat Hospital, 2205 Beltline Road, S.W., Decature, Alabama 35603

Sheryl C. Wilson · Proseminar Institute, Research Division, Cushing Hospital, Framingham, Massachusetts 01701

Preface

After a prolonged relegation to a position of near disgrace, the "internal pic-tures" have recently been greeted with a burst of enthusiasm by psychologists of varied persuasions. Clinical and experimental psychologists alike have increasingly and convincingly documented the power of human fantasy and imagination.

This volume further explores the enormous potential of this fundamental human gift, particularly in the clinical and educational domains. A wide gamut of related topics is covered. All chapters are written by experts in the field, many of whom are internationally known. This book, we believe, will prove to be invalua-ble to psychologists, psychiatrists, psychotherapists, educators, and, in fact, to all interested in comprehending the nature and function of fantasy and imagination.

Anees A. Sheikh
John T. Shaffer

July, 1979

Contents

Chapter 1
The Outside and the Inside: Compartmentalization or Integration?
Barbara L. Forisha.. 1

Chapter 2
Image for Effective Psychotherapy: An Essay on Consciousness, Anticipation, and Imagery
Akhter Ahsen.. 11

Chapter 3
Imagery and Affect in Psychotherapy: Elaborating Private Scripts and Generating Contexts
Jerome L. Singer... 27

Chapter 4
Cerebral Asymmetries, Emotional Experience, and Imagery: Implications for Psychotherapy
Robert G. Ley 41

Chapter 5
Guided Imagining and Hypnosis: Theoretical and Empirical Overlap and Convergence in a New Creative Imagination Scale
Theodore X. Barber and **Sheryl C. Wilson**............................. 67

Chapter 6
Imagery Processes and Hypnosis: An Experiential Analysis of Phenomena
Peter W. Sheehan.. 89

Chapter 7
Psychosomatics and Mental Imagery: A Brief Review
Anees A. Sheikh, Phyllis Richardson, and **L. Martin Moleski**............... 105

Chapter 8
Mental Imagery and Psychotherapy: European Approaches
Charles S. Jordan 119

Chapter 9
Emotive Reconstructive Psychotherapy: Changing Constructs by Means of Mental Imagery
James K. Morrison 133

Chapter 10
Death Imagery: Therapeutic Uses
Anees A. Sheikh, George E. Twente, and Dwight Turner 149

Chapter 11
The Experience of the Holistic Mind
John T. Shaffer 171

Chapter 12
Between Wakefulness and Sleep: Hypnagogic Fantasy
Peter McKellar 189

Chapter 13
Art, Mental Imagery, and Cognition
Gisela E. Speidel and **Alexander Pickens** 199

Chapter 14
Visual Thinking in Education
Rudolf Arnheim 215

Author Index 225

Subject Index 233

1

The Outside and the Inside: Compartmentalization or Integration?

BARBARA L. FORISHA

The division of outer and inner, public and private, rational and emotional, cuts a wide swath through all of American culture, and just as it sets institution against institution, individual against individual, masculinity against femininity, so it splits the individual within himself/herself. Americans pay obeisance to the public, the rational, and the scientific, and legitimatize the outer sphere; they retreat with embarrassed justifications and sheepish grins to the private, the emotional, and the aesthetic, only when the inflexibility of their public behavior has led them up against the proverbial brick wall. The private sphere remains, however, unacknowledged and illegitimate and only a refuge when more valued behavior has failed. The private sphere remains in the dark, the public usurps the light. Thus, in American mythology, the private always yields to the public, the artistic to the scientific, the feminine to the masculine. In like manner, individuals offer up their emotional selves on the altars of rationality.

This pervasive compartmentalization of human life, this distinction of outer and inner (light and dark, good and evil, right and wrong, or male and female) has also compartmentalized psychologists and their authoritative evaluation of "what counts" in the description of human beings. For most of this century inner has yielded to outer, and words have been proclaimed the proper measure of human

Barbara L. Forisha, Department of Psychology, University of Michigan — Dearborn, Dearborn, Michigan 48128.

1

beings, and any subjective testimony to the validity of imagery has been swept aside. We have not only maintained that we are outer, public, rational, and scientific, but also *verbal*. Until the late 1950's, images were banned from the portals of legitimacy.

However, dark/light, right/wrong, masculine/feminine as well as an entire multitude of either/or's prized by our culture have never been good for anybody. Keniston, for one, laments the separation of accuracy, realism, verifiability and objectivity from the sphere of aesthetic experiences, intuition, fantasy, private illumination, and subjectivity (1965, p. 257). In drawing a line through the middle of human potential, we have placed the outer against the inner, male against female, and reason against emotion. In so doing, we have separated our heads from our hearts and denied the validity of our inner experience.

Yet despite our cultural compartmentalization, theorists argue that high levels of human development occur with the integration of conflicting elements of self (Ahsen, 1968; Loevinger, 1966; Perry, 1968; Rank, 1945; Werner, 1948). Researchers in creativity have come to similar conclusions. As MacKinnon states, the "creative person has the capacity to tolerate the tension that strong opposing values create in him, and in his creative striving he effects some reconciliation of them" (1962, p. 490). May states more poetically that creative individuals join being and nonbeing: "They knock on silence for an answering music; they pursue meaninglessness until they can force it to mean" (1975, p. 93).

If integration of polarities, rather than compartmentalization, accompanies emotional well-being and creativity, what does this say about the ongoing controversy surrounding the relative importance of imagery and words? Various researchers from the time of Galton (1883) through modern theorists such as Bruner (Bruner, Oliver, & Greenfield, 1964) have seen words and images as separate and opposing modalities, such that strength in one requires weakness of the other. Yet numerous other psychologists, both clinicians and researchers (e.g., Paivio, 1971; Schachtel, 1959), have argued that full cognitive as well as emotional functioning requires the interplay of these two modalities.

When separated from each other, both words and images may imprison us. Words give us the categorical structure for our world and give us the form through which we learn to identify rather than see. As Sapir pointed out some years ago, language "actually defines experience for us by reason of its formal completeness and because of our unconscious projection of its implicit expectations into the field of experience" (1931, p. 578). As Bowers and Bowers point out, language can be very limiting, "subtly forcing us to exclude from consideration and even from consciousness those aspects of our subjectivity that evade easy articulation." Language thus becomes "the enemy of the as yet unimagined" (1972, p. 265). Schachtel has also argued that our "unseeingness" is often due to "the encroachment of an already labelled world upon our spontaneous sensory and intellectual capacities" (1959, p. 243).

Yet, verbal processes can be liberating: they increase our capacity for communication, provide means for consensual validation of our beliefs, and "give logical direction to the stream of thought, preventing unconstrained leaps of imagination from lapsing into daydreaming" (Paivio, 1975, p. 161). However, verbal processes alone fragment experience by dividing it up into preconceived categories, which separate us from our immediate experience. With words, we drop intellectual nets and boxes upon the world (Watts, 1969, p. 46). As Hall states, we tend to deny the integrative part of self by enshrining language alone (1977, p. 9). "One reason for this," he states, "is that much of the truly integrative behavior that falls under the rubric of culture is under the control of those parts of the brain that are not concerned with speech. What we are discussing are super geestalts, so important and so centrally located in the scheme of things that they are almost impossible for us to formulate verbally" (1977, p. 153).

There are suggestions that the integrative behavior of which he speaks includes the use of imagery. Nebes, in his review of right- and left-hemisphere functions, associates verbal processes with the left hemisphere and imaginal processes with the right. He follows the lead of other investigators in suggesting "a model of hemispheric action in which the minor hemisphere is seen to organize and treat data in terms of complex wholes, being in effect a synthesizer with a predisposition for viewing the total rather than the parts. The left hemisphere in this model sequentially analyzes input, abstracting out the relevant details to which it associates verbal symbols in order to more efficiently manipulate and store the data" (1974, p. 12). Richardson states the case explicitly: "Verbal or mathematical processes involving sequential processing take place in the left hemisphere while spatial or imaginal processes involving parallel processing occur in the right hemisphere" (1977, p. 112).

If imagery is then more global, holistic, and synthesizing, the recognition and utilization of imagery may indeed free us from the structures imposed by verbal processes. Further, imagery has been connected with the emotional meaning we give to experience, meanings which are often not given verbal structure. Bugelski (1970), for example, sums up a number of studies which strongly suggest that meaning is dependent on imagery. He goes on to say that all words arouse images which are accompanied by emotional responses which give meaning to our words. Arieti (1976) concurs in stating that images enable human beings to retain emotional dispositions toward absent objects (p. 45). Thus, in the use of words, we utilize our heads, with imagery we may explore our hearts. The recognition of the omnipresence (Doob, 1972) of imagery can indeed liberate us from the sterile imprisonment of logic and abstraction.

Yet imagery, without logical thought, can also create its own prison. Imagery, too, is not without structure as Gordon reminds us. She states that the image brings some order that "is meaningful and relevant to our physical and psychological needs out of the terrifying chaos that is the world of sight, sound, smell, taste, touch, and movement. Through the image we sift, select, and render down to a manageable scale both the world of objects and our own human experience" (1972, p. 75). The structures provided by imagery may however be disruptive, distorted, and/or deformed (Arieti, 1976; Gordon, 1972; Hudson, 1975; Singer & Antrobus, 1972). When imagery is rigid and intrusive, the meanings which we give our current experience may flow from images of the past, inappropriate to present experience. As Gordon states, we may be carrying with us "a bagful of antiquated and obsolete views of the world" (1972, p. 76). Words separated from imagery cannot be liberating, and, imagery without awareness and the interplay of logical process, cannot free us from our past.

Thus, neither words nor images stand solely in the light or in the dark. Both explore regions closed to the other and open doors through which the other may not enter. Either words or images alone become polarized and constrictive, limiting our view to a partial experience of reality. Both may become forms, drained of process, or structures which bear more relation to the past than to the present. Experiences in either modality may enlighten or imprison us, yet with the interplay of both modalities begins the journey to a full use of human potentialities and the integration of the dichotomies which have fragmented our individual and cultural experience.

Yet Western culture has tended to exalt our imprisonment with words in eulogizing our "reason" and placing "rational man" at the pinnacle of its value system. Thus, in our culture, we need to emphasize the importance of imagery, to bring imagery back into its own — and yet to do so without throwing out our capacities for logical thought. In accomplishing this, we will find that we liberate ourselves from past verbal and imaginal structures and also open ourselves to that "momentary feeling of disgust, or awe, an intuitive hunch, a fantasy, all of these subarticulate experiences," which, "if seized upon and elaborated, can create a new form, a new insight into reality" (Bowers & Bowers, 1972, p. 265). We need to seek a new integration, and for most of us, rational and head oriented, this step begins with an openness to our imaginal experience. As Bugental states:

I am inclined to think that once we release the constraints of self-bondage and learned inhibitions and fears of our own being, we may be able to find tremendous stimulation and greatly increased creativity in allowing awareness to be aswirl with a multitude of percepts mixing and interlocking in as many ways as possible, while our intentionality gradually draws from this boiling broth that which best expresses our being at any given moment (1965, p. 224).

Then the wish, the fantasy, the image must be converted into will and action (May, 1969) and the modalities of words and images brought together.

This integrative process is seen in the subjective accounts of creative individuals. The story of Poincaré is familiar: he *saw* the solution to his mathematical problem (Ghiselin, 1955). Wolfe relied heavily on his imagery in his writing and wrote that he was astonished at the "power of memory to evoke and bring back the odors, sounds, colors, shapes and feel of things with concrete vividness" (Ghiselin, 1955). Nietzsche, Einstein, and others also state their reliance upon imagery for inspiration (Ghiselin, 1955). Koestler summarizes by saying that in the work of scientists, "thinking in pictures" dominates creative work. "In fact, the majority of mathematicians and physicists turned out to be 'visionaries' in the literal sense — that is visual, not verbal thinkers" (1964, p. 322). This may be said, too, of poets, artists . . . and potentially most of humankind. Yet, the inspiration without the logical verification becomes "ecapist" (May, 1975), and the imaginal breakthrough must be validated through other modalities and thus the paradoxical modes of thought must be brought together.

In personal growth experiences, the same interplay of images and words occurs. In a momentary flash, I saw myself at three or four, passing cookies to my mother's friends, and was overwhelmed by unexplored feelings toward my mother, the hostility and anger of circumscribing love which I had never previously recognized. In a later incident, I suddenly perceived myself as an infant with my father's large face looming over the crib and for the first time came to a full emotional awareness of my terror of my father . . . and of men. Yet these dark spots are balanced by the light of positive childhood experiences, and the personal process of weaving an integrative whole out of both the dark and light, the outer and the inner, the masculine and feminine still continues in my own life.

Such experiences liberate us from past meanings which may no longer be appropriate to our current reality. In recovering, as Perls states, the "original scene, " we are freed of the unconscious impact of autonomous and unrecognized emotional complexes. On many levels, as clinicians, leaders, teachers, we may also utilize imagery to facilitate growth and liberation in others. Such use of imagery need not always recover the "original scene" but can open avenues of self-exploration which are blocked by the structures imposed by verbal realities. This imagery may be visual, kinaesthetic, or auditory, or an integration of all modalities. By leading others to move away from their more common, verbalized point of view, new insights often surface in them.

Two examples follow from my own groups. Both involve small and as yet incomplete recoveries of awareness, and both precede a later integration of this material. Each is the story of a young woman in her 20's.

In the first incident, which occurred several years ago, Ann was momentarily unable to express her feelings but was aware of discomfort surrounding pending decisions in her life. I asked her to imagine herself seated in a circular movie theater with a blank screen surrounding her and led her through several moments of breathing and relaxing exercises. Then I said that she would see on the screen whatever she desired at the moment; suddenly, she saw a tale of adventure, bright colors, and exciting action. However, as she continued to watch, she reported that the bright sky was being obscured by dark clouds, that the light was dimming, and that darkness was enveloping her. She reported an emotional reaction of fear to this happening. Imaginally, I handed her a washcloth and asked her to go through the motions of scrubbing the dark away. She began to do this and said it was lightening. But her task was interrupted by a new reaction as fear surfaced again, "I am scared of the light." This realization was followed by further work on the fear we experience of freedom, and on the self-limiting conflicts we induce to restrict our freedom. Ann keeps the dark about as protection from choice . . . but less so today than yesterday.

In another, more recent setting, Cheryl stated that she was too distracted to be fully present with us . . . that she wished she were not but she was and that was the end of it. I asked her to move to the middle of the room and to objectify and see all her distractions surrounding her and to identify for herself each of these concerns. "Now, pick each one up and throw it out," I said. Cheryl followed the instructions rather gleefully. "There," she said, "goes tomorrow's test . . . there goes the shopping I haven't done . . . there goes my father's unhappiness" and so forth. Then, she came to the last one: "Now, I will throw out my friend's arrival tomorrow . . . no, I don't want to . . . I want to keep that about." Once again, there was a recovery of awareness of self-imposed restrictions . . . and further exploration of her need to take responsibility for others which yet she experienced as interfering with her enjoyment of the moment.

In both instances, imagery was a tool in recovering polarized desires and bringing to the surface the dichotomies experienced by most of us in many different ways. For many of us, such conflicts remain beneath the surface. The acceptable desire is brought to the light, the unacceptable desire is kept in the dark; the split is unrecognized but the discomfort of conflicting needs is experienced. The re-entry of both sets of desires into awareness begins the process of change. In being all that we are, we indeed do change. Recognition is the beginning of integration; imagery is a tool of liberation from the past.

Imagery is also a tool for facilitating present awareness. When we are liberated from past forms, both verbal and imaginal, we can utilize imagery in the present to enhance our current experience. One exercise which I use frequently is a modification of the familiar gestalt exercise of leading people on a journey up the mountain, an exercise which illuminates our approach to life. However, instead of asking the group to imagine that they are proceeding to the top of the mountain, I ask them to imagine that they are stopping at a point halfway up the mountain as soft darkness falls — a position from which they can see neither the goal toward which they are heading nor the beginnings from which they have come.

Many individuals have voiced their uneasiness at thus being asked to give up their goal orientation and their linear time perspective. But we stay awhile at this place on the mountain, and I suggest that they may find many things that they like at this place: "Listen to the sounds about you, welcome them rather than shrink from them; take off your shoes and feel the earth; lift your face and feel a light rain and the gentleness of the wind; with touch and smell and hearing let yourself explore your immediate environment and notice the details of your experience." Sometimes I ask them to stay there as a storm develops, and to utilize the energy of harsh wind and rain, to remain rather than to leave, to be open to adventure rather than to run and hide. And then we watch, in the early morning, as the sun rises above the mountain top and find our sense of direction illuminated once more.

During the course of this exercise, some individuals experience a terror of the unknown and the dark, and a sense of emptiness without a goal in sight. But most overcome this uneasiness and find that our sense of not knowing can yield to an awareness of sensations, perceptions, and emotions which are often obscured or denied by our goal orientation. Yet, the experience of timelessness and spaceless-ness and a renewed awareness of immediate experience comes cyclically with a returning direction and future purpose. The linearity of our usual thought alter-nates and interacts with the immediate experience of diffuseness and timelessness. If we perceive this, we can utilize such moments, often imaginally, to refresh and renew our commitment to more tangible pursuits. The full experience of the pres-ent broadens our perspective and reduces our attachment to the seriousness of our current concerns. "Authenticity does not call for one to abandon the familiar world," Bugental states, "rather to recognize he is very much in the world indeed, while yet recognizing that the familiar world is an incomplete arena for the human experience" (1965, p. 34).

In imagery, we may also broaden, change, and shape our view of reality when we are open to perceiving what goes on within. Two images, which both surfaced in the last five years, have been important in shaping my current views. Both came to me in a momentary perception, yet the integration of each into my way of being in this world, is yet incomplete.

A few years ago, in a quiet moment in the classroom, I was momentarily aware of standing on a beach of sand of pale but luminescent colors. As I stood there, I was aware of the continual motion of the sand, so that I was never standing in ex-actly the same way or in the same place, and yet I remained at the time, steady and in place. My interpretation of this experience was in terms of the paradoxical nature of change and continuity, the lack of seriousness with which we must take the particular minutiae of our experience, but, with this in mind, the steadiness of the overall gestalt of our experience.

A newer image, which I have attempted to verbalize elsewhere, was more visual in nature and less kinaesthetic, and yet I was also part of what I saw as well as an observer. The image, itself, is not new as a metaphor, but the meanings which it symbolized for me received a new vividness in my experience. I will report it as I have written it previously:

The image is of a varicolored, multitextured tapestry with each thread weaving its own path, describing the course of its own destiny, contributing to the aliveness and complexity of the whole. Some threads have only little kinks in their straightness, slight shading to their hues, where others swerve and bend and double back, changing color as they change shape. Yet each highlights the other, the dark calling forth the light, the crooked illuminating the straight, each strand part of the overall pattern which emerges as the whole. No thread is perfectly straight nor perfectly crooked. No strand approaches the ideal of threadness. Yet each is essential to the complex pattern of the tapestry.

Later I continued as interpretation:

We cannot see the necessity of perceived evil in calling forth the good, nor the imcompleteness of the good without the shadow of evil. Even as we each pursue the course heralded by our visions, we cannot be sure that others, doing differently, are not also following theirs ... We need remember that no path is truly straight and all the bends and curves and detours and excursions of our lives, as well as those of others, compose the richness and the complexity of human life — the total picture beyond our grasp (Forisha, 1978).

Thus, with the use of imagery, we may recapture our past, enrich our present, and shape our directions toward the future. With imagery, we can recapture the inner elements so long disowned by Western cultures, and join the inner with the outer, bringing together the dark and the light, as part of the integrated process of being who we are in this world. Yet we must live with the paradox of our global visions and the compartmentalization of our learned structures and recognize that only incompletely do we ever succeed in achieving integration — but for full human development there is no other choice.

REFERENCES

Ahsen, A. *Basic concepts in eidetic psychotherapy.* New York: Brandon House, 1968.

Arieti, S. *Creativity: The magic synthesis.* New York: Basic Books, 1976.

Bowers, S., & Bowers, P. G. Hypnosis and creativity: A theoretical and empirical reapprochement. In Fromm, E. & Shor, R. (eds.), *Hypnosis.* Chicago: Aldene-Atherton, 1972, pp. 225-291.

Bruner, J. S., Oliver, R. S., & Greenfield, B. M. *Studies in cognitive growth.* New York: John Wiley, 1966.

Bugelski, B. R. Words and things and images. *American Psychologist,* 1970, *25,* 1002-1012.

Bugental, J. *The search for authenticity.* New York: Holt, Rinehart and Winston, 1965.

Doob, L. The ubiguitous appearance of images. In Sheehan, P. (ed.), *The function and nature of mental imagery.* New York: Academic Press, 1972, pp. 311-332.

Forisha, B. The Gestalt growth experience. Unpublished manuscript, 1978.

Galton, F. *Inquiries into human faculty and its development.* New York: Macmillan, 1883.

Ghiselin, B. (ed.) *The creative process.* New York: Mentor Books, 1955.

Gordon, R. A very private world. In Sheehan, P. (ed.), *The function and nature of mental imagery.* New York: Academic Press, 1972, pp. 64-80.

Hall, E. T. *Beyond culture.* Garden City, N. Y.: Anchor Press/Doubleday, 1977.

Hudson, L. Human beings: *The psychology of human experience.* Garden City, New York: Anchor Press/Doubleday, 1975.

Keniston, K. *The uncommitted: Alienated youth in American Society.* New York: Harcourt, Brace and World, 1965.

Koestler, S. *The act of creation.* New York: MacMillan, 1964.

Loevinger, J. The meaning and measurement of ego development. *American Psychologist,* 1966, *21,* p. 195-206.

MacKinnon, D. W. The nature and nurture of creative talent. *American Psychologist,* 1962, *17,* 484-495.

May, R. *Love and will.* New York: W. W. Norton, 1969.

May, R. *The courage to create.* New York: W. W. Norton, 1975.

Nebes, R. D. Hemispheric specialization in commissurotomized man. *Psychological Bulletin,* 1974, *81,* 1-14.

Paivio, A. *Imagery and verbal processes.* New York: Holt, 1971.

Paivio, A. Imagery and synchronic thinking. *Canadian psychological review.* 1975, 16, p. 147-163.

Perry, W. G. Jr. *Forms of intellectual and ethical development in the college years.* New York: Holt, Rinehart and Winston, 1968.

Rank, O. *Will therapy and truth and reality* (Trans. by J. Taft), New York: Knopf, 1945.

Richardson, A. Verbalizer-visualizer: A cognitive style dimension. *Journal of Mental Imagery,* 1977, *1,* 109-126.

Sapir, E. Conceptual categories in primitive languages. *Science, 1931, 74,* p. 578.

Schachtel, E. G. *Metamorphosis: On the development of affect, perception, attention and memory.* New York: Basic Books, 1959.

Singer, J. and Antrobus, J. S. Daydreaming, imaginal processes, and personality: A normative study. In Sheehan, P. (ed.), *The function and nature of mental imagery.* New York: Academic Press, 1972, pp. 175-201.

Watts, A. *The two hands of God,* New York: Macmillan, 1969.

Werner, H. *Comparative psychology of mental development.* Chicago: Follett, 1948.

2

Image for Effective Psychotherapy: An Essay on Consciousness, Anticipation, and Imagery

Is there a place of discerning activity in the mind? Can the confusing possibilities in consciousness be given direction by an energetic content through which a fruitful order of experience can be enjoyed? As curiosity begins to play with doubt, touching the ever widening boundaries of relative thought, one needs to re-establish contact with the source of this active center. Effective psychotherapy is concerned with making contact with this effective side of the mind. One needs to know consciousness apart from the mechanistic and partial, to recognize it as an entity which comprehends total well-being.

Study of consciousness as a totality has suffered from neglect since the beginning of this century. Currently, it has regained respectability among researchers (Mandler, 1975; Ornstein, 1972) by becoming the object of impressive research again. Serious experimental work on imagery has emerged on the scene concerning the apparatuses of consciousness, such as attention, preattention, focal attention, short-term memory, anticipation, expectancy, perceptual elaboration, and constructions such as cognition and limited capacity notions. New research on imagery and its relationship with consciousness has led to the replacement of Freudian terms "conscious" and "unconscious," which defined distinct boundaries in consciousness (Miller, 1962), by such terms as "nonconscious," "preattention," etc., since ready access to the so-called inaccessible "unconscious" has been demon-

---

Akhter Ahsen, Eidetic Analysis Institute, 22 Edgecliff Terrace, Yonkers, NY 10705.

strated through the general imagery and eidetic processes (Ahsen, 1959, 1977a; Mandler, 1975; Sokolov, 1960). To identify consciousness with the limited span of conscious attention or mere thinking is to define it too narrowly. Such a definition dwells on the end *result* in consciousness rather than on the wide spectrum of *processes* of consciousness (Miller, 1962). This view is confirmed in general imagery research and very convincingly in the famous Sokolov experiment (1960), which showed that although habituation had occurred to the stimulus (beep), when the stimulus was changed slightly (the beep became softer), all the initial alerting reactions recurred. Sokolov's findings suggested that a person is specifically aware of the stimulus, that although he/she may become habituated to something and drop its details out of consciousness, he/she somehow continues to match the current representations to the stored detail, and if any detail in the stimulus changes, a full-blown orienting response occurs again. Other experimental research suggests that the image process plays an important role in this nonconscious awareness of the stimulus (Ahsen, 1978).

Anticipation

Interestingly, Neisser, one of the important writers on modern cognitive theory, holds that constructive processes participating in memory "themselves never appear in consciousness, their products do" (1967, p. 301). But this position becomes untenable in the face of new imagery research. This history of new research goes back to the experimental work on expectancy response by Curtis (1937), Mowrer (1938), Upton (1929), Wever (1930), and Schlosberg (1934), among others. In my own experimental/clinical research and that of my contemporary colleagues in imagery, the fact has emerged that descriptive details of what happens in thought are revealed in imagery, and that what is present in consciousness is only a fraction of what can appear in a detailed way in the image process. With proper linking of imagery to anticipation, the volume of available as well as potentially conscious structures increases manifold (Ahsen, 1977b). It has become evident that structures not of conscious thought but of imagery processes and anticipation mobilize the innate potentials of consciousness; and it is this fact that holds astonishing promise for psychotherapy.

The work of Craik and Lockhart (1972), Festinger, Burnham, Ono, and Bamber (1967), Mandler (1974), Posner and Keele (1970), and Shallice (1972) contains important elements of this direction of research. They emphasize different processing depths, dealing with focal attention, phenomenal experience and information processes, processes that interfere, corrective processing, rehearsal, awareness, inattention, exploration, storage, retrieval, and so forth. Importantly, since imagery resembles more a form of anticipation than a passive and archaic trace, the study of anticipation serves as the central pivot of this critical drama of consciousness. But unfortunately, this view has long been overshadowed by the influence of cognition theory, which tends to favor conscious thought over anticipation, under-playing the true role of the image process in mental activity. As Mandler put it, "Unfortunately, partly by accidents of history, cognitive psychologists tend to be somewhat careless about specifying how organisms come to act" (1975, p. 236) in reality. Still, many researchers, including Mandler (1975), do not want such a total study of the consciousness process to go beyond the personal into "some magical burgeoning of internal awareness," and define it narrowly as "internalizations of actions" (p. 238). As one can see this one-dimensional location of the reality in the outside amounts to an unwarranted rejection of the innate biologic and mythic behavior of the organism, and it could well be another limitation of current research.

The failure to recognize the importance of anticipation behavior may stem from the way anticipation and attention are understood in a particular theory of con-sciousness. Attention is treated as a mechanistic focus or a scanning mechanism, as Mandler's quote (1975) suggests: "Clearly many cognitive structures that lead to certain outcomes and the anticipation of these outcomes (a scanning ahead of a particular structure) may switch the system from one structure to another" (p. 242). Multilevelled structures which are operationally ready to ignite biologically relevant activity are attached to anticipation and not to focal attention; for exam-ple, consciousness was nonconsciously still attached to the sound in Sokolov's ex-periment. Since focal attention does not centrally fit into the mental schema prop-erly, we should be prepared to restrain the term "attention" somewhat and extend . the term "anticipation" to cover images and other processes which facilitate such nonconscious phenomena (Ahsen, 1978).

Mega Anticipatory Kinetic Response

Long ago, even before behaviorism won its popularity in the psychological field, it was established that no convincing evidence existed of the central importance of operant or classical conditioning among humans, pigs, or rats. This fact, along with the existence of another fascinating phenomenon, that is, anticipation, was dem-onstrated in the astonishing experiment by Curtis (1937). He showed that a com-plete and spontaneous change in conditioned behavior in the pig (flexion of foot) occurred involving anticipation, apprehension, anxiety, excitement, and relief when the shock was administered. He also found that when the shock was designfully postponed, the total response moved toward the next phase, which Curtis, suspecting it to contain a definite internal image, called "hallucinatory reac-tion." In the pig, the tension mounted to the point that the animal could no longer contain it, and went through the flexion as if the shock had been administered; this behavior suggests experience of an image. This finding concerning anticipation and its relationship with the image was supported by a host of other studies, in-cluding those of Mowrer (1938). Earlier, Upton (1929), Wever (1930), and

Schlosberg (1934), had reported evidence of a mounting subjective experience in the form of tensions which, however, they had never intended to be viewed as part of conditioning. In Curtis' experiment, even the conditioned foot flexion changed, and the subjective experience was characterized by the fact that the noxious stimulus of shock was now being used as a signal for eventual relief. This change was reported to have emerged entirely from internal sources of the organism and was not regarded as explicable in terms of conditioning.

These studies remained confirmed, but recently, after the passing of 40 years, Mowrer (1977) suggested that the "hallucinatory reaction," as the new unlearned response, was perhaps connected with the *robustness of the organism,* since this reaction was not successfully produced in albino rats which, according to him, were too docile and stupid, but was definitely procurable in Lashley-strain rats which had some wild rat "blood" in them. In my opinion, this specific implication in Mowrer's remark is important in the light of current needs in psychological theory and practice. To stress the importance, I would like to assign a specific term to this robust behavior of the organism: Mega Anticipatory Kinetic (MAK) Response. I propose to describe this powerful response of the organism as anticipatory in essence, imagistic, moving, combative, or kinetic in character. I shall define the MAK Response as a high anticipation response dependent on robustness, and initiated by an external and/or internal tension impacting on the organism.

What is this mega anticipation? It is a state of powerful expectancy simultaneously related to outer and inner stimuli, and the stimuli may be conscious or preconscious, clearly formed or amorphous but ready to become identified. This anticipation is a preparatory set with a powerful orientation of consciousness toward something, containing a variety of orientations dependent on permanent determinants in motivation and expression. Its overt manifestation is only one description of its appearance under one set of conditions, but under average circumstances it remains covertly operative all the time in the organism.

It is now known that neurons, when not kept active, fire spontaneously, and that during learning of a prolonged task, neurons which are not necessary for the learning task become active and fire anyway, producing images besides those that concern the task directly (Ahsen, 1968, 1978; Milner, 1970; Pribram, 1971). This form of imagery behavior in a paradoxical way works against focal attention or conscious thought; that is, general consciousness works against narrow, rigid consciousness. This fact explains how one grows more efficient at a task, and also how one grows stiffer and less creative (Ahsen, 1978): it is known that older subjects display more rigidity than children, who are more open to the random activity of neurons. This open and organismically moving psychological orientation is distinguishable from efficient, specific task activity.

The implications of new evidence in research deal with this creative behavior of the organism. As Lashley (1960) demonstrated long ago, brain operations resulted in no clear-cut loss of single habits, even when up to 20% of the cortex was removed. This we are able to understand more clearly today. Current neurological research has shown that dendrites and cell bodies lie closely together and tend to be excited together; if the axons, lying side by side, end at the same place, the impulses reaching the axons can sum their effect on cell bodies of neurons or dendrites, past the synapse at the next level. This typical arrangement is known to exist all the way from the skin to the cortex. For instance, skin stimulation produces an excitation, with high reliability, in the corresponding region of the somesthetic cortex; and we find a divergent conduction of excitation from the sensory to the association cortex (Milner, 1970). The fact that neurons lead in different directions, making transmission less reliable, is not a defect but an intelligent condition which allows the central process to work out its effects more efficiently at the level of the MAK Response. This unreliability of the divergent condition is a basis of enrichment of the associative cortex and energetic functioning of the organism.

Mowrer's recent statement (1977), Clark Hull "once told me that he did not find my notions about 'expectancy' at all 'useful' and saw no future for this line of inquiry" (p. 314), is very intriguing. Present evidence, especially neurological findings, in fact, suggests a complete rejection of behaviorism. Even long before current neurological evidence emerged, it was known, as Mowrer (1938) put it, that "apparent conditioned responses can be suddenly established and equally suddenly abolished in human beings (and probably also in animals) merely by controlling the subject's state of expectancy or preparatory set" (p. 88). This view has been confirmed by contemporary imagery research. During a taped discussion concerning therapy through imagery experience with Joseph Wolpe at Eastern Pennsylvania Psychiatric Institute (Ahsen, 1967), I pointed out its importance in the field of psychotherapy. The obvious proof of it lies in the imagery processes, where not only conditioning responds in a resilient way, but more importantly something opposite to conditioning usually happens. In the mind, under the imagery impact, long established associations break down and new ones are formed in seconds. The mental structures spontaneously, without training, give rise to and establish new associative ties for the guidance of the organism. This fascinating fact can be demonstrated through a technique called the Age Projection Test or the Symptom Oscillation Test (Ahsen & Lazarus, 1972). For instance, during formation of self-images at various age levels (Ahsen, 1977a; Dolan, 1977), a subject had spontaneously seen himself wearing a particular shirt at a specific age level, while the image-shirt, in fact, belonged to an age level about 8 years earlier. While concentrating on this new juxtaposition representing a spontaneous breakdown and change in the original conditioning of the earlier self-image and the shirt, the subject realized that this shirt pertained to a very secure time in his life, and the shift in juxtaposition represented a symbolic rejection of the later years in his life which had been particularly traumatic for him. The appearance of the shirt at the wrong age level in the image, was construed by the subject as an emotional indication of his desire to withdraw from the traumatic time of the present to an earlier, more secure age, to achieve a state of positive well-being through a regression, that is, by "progressing" the secure shirt to a later time frame. While discussing this aspect with Wolpe, I posed the question in psychological terms: why was the original conditioning of shirt and age level suddenly abolished and replaced by an altogether different structuration with a "symbolic" significance, and how was all this achieved without any conscious awareness, thinking, or training? I suggested that the original conditioned state was obliterated, because it was replaced by a new expectancy state involving a more valid image state, a high condition of being.

Life, when healthy, moves in its own true grand style. Life in its natural form is made of a series of self-realizing events that represent effective experiential units for fruitful living. Conditioning thus represents only temporary seduction toward forced behavior, away from natural propulsion. When one pattern of habitual activity is proven useless and in its place another pattern is required by the organism, the old associations promptly break down and new ones are formed with equal promptness. At this point, the importance of the new structuration process and its relationship with mega anticipation in the MAK Response become evident. The MAK Response is expressed through a total and heightened inner state which guides development of appropriate behavior in response to the situation.

In general, we know that the mental structures manifest depressed and elated states related to depression and elation, and during these states, the mind relates through depressed and buoyant images. If there are albino rats which are too docile and stupid to give us a true measure of adaptive behavior, there are also albino images in the mind, that is, depressing images without the wild "blood" of nature in them. The buoyant and depressed images serve the anticipation process by acting as releasers or barriers. When the psyche is so gripped by a high image that a mega state of anticipation is born, then we begin to see the importance of imagery processes for effective therapy. We are then talking of a truly high condition in the psyche.

At this point, the relationship between mega anticipation and buoyant imagery becomes clear. Traditionally, the problems of aggression imagery have been studied in the context of a variety of schools. Psychoanalysts, for instance, hypothesize the existence of unwanted "aggressive impulses" in the unconscious and propose to "resolve" them through developing a mature distance from them (where Id is, Ego shall be). Behaviorists, on the other hand, concentrate on "aggression" as an important positive aspect of life and propose that if the subject truly "learns" to be "aggressive," he/she would be effective as an organism. Neither of these groups deals with the active states in the organism in their naturally buoyant and energized side. One school wants to suppress, the other wants to condition the human psyche. The organism is, in fact, buoyant by nature and is propelled and guided by this energizing process in a fundamental way. The organism is centrally provided with a "buoyant" will to success, only in the absence of this buoyancy does an organism collapse, that is, submit to control and life through suppression. This central core of mega anticipation and will to buoyant life is explained below through the case history of Reiner, a dog living with a middle-class American family.

The Case History of a Dog Called Reiner
(In Terms of MAK Response)

Reiner is a nice, well-behaved dog, young in years and capable of vital, energetic behavior. Three years ago, for a period of 2 years, he was regularly taken out for a 15-minute walk every day, at 6:30 p.m., by the father of the family, Mr. Tompkins. When Mr. Tompkins would be away at his job, Reiner would spend this time lying in the basement. With clocklike regularity, at approximately 6:00 p.m., the time of Mr. Tompkins' return, Reiner would *come* upstairs and *pace* the floor. Then he would sit *near* the door, at times looking around, especially toward Mr. Tompkins, if he was home, in *anticipation* of the evening walk. Reiner would also emit pleasure sounds and show *playful* behavior in the general vicinity of Mr. Tompkins. As soon as Mr. Tompkins would say the words "walk" or "leash," Reiner would respond by *jumping up and down* and then running to the basement, where his leash was kept. After the leash was procured, he would slip excitedly into the collar and then would go out for a 15-minute walk with Mr. Tompkins.

This was the pattern for 2 years. The third year, Mr. Tompkins had to be out of town for almost a whole year. During this time, Reiner underwent a sequence of behavior changes and adjustments, totally spontaneous in nature. The behavior changes occurring during the first 2 years and the year following are listed below in order of appearance, and their significance is discussed briefly.

1. *High Event.* The first 2 years in the Tompkins household were a very happy and buoyant period for Reiner. The evening walk was the high event, and it represented the essence of his life. He looked forward to it, with no previous training whatever. He did not need to be taught to enjoy pleasure and freedom, it came to him effortlessly. The evening walk was truly a high event bringing release and fulfillment of his nature.

Learning. The dog showed willingness to learn almost anything within his capabilities, if it was presented as a *condition* for the walk; for example, he would wear the collar peacefully, even excitedly. He even developed spontaneously the behavior of picking up the ball when thrown during the walk, because it pleased the master. The evening walk was very central to the learning of these responses.

2. *High Anticipation.* During the 2 years prior to Mr. Tompkins' departure, the dog showed a consistent mood of anticipation of the evening walks. He knew that the high event was always predictable, that it occurred without any significant break in the pattern. The dog was aware of this predictable reality at the various levels, and he offered various postures toward it in the form of a totally internal

process, probably imagistic in nature, as Mowrer (1977) put it.

Image Buoyancy. The dog's primary behavior at the time of the evening walk reflected heightened buoyancy at many levels. It directly derived its character from his internal imagery experience involving the high event and was reflected in intense pleasurable behavior which was both reality related and fantasy based. To whatever was directly or indirectly connected with the high event, the dog responded with positive anticipation. The idea of the walk prompted even an element of fore-enjoyment and reverie: already at the utterance of the words "walk" or "leash," the dog would jump up and down excitedly. Just as poets have written that they "enjoy" the daffodils in poetic fancy, the dog enjoyed the high event in fantasy.

3. **High Futurism.** The dog appeared to have a firm belief in the future reality of the evening walk, that, from the start of each day, events would lead up to the high event. This was proven by the dog's general behavior and by the fact that his whole behavior changed when Mr. Tompkins suddenly stopped taking him out for the walk. He started to become sullen from the first hours of the morning and remained withdrawn and depressed from then onward. If he had not believed in the continued future reality of the walk and was not clearly protesting against the unfortunate turn of events, he would not have responded with moroseness from the beginning of the day. He was truly futuristic in his attitudes.

Insight. The dog however did not give in to depression immediately after Mr. Tompkins' departure. He continued to hope for some time and this hope was mirrored in some positive activity. By his look, he would implore the daughter and son to take him out for the evening walk, and he would try to follow them out the door. The dog knew what he wanted. He tried to coax them into responding affirmatively by efforts to please them and by wagging his tail. Finally, after continued rejection, he showed separation from them characterized by clear signs of anger, intolerance, and sullenness.

The dog was still aware of the reality of events and adjusted accordingly. When the daughter took him out for a walk, he was very pleased and friendly with her, and there was a marked change in his behavior already the next morning after the first outing. But when she stopped taking him out, he again became sullen. However, he was not as indifferent toward her as he was toward the son, who never took him out and from whom he became completely detached.

4. **Reality Replay.** In place of a walk in the evening, the dog now sat in the living room before a huge picture window which looked into the woods, watching leaves and birds and sometimes acting in an hallucinatory way, as if he were outside. But his excitement and buoyancy revealed that he was still aware of reality: he seemed to know that he was inside the house, and not outside, really; he knew exactly what he was missing and why and had not been confused into a total acceptance of new conditions. In short, he had not yet been conditioned into an acceptance of a new hopeless interpretation of life, that once life goes away it never

returns and whatever loss has filled in the vacuum, must be embraced with total resignation. In fact, such a total conditioning could never occur in him, due to the fact that he was a whole organism, having an unconditional gift of life within.

Sokolov-Signal. In the last stages, the dog became depressed and was guided by the final preattentive scanning signal, called here the "Sokolov-Signal." This signal did not appear in full detail like a vivid, conscious picture but as a brief scanning signal containing a picture of the reality which he had lost. All other expectations were arranged behind this signal, which was nonconscious and all but invisible at the surface, but it was vigorously operative under the surface, as suggested in Sokolov's experiment (1960). The dog was with and without hope at the same time, looking for the return of reality. On the surface he was withdrawn and slept most of the time in a state of depression, but under the surface he was still watching the flow of events. This permanent negative posture of depression toward a permanent negative environment concealed a state of anticipation. In this light, his depression could not be called a meaningless phenomenon but a highly meaningful Sokolovian signal, a watching without watching.

The MAK Response in Reiner revealed some fundamental levels of behavior and imagery processes connected with anticipation. The behavior of the dog, from the explicit anticipation of the walk to the implicit anticipation during rejection and depression, contained many cogent structures. These structures originated entirely from a great spontaneous source — mega anticipation — which has little to do with the training or learning. The dog's elated and buoyant behavior manifested during the walk spread over only a 15-minute period; however, the anticipation behavior extended beyond that, over the 30 minutes prior to the walk and even into the next morning, as analysis under futurism showed. If closely examined, all these behaviors — his anticipation, fore-enjoyment, reverie, even enforcement behavior, and his behavior during the actual walk — were completely unlearned, originating spontaneously from his personal nature. Reiner's enforcement behavior even gave evidence of discerning intelligence: he cleverly chose the second best, the daughter rather than the son, when he could not have the best, the father. Although reality replacement briefly occurred while sitting before the window, he remained aware of reality, aware that he had been forced into a negative condition of existence. Yet, his capacity for reality replay in his mind was always kept ready in case the reality signal (Sokolov-Signal) changed and circumstance gave his evening walk back to him. The dog in the middle of these many structures, in fact, acted like a strategist and a poet. In himself he was hopeful about the future. In the deepest depression, he was still alive: he would wait and see. He was attentive and yet not attentive, oriented toward reality yet nonconscious.

The case history of Reiner provides an interesting lesson: a dog does not lose hope of life but man does. In contrast to the animal, man goes one step beyond, into a condition of self-imposed fixation on negativism and hopelessness. While nature keeps reality awareness spontaneously available to the dog, man takes one step beyond nature: he *interprets* the cause of his depression in a fixated manner and adds the weight of his powerful memory to it, turning it into a symbolic trauma. Man can brood over a transitory trauma and can isolate himself from true nature into memory mechanism. He can go even one more step beyond memory and develop a new level of cognitive interpretations to justify his memory fixation.

Besides fixation and secondary interpretation, an important distinction between dog and man lies in the fact that contrary to the dog, man can earn freedom from fixation through scientific investigation. The dog possesses natural grace, but man can set up a scientific process for investigation of his plight and find a way out of loss back into hope. The ultimate distinction accorded man thus is that he can scientifically replay and investigate important pieces of inner reality in the form of inner imagery potentials and thus destroy his fixation on memory mechanisms. He can scientifically arrive at the signals of his true nature and release his life in its original form, as it was given to him before the memory took over.

The scientific replaying of inner reality, through the imagery process, can give man knowledge of his nature. Through imagery, the original balance in his psyche can be replayed and the lost happiness can be retrieved into consciousness. This replay of inner reality through imagery is vital in man's attempt to retrieve his true nature.

The mega anticipatory kinetic response, the MAK Response, embodies the energetic resources of the organism, separate from memory fixations. The observable tension in the mega anticipatory response mentioned by Mowrer and Curtis contains more details than a casual observer would suspect, since it is comprised of many levels of natural structures of energetic behaviors. Mega anticipation in the final analysis is not just a shield or mere tension which needs to be discharged, but a condition of holistic buoyancy containing awareness, strategy, reality discernment, and play with imagined reality in order to explore absent reality (see the relationship of eidetics to rehearsal in Ahsen, 1977b; Allport, 1924). When the organism deals with the situation in a genuine, vigorous way, anticipation appears in full-blown form, as a high expression of potentials manifested in imagery form.

The MAK Response, which thus centrally involves imagery, provides us with a new look into energetic potentials of the organism and the possibility of designing a scientific psychotherapy based on related imagery research. Encounter, mobilization, replay, and energetic rehearsal behaviors of imagery, all appear to emerge from around the MAK Response. We can clearly describe the individual's health, based on the nature of participating imagery, whether it is buoyant, energetic, and positive, or depressed, narcotic, and negative. When an individual experiences a high-consciousness image, he accordingly enters into a mega anticipation reflecting a process containing great potential.

In my own clinical practice, I repeatedly came across specially active, motivating forms of images distinguishable from other types, which forced me to use the Marburg School's term "eidetic." If we define *all* images as equally good mechanisms for regulating behavior, we do not recognize that passive or resistant or downright negative and destructive images do exist. There is clinical evidence, that images which are not merely passive and stupid but definitely catastrophic in nature unfortunately do exist. Images associated with phobias, obsessions, etc., which clearly choke and drain the natural driving force of the organism, are a point in question. Since the nature of images varies widely, we need to develop a clear image theory which explains energetic resources of the mind and accounts for the general paradoxical behaviors of imagery. Whether we call the healthy images "eidetic imagery," "buoyant imagery," or just "positive imagery," we need to focus clearly on the existence of these positive images, since the future of effective psychotherapy appears to be tied to them. Research in general imagery and psychotherapy has revealed that in states such as sleep or drowsiness or negative imagery, the positive qualities of anticipation are largely inhibited and attention is minimally activated. When attention, with all its integrative attributes, is not maximally activated and heightened, the person acts like a drugged subject or one in sleep who experiences the pea as a camel's hump. This essential difference between negative, narcotic attention and high consciousness imagery is manifested not only in sleep and some twilight forms of consciousness, but also in those special forms of imagery which do not allow the full potential of consciousness to come into play, for instance, in negative memory images and images with negative symbolic potential. The distinction, that certain images definitely allow heightened expression of the organism, thus becomes centrally important for psychotherapy. The highly interactive potential experienced during positive images renders possible psychotherapy procedures of high value. The behavior of these positive images is described below.

High Consciousness Images

These images reflect high consciousness which involves the organism in a total and profound manner. To demonstrate the access to this healthful imagery process, descriptions are provided of images in terms of their capacity for release or creative interactive potential, factors which are the very soul of the psychotherapeutic process (Ahsen, 1968, 1977a, 1977b, 1978).

Nature Images. The mind processes are found within nature, and only in the context of nature can they be fully revealed. Separated from nature, the mind becomes a hollow mold of activity, without luster and authenticity, seeking mere empty forms without the pleasure of being. What is really higher: the natural or the mechanical? If one is asked to concentrate in one's mind on a mechanical object, like a ticking clock, and on a natural one, like a trotting horse on a dirt road, and then to compare the two images, one can see the important distinction. The two sets of images create two different conditions in the mind: the one is mechanical, restraining, and chopped, the other is releasing and wholesome. A characteristic hollowness is created in the mind by a mechanical object. That our shackled minds in the isolating world need to be revived through images of nature was first emphasized in the Vedic tradition. The scientific investigation also has led to the conclusion that the fascinating pure sensations of the mind are retrievable in their original form. These natural sensations, deserving the highest tribute, would be fascinating to experience. H. Klüver once emphasized the great potential which eidetic phenomena offered in this important area, and he referred to Carpenter's observation in *Principles of Mental Physiology* (1896) that it is "consistent with ordinary medical experience and accordant with physiological probability . . . that real sensations are producible by mental states" (Klüver, 1928, p. 93). Staudenmaier's work as well as Ebbecke's research on cortical excitation using records of his own subjective phenomena applicable to the study of sensations offered remarkable techniques for evoking subjective phenomena in all sense fields (Klüver, 1928, p. 93). This view is consistent with the known yogic position, that there exists a whole area of high sensory experience dealing with breathing rhythms, postures of the body, concentration, color, touch, and other sensations. One can reproduce natural experience of the sense organs in those areas and regenerate the original mythic capacity of the mind.

The potent images which flow from nature serve as the prime source of healthy experience. In these images, we again discover our souls. These images of nature represent the gratifying vision of the true world.

Progression: Negative images behave in a unipolar fashion, that is, they exert only a negative influence on consciousness and provide no freedom, depth, or variation. In short, they provide no release or progression. These images which occur, for example, in obsessive thought and phobias, dominate consciousness and move it toward narcosis and depression. Similarly, most memory images carry a preconceived interpretation of the event and are therefore resistant to new structuration.

Progression is a marked characteristic of the high image process, especially when the process starts from a valid nucleus of life (for detailed discussion, see Ahsen, 1977b). This important attribute of the imagery process derives directly from the buoyant and heightened state of consciousness, and it is of central importance (Sheehan, 1978) for the growth and expression of consciousness.

The images which contain the potential of high consciousness develop from an inert state to activation in a progressive fashion, when attention is paid to them. As the inert state is repeated by projecting the images over and over again, the images move toward a state similar to a flare during explosion and a new image leaps out of the previous image state, in the typical manner of a new pattern emerging out of an old pattern (Sheikh, 1978).

The progression can occur spontaneously, or, as in the face of defenses, it can be made to take place, through sheer repetition, using tantalizing techniques. While projecting an image, for instance, one can actively interact with it by projecting into it various emotions like anger, love, and so forth. By introducing new situations into the image, one can cause a high interactive condition to enter into the image, which, in turn, can cause the whole state to become energized. In brief, all interactive techniques lead to energized progression and finally to high-image states.

Creativity. We can stop thought and study its logical structures by repeatedly examining its rational process, but we are rewarded in a limited way; on the other hand, when we arrest imagery and concentrate on its structures by repeatedly seeing the perceptual details, a rich unfolding of information accompanies the process. If we cannot playfully interact with an unfolding experience, we are in the grip of compulsive and obsessive structures which are limiting and destructive to health. Thus, even if thought appears to give us some superficial details, its potential is far inferior and in some cases even dangerous, when compared with the potential of the image process which is inherently expansive and creative.

The imagery processes comprise the energized response system of the organism. This system contains whatever is centrally in need of response and has all the resources of the organism at its disposal. Since this system contains the very essence and vitality of the biological organism, it is to this system that an organism addresses itself in the hour of expression. Pavlov called this creative system the first signaling system. In his concept of the biological structure, this first signaling system feeds the second signaling system of developmental memory and learning. Behaviorists have generally rejected the first signaling system as unconscious and unreachable and have instead concentrated on the external behavior. However, today, researchers in the area of imagery have clearly established that the processes of the first signaling system are freely available. Since these processes are actually preattentive, one can come into contact with them at will, if one knows how to use imagery processes. At this point, Pavlov's comment concerning the importance of the first signaling system and its obvious relationship to creativity, comes to mind: there are "two categories of people — artists and thinkers. Between them there is a marked difference. The artists . . . comprehend reality as a whole, as a continuity, a complete living reality, without any divisions, without any separations. The other group, the thinkers, pull it apart, kill it . . . . This difference is especially prominent in the so-called eidetic imagery of children . . . . Such a whole creation of reality cannot be completely attained by a thinker" (1941, p. 113).

In an ordinary imagery state as in the rational process, a person may search in panic for a solution, but no solution may come through. On the other hand, energized imagery is characterized by a definite alertness and an inherent capacity for solutions channelled from the deepest potentials of the organism. During high consciousness imagery states, the individual feels vital and confident; and his imagery experience gives him the feeling of being in command of the situation (Twente et al., 1978). This aspect of the high mental process has been widely recognized by psychotherapists and is generally associated with "creativity," "intuition," and "breakthroughs."

Conclusion

In ordinary limiting states of consciousness, as, for instance, in memory, one uses partial, biased, and distant envisioning of the original experience. The central function of high consciousness imagery is to contribute fundamental enrichment to one's experience. Seen from this angle, mega anticipation and MAK Response provide a central point of reference for the development of a new dynamic theory of consciousness dedicated to activation and energy. The precise contribution of various imagery levels, including memory, can be developed in relation to this fundamental core. Most psychotherapy issues can be systematized around this concept and can be assigned their rightful place on the basis of their relevance to activation and the way it exudes its essence.

High consciousness images represent total activation of the organism. Interaction with these images provides a view into the innermost psychical dynamics, a personal encounter with energy and freedom. These energetic and buoyant images comprise the vital core of the organism and need to be released, if the individual is to evolve an effective life vision.

REFERENCES

Ahsen, A. Hemispheric experiments on eidetic images of parents. Presented at the Pakistan Science Conference, 1959.

Ahsen, A. *Basic concepts in eidetic psychotherapy.* New York: Brandon House, 1968.

Ahsen, A. *Eidetic parents test and analysis.* New York: Brandon House, 1972.

Ahsen, A. *Psycheye: Self-analytic consciousness.* New York: Brandon House, 1977.(a)

Ahsen, A. Eidetics: An overview. *Journal of Mental Imagery,* 1977, *1,* 5-38.(b)

Ahsen, A. Eidetics: Neural experiential growth potential for the treatment of accident traumas, debilitating stress conditions, and chronic emotional blocking. *Journal of Mental Imagery,* 1978, *2,* 1-22.

Ahsen, A. & Lazarus, A. A. Eidetics: An internal behavior approach. In A. A. Lazarus (Ed.), *Clinical behavior therapy.* New York: Brunner/Mazel, 1972.

Ahsen, A. & Wolpe, J. Taped discussion on imagery process and conditioning. Eastern Pennsylvania Psychiatric Institute, 1967.

Allport, G. W. Eidetic imagery. *British Journal of Psychology,* 1924, *15,* 99-120.

Craik, F. I. M. & Lockhart, R. S. Levels of processing: A framework for memory research. *Journal of Verbal Learning and Verbal Behavior,* 1972, *11,* 671-684.

Curtis, Q. F. The experimental neurosis in the pig. Read before the American Psychological Association, September, 1937.

Dolan, A. T. Eidetic and general image theory of primary image objects and identification processes. *Journal of Mental Imagery,* 1977, *1,* 217-228.

Festinger, L., Burnham, C. A., Ono, H., & Bamber, D. Efference and the conscious experience of perception. *Journal of Experimental Psychology Monograph,* 1967, *74,* No. 4.

Hull, C. L. *A behavior system: An introduction to behavior theory concerning the individual organism.* New York: John Wiley & Sons, 1952.

Klüver, H. Studies on the eidetic type and on eidetic imagery. *Psychological Bulletin,* 1928, *25,* 69.

Lashley, K. S. In search of the engram. In F. A. Beach, D. O. Hebb, C. T. Morgan & H. W. Nissen (Eds.), *The neuropsychology of Lashley.* New York: McGraw-Hill, 1960.

Mandler, G. Memory storage and retrieval: Some limits on the reach of attention and consciousness. In P. M. A. Rabbitt & S. Dornic (Eds.), *Attention and performance V.* London: Academic Press, 1974.

Mandler, G. Consciousness: Respectable, useful, and probably necessary. In R. Solso (Ed.), *Information processing and cognition,* Loyola Symposium. Hillsdale, N. J.: Lawrence Erlbaum Associates, 1975.

Miller, G. A. *Psychology: The science of mental life.* New York: Harper and Row, 1962.

Milner, P. M. *Physiological psychology.* New York: Holt, Rinehart & Winston, 1970.

Mowrer, O. H. Preparatory set (expectancy) — a determinant in motivation and learning. *Psychological Review,* 1938, *45,* 61-91.

Mowrer, O. H. Mental imagery: An indispensable psychological concept. *Journal of Mental Imagery,* 1977, *1,* 303-326.

Neisser, U. *Cognitive psychology.* New York: Appleton-Century-Crofts, 1967.

Ornstein, R. E. *The psychology of consciousness.* San Francisco: Freeman, 1972.

Pavlov, I. P. *Conditioned reflexes and psychiatry.* Trans. and ed. by E. Horsley Gantt. New York: International Publishers Co., 1941.

Posner, M. I. & Keele, S. W. Time and space as measures of mental operations. Paper presented at the Annual Meeting of the American Psychological Association, 1970.

Pribram, K. H. *Languages of the brain.* Englewood Cliffs, N. J.: Prentice-Hall, 1971.

Schlosberg, H. Conditioned responses in the white rat. *Journal of Genetic Psychology,* 1934, *45,* 303-335.

Shallice, T. Dual functions of consciousness. *Psychological Review,* 1972, *79,* 383-393.

Sheehan, P. W. Eidetic imagery and the therapeutic development of consciousness. (Review of *Psycheye: Self-analytic consciousness* by A. Ahsen). *Contemporary Psychology,* 1978, *23,* 430-431.

Sheikh, A. A. Eidetic psychotherapy. In J. L. Singer & K. Pope (Eds.), *The power of human imagination.* New York: Plenum Publishing Corp., 1978.

Sokolov, E. N. Neuronal models and the orienting reflex. In M. A. B. Brazier (Ed.), *The central nervous system and behavior.* New York: Josiah Macy, Jr. Foundation, 1960.

Twente, G. E., Turner, D. & Haney, J. Eidetics in the hospital setting and private practice: A report on eidetic therapy procedures employed with 69 patients. *Journal of Mental Imagery,* 1978, *2,* 275-290.

Upton, M. The auditory sensitivity of guinea pigs. *American Journal of Psychology,* 1929, *41,* 412-421.

Wever, E. G. The upper limit of learning in the cat. *Journal of Comparative Psychology,* 1930, *10,* 221-233.

3

Imagery and Affect in Psychotherapy: Elaborating Private Scripts and Generating Contexts

JEROME L. SINGER

Most psychotherapy and behavior modification (except for operant techniques and token economies in institutions) takes place in a small room under conditions in which therapist and patient are alone and engaged in conversation with each other. What goes on between these two people is designed not necessarily to affect the nature of their relationship to each other but to lead ultimately to some significant alteration in the patient's pattern of thought and overt behavior in dozens of settings or interpersonal relationships outside of this small room. It is true that in some therapeutic techniques it is emphasized that change in the patient's behavior in the outside world will hinge very much on the pattern of the relationship that evolves with the therapist. This view is clearly the theory behind the psychoanalytic concept that a miniature version of the client's neurosis must be created in the transference situation and then, in effect, cured in relation to the therapist before the client can effect a broad-ranging personality change. In some cases, as in the form of treatment pioneered by Helmut Kaiser, the focus of treatment is almost obsessively upon the relationship and pattern of interaction between therapist and patient.

Of course, some clients come simply to "purchase friendship," and others, as some long-term classical psychoanalytical patients, come to find, in the quiet comfort of the office, daily surcease from the pressures of life's complexities. For the

Jerome L. Singer, Department of Psychology, Yale University, New Haven, Connecticut 06520

most part, the ultimate object of a therapeutic transaction is to lead to major changes in the way the patient confronts a great many day-to-day situations that occur in places far removed from the sheltered office. For the psychotherapy to be effective, therefore, the patient must be able to present, in the session, descriptions and details of many kinds of occurrences and interpersonal interactions that are important in his/her daily life. It is necessary, also, for the psychotherapist to process this material. Bringing the outside world into the therapy room as a basis for an interaction between patient and therapist that will lead to changes in the outside-world behavior of the patient necessitates extensive reliance not only on verbal communication between the two, but also involves the imagery systems of both participants. Imagery is viewed here as the chief method by which human beings can transcend time and space, and provide in miniaturized form for themselves and for communication to others the complexities of experiences which occurred elsewhere.

The imagery system has, of course, a variety of very specific uses in the forms of psychotherapy and behavior modification (Singer, 1974, Singer & Pope, 1978). The essential nature of this system lies in making possible effective communication between patient and therapist, but there are at least a dozen specific ways in which the human capacity for duplicating external events in the miniaturized private form of the image becomes a critical part of the change process. In psychoanalysis, the reconstruction of dream images recalled from the previous night's sleep or even from several days before is obviously a central part of the treatment. In the elucidation of transference, fantasies are critical in most forms of Freudian or Neo-Freudian psychoanalytic-treatment procedures. Singer (1974) and Singer and Pope (1978) have sketched ways in which imagery can be effective in circumventing defensiveness, in increasing effective rapport and communication, and in helping patients to identify their own creative potentialities more fully. Horowitz (1978) has elaborated even more extensively on the ways in which imagery can effectively be employed within the framework of a psychodynamic-treatment format. Either directively, by suggesting a use of imagery, or interpretatively, by calling attention to defenses, Horowitz pointed out approaches to helping patients move beyond verbal, abstract summaries toward concrete, emotionally charged associations.

Reyher (1978) has gone even further in proposing a shift in psychoanalytically oriented therapy from the use of a verbal, free association towards an emphasis on a purely imagery association method. Reyher's Emergent Uncovering method, supported by some empirical data, indicates that image associations are more likely than verbal sequences to generate powerful emotional reactions and to circumvent defensiveness and therapeutic delay.

A variety of approaches developed in Europe (see Singer, 1974) and related probably originally to the work of Schultz (Autogenics) or Jung (Active Imagination) have evolved and are perhaps most clearly exemplified in the elaborate Guided Affective Imagery method of Leuner (1978). In these approaches, imagery is put at the center of psychotherapy. Less emphasis is placed upon interpretation or insight. In effect, the guided-imagery practitioners propose that the ongoing nature of the private symbolic processes, when allowed freedom of development under controlled therapeutic conditions, are inherently curative (Singer, 1974). Although direct linkages are not easy to spell out all the time, it is possible that the therapeutic effectiveness of such procedures may be explicable ultimately in terms of common psychological processes which operate for either the psychodynamic methods or the behavior modification procedures (Meichenbaum, 1978; Singer, 1974).

Perhaps the most varied and proliferating uses of the imagery system in treatment are now evident in the various forms of behavior modification. This development has a certain irony, since these procedures, after all, are descendants of John B. Watson who presided over the banishment of private imagery from psychology in the second decade of the century. Nevertheless, as exemplified in the work of Cautela (1978), imagery is being used to desensitize individuals suffering from irrational fear: in the case of aversive imagery, it is utilized to help individuals gain control over unwanted wishes or behaviors in covert modeling, it is called upon to help individuals gain assertiveness or self-expression; and, in general, it is used to increase the repertoire of cognitive skills and strategies (Meichenbaum, 1977, Singer, 1974).

There is a danger, however, that imagery can come to be regarded by psychotherapists as an almost magical symbol, a new panacea, in this most faddish of the areas of applied psychology. The purpose of the present chapter is to take a closer look at the process of imagery, its relation to basic systems of personality, its particular relationship to the affect system, and its special role within the psychotherapeutic setting.

A Systems Approach to Personality

I begin with the assumption that the processes that produce psychological distress or deviance and the therapeutic measures instituted to modify these stem ultimately from the same basic principles of psychological science. The time is past when each new psychotherapy required its own more or less elaborate theoretical substructure. Instead, it seems appropriate that we formulate our thinking about what goes on in the clinical situation in relation to basic scientific findings available about the systems of the individual personality. In this paper, I will limit emphasis to those systems that are most frequently involved in psychotherapy and behavior modification and mention only in passing the other major systems which operate together to produce what we define globally as human behavior or thought. An early presentation of a systems orientation, as it applies more specifically to the affects as motivating forces, can be found in Izard and Tomkins (1966).

Essentially, followers of this orientation propose that a limited but differentiated number of basic systems are operative in defining the individual and his/her pattern of response to a variety of situations. The brain system, with its essentially silent operation, is being increasingly recognized, not only because most other important systems are controlled through the brain, but also because within brain structure, specific levels of neurochemicals secreted at nerve endings seem to be critical for the likelihood of experiences of general pleasure or depression as well as for reduction in pain or distress. The other silent systems which involve homeostatic balances governed chiefly by the autonomic nervous system (hormonal responses) as well as the body's basic rhythmic cycles, are better understood today. With the advent of new technology for assessing biofeedback, some degree of identification of signals from these systems is now possible and it is likely that they, for instance, heart rate and temperature, can come under greater control (Schwartz & Shapiro, 1976, 1978).

Until the 1960's, the drive system was the focus of attention in both psychoanalysis and the dominant learning theories of psychology as a fundamental motivating force. *Hunger, thirst, sex, relief from pain,* and, somewhat more speculatively, *aggression* were characterized as drives, and much of the attention in psychotherapy was centered on the "vicissitudes of the instincts," especially of sex and aggression, and on their role in determining personality development and the possibility of change.

A confluence, in the 1960's, of revised motivation theory, neuropsychological modeling, computer simulation, and empirical research led to a shift in emphasis, in the motivation of personality, away from the more peripheral and somewhat dubious drive models towards the concept of a differentiated affect system and the cognitive and information-processing capacities of the human being (Singer, 1974; Tomkins, 1962, 1963). The affect or emotional system has been increasingly recognized to have a major role in human motivation, since it serves as the critical amplifier of signals from the other systems and also provides the basis for self-generated rewarding or punishing experiences (Izard, 1977; Tomkins, 1962, 1963). It is increasingly clear that the emotions represent differentiated processes with special properties linked to facial musculature, to facial skin sensitivity, and also to broader bodily representations, as well as to central cognitive processes (Ekman & Friesen, 1975; Izard, 1978; Tomkins, 1962, 1963, 1978).

A critical step has been taken by Tomkins who proposes that the affect system in its operation is closely tied to the cognitive system, the major system by which we process, store, and retrieve the complex stimulation presented to us in the external environment or generated out of our long-term memory system by the continuing activity of the brain itself (Singer, 1966, 1974). It is, of course, the cognitive system which serves as the general overriding rubric for processes of attention, perception, memory, image construction, fantasy, and dreaming. Thinking, whether in the form of direct problem-solving activity or in the form of daydreaming, may be viewed as an apsect of the cognitive system under circumstances in which information processing is directed not so much at material generated outside the person, but at material generated by his/her own long-term memory system (Singer, 1966, 1974).

There has been increasing interest recently, even amongst social-learning theorists, in conceptions of what might be termed superordinate systems of personality. The notion of a self-system or some type of central executive is gaining increasing favor, and there are more and more efforts to specify operations for defining the unique characteristics of self-appraisal, self-efficacy, and self-reinforcement (Bandura, 1977). To clinicians with a background in psychoanalysis or Sullivan's interpersonal theory, this attention to central processes of ego or self is scarcely new. The difference may lie in the fact that recent efforts have been more closely tied to experimentally reproducible operations which permit us to identify specific patterns of behavior that seem traceable to unique properties of a concept of self (Bandura, 1977, in press).

Finally, of course, the human being must act. We must talk to others, must move about in the world, and, indeed, must also inhibit many motor or verbal activities. In the pattern of movement and inhibition of movement in the physical environment and also in relation to other persons in the broader social systems within which we all operate, we come full circle. Action can, in effect, not be taken back once executed; but if it is inhibited before full expression, it may become the basis for specialized body orientations or body awareness. The unique properties of the affect system as represented through facial or muscular activities are especially important if inhibited or only partially expressed (Tomkins, 1978). Linkages between explicit and implicit action or affect are now more effectively being teased out with new instrumentation (McGuigan, 1978; Schwartz et al., 1973).

Images and Scripts

In this chapter, I am emphasizing the special role of imagery processes in psychotherapy. The clinician must ultimately view the client in relation to the broader range of systems sketched above. Nevertheless, for many types of psychotherapy, the major work of producing cognitive and behavior modification changes rests to a considerable degree on an engagement of the client's cognitive and affective system.

A part of a major shift in conceptualization of human motivation from the somewhat more peripherally oriented drive model towards the cognitive-affective model, is the change in the representation of human striving from the image of the infant aroused by pressures of hunger or thirst (Rapaport, 1960) to that of the active individual trying continuously to organize and make sense of the environment and to match new imputs against well established schema (Neisser, 1967; Singer, 1974). We have moved from the psychoanalytic model of an infant or baby processing everything orally to a more Piagetian notion of the importance of the eyes, ears, and broader sensory apparatus of exploration and curiosity as well as of oral gratifications. The basic units of analysis thus become not so much drives and cathexes but schema (Piaget, 1962) or scripts (Schank & Abelson, 1977; Tomkins, 1978). The basic working units which we process from our environment or which we retrieve from long-term memory are not just single pictures or words or body associations but organized sequences of images, or verbal phrases, and sometimes even combinations of nonverbal representations with verbal series.

Indeed, this view is really not that different from what perhaps was intended by Freud in his emphasis on the fantasy, often unconscious, which became the basis for thought and action. In the psychoanalytic usage, however, the emphasis was perhaps on the more unrealistic or primitive aspects of this representational sequence, and there was too little attention paid to the inherently adaptive, organizing properties of image sequences and the fact that they may indeed represent an effective basis for interpretation and action in relation to the "real world."

I have already suggested that information is organized in keeping with a dual coding system (Paivio, 1971). This view has gained increasing support with the emergence of an extensive body of research on the differential functions of the left and right hemispheres of the brain. We are still far from comprehending all of the implications of the finding that the left side of the brain seems more specialized for sequential thought processes, verbal and ordered thought, while the right brain seems more linked to representational systems of a parallel nature, global or diffuse representations, and possibly intuitive experiences (Gazzaniga, 1970; Ornstein, 1977).

For present purposes, it is important to specify that we organize our experiences with the physical and social environment into modality-specific representations (images), or verbal labels, and sometimes combinations of both. These may be separately stored and may have different rules for retrieval. Thus, verbal material is far more efficient, since it encompasses a greater variety of specific situations within a single label - thousands of different chairs are represented by that single term. The imagery system provides the basis for considerably more *detail* about a specific event or interpersonal transaction from the past. An image is harder to retrieve from the memory system, because the brain has indeed stored literally millions of such potential representations. Experimental work by Seamon (1972) has indicated that optimal memory function occurs when we store not only a "picture" or "sound" but also a fairly precise label for the event.

Retrieval of words is made easier by the fact that they fall relatively neatly into categories and subclasses. The specific events of our life, the scenes witnessed, the early childhood fantasies associated with terrors and experiences of the uncanny often have not been classified under some general category and labelled verbally. Thus, they cannot easily be retrieved on demand and may influence us without our ability to connect their occurrence with particular verbal systems. A major method of psychotherapy has therefore been the use of the somewhat child-like, regressive couch setting to produce an atmosphere in which the retrieval of childhood experience becomes more likely (Singer, 1974).

Indeed, one way of looking at psychoanalysis, as Dollard and Miller (1950) long ago suggested, is that it seeks to provide efficient verbal labels for a variety of linked experiences from childhood. Once one recognizes that one's current attraction to older persons of the opposite sex, one's earlier crushes on school teachers or on aging movie actresses or actors, and one's fleeting memories of attachment to mother and fear of a menacing Big Daddy can be considered manifestations of an Oedipus Complex, then one seems to have made a major step towards organizing what might appear as chaotic experience. Whether such labelling genuinely produces personality change or more effective behavior is another question. More likely, the identification of the commonalities in these events and their linkage to a verbal label makes for still another step in a process of cognitive control of behavior. The individual now can quickly identify recurrences in current life situations that reflect the influence of these earlier patterns and try to introduce alternative responses or at least to avoid impulsive emotional response or overt behavior (Singer, 1974).

Images and Ongoing Thought

Although investigators, such as Shepard (1978), have made important strides in developing methods for measuring the special properties of the single image, insufficient attention has been given to the fact that human thought is continuous and that we may be constantly replaying our scripts and images in the course of our stream of thought (Pope & Singer, 1978; Singer, 1975a, b).

Klinger has proposed that fantasy, as he terms it, is best regarded as a "respondent process," the basic core of most activity. "It is possible to think of behavior in terms of a four-level continuum. . . . On one level, using perhaps the greatest diversity of functions, is fully conscious, voluntary motor behavior. Here, the motor activity is served not only by effectors but also by sensory, perceptual, and cognitive processes. On the next level, we might place operant thought. It is volitional, directed towards specific objectives, and more or less ethical, but it incorporates no overt use of effectors. Going to the third level, we arrive at respondent mental activity. This is nonvolitional, undirected in any deliberate sense. Here is where we would place fantasy. Finally, at the remaining level, we can place the blank state during which the person remains conscious but entertains no figured imagery of any kind" (Klinger, 1977, p. 223).

Klinger goes on to elaborate on the fact the ongoing thought process is itself governed by the principle of what he calls "current concerns." These reflect the major motivational orientations which determine which activity of the continuing processing of the brain will be noted and further organized by the individual.

Pope and Singer (1978) have expanded the notion that human beings are constantly playing and replaying stored material as they go about their business of the day, and they have attempted to draw from this idea a formulation of basic principles of ongoing thought. Singer (1966, 1975a, 1975b) has suggested that ongoing thought might be viewed as an alternative stimulus field which in a sense must be organized and responded to selectively in much the same way as the external environment of sound and light signals or interpersonal communications to which we are subjected. Pope and Singer write:

> The mind itself is not static, not a large storage bin, nor a passive blank slate; it is an organ of activity, process, and ongoing work. To a great extent, this active organ concerns itself with the processing of sensory input. The sense organs, then, exert considerable influence over what material will be ultimately available to consciousness. The material that reaches consciousness from immediate sensory input may be conceptualized as at one pole of a continuum of awareness that runs from a public pole (physical stimuli from the environment, clearly measurable or capable of consensual description by other people as well as by the individual) through internal bodily stimuli (not so readily accessible to the public, but still on the whole traceable to physically measurable characteristics) to the private pole of the continuum (images, associations, and other materials related to short-and long-term memory).
> Attention is the process by which the material available is screened and selected for introduction into the stream of consciousness. There appears to be a distinct bias toward attending to sensory material, a characteristic of obvious survival and adaptation value. When the environment becomes predictable, dull, or barren, however, the tendency is for the consciousness to move toward the more private end of the continuum, for memories, associations, and imaginary materials flow into the stream of consciousness The quality of being predictable, dull, or barren does not inhere solely in the environment but depends to a great extent on the individual's image or scheme of incoming stimuli and on how well these representations are able to match or anticipate the environmental stimulation (Pope & Singer, 1978, pp. 106-107).

Other determinants of the ongoing stream of consciousness are, of course, the current concerns of the individual as suggested by Klinger (1977), and also the basic unfinished business of the person's immediate life. The long-term unfinished business of major early fantasies and wishes that have persisted without resolution must be considered as well. The repercussions of significant trauma may take years before they no longer recur in the ongoing stream of thought (Janis, 1969).

There are probably also special structural characteristics of ongoing thought whose properties have as yet been relatively little studied. For example, rhyme or clang associations or other kinds of symmetrical forms may be hard to eliminate from thought once they have appeared. We also have developed differential sets towards processing internal material: the consistent evidence of introvertive-personality styles or orientations, such as thoughtfulness or self-awareness, identifies individuals who have developed a habitual style of paying more careful attention to their ongoing stream of thought (Singer, 1966, 1975a, 1975b).

In effect, then, the ongoing stream of consciousness provides a continuing, *alternative* environment to which we can respond and through which we may repeat and rehearse both verbal phrases and images which have been stored. Such "practice" increases the probabilities that we can quite easily retrieve certain material later on, or that such especially rehearsed "scripts" will be more influential in the course of our subsequent decision processes when we attempt to make connections for an organized thought sequence. Undoubtedly, the importance of images as part of adaptive thought and, indeed, the highest level of scientific thought has been undervalued in the past, and examples of how important scientific theory has been advanced suggest that images often preceded the development of verbal or mathematical formulation (Shepard, 1978).

Images and the Affect System

If we view imagery processes as part of an alternative environment which the individual confronts, then we can also see why images may be especially closely related to the occurrence of emotions or affect. A major implication of Tomkins' (1962, 1963) theory is that the inherent arousal of affect is tied to the nature of the information-processing task confronting an individual. Thus, extremely novel stimulation, presented at a rate too rapid for matching and assimilation to established schema or scripts, will lead to the startle response or to the experience of fear and dread. Material that is presented at a moderate pace which has at least some point of reference to earlier learned material is more likely to lead to the arousal of the positive affect of surprise and interest and keep the individual moving towards exploration. High levels of persistently unassimilable material are likely to arouse the affect of anger while somewhat more moderate, but persistent levels of material difficult to assimilate will arouse distress, sadness, or the weeping response. Novel material that has aroused considerable interest but is then resolved by matching, will lead to the experience of joy or the smiling response. A detailed discussion of some of the implications of this position for the role of imagery has been presented elsewhere and cannot be reviewed in detail here (Singer, 1974). The important thing to note is that our own images and private fantasies have the inherent capacity to arouse complex affective reactions.

Words, however, by their special abstracting power, integrate so many potential images that they may lose the capacity to reproduce the original affective responses. That is why Schachtel (1959) has called attention to the fact that, mature adults, through the use of language and a great variety of shortcuts and abstractions inherent in the lexical system, frequently lose touch with the images formed through smell, touch, taste, hearing, and sight. The greatness of Shakespeare lies in part in the tremendous range of vocabulary he employed, in his constant use of words evoking smell, touch, tastes, sounds, or sights, which permitted him to reinvoke images with which we had lost touch (Singer, 1975a).

The imagery system increases the likelihood that we will experience more fully a range of emotions. In producing an image, we are in part, at least temporarily, blocking out external stimulation and attending to a new self-created context. This context may in itself have elements of strangeness and novelty. We can, as we all recognize, be surprised by some of the things we see in our own imagery, and we can also experience the delight of gradually assimilating these to more established schema much in the same way as during the assimilation of externally generated material. The extensive research concerned with the ongoing stream of thought and the daydreaming process, as well as with the nature of visual imagery (Shepard, 1978) suggests that our images follow the same modality specific patterns as the perceptual process. They are, however, not direct reproductions of external material any more than perception is (Neisser, 1967). Rather, they are approximations of previously experienced events and require further elaboration to be processed. This very activity, therefore, evokes some degree of effort but also increases the likelihood of affective experience of the kind outlined by Tomkins.

Imagery and the Reconstruction of Content

Within the context of the psychotherapy situation, then, the special role of imagery may be its strength in evoking a varied but relatively intense affective response. A patient comes into the therapy situation and mentions, "Things are not going well in my marriage. My wife and I have tried working on our relationship but it doesn't seem to be helping." This abstract account leaves both the therapist and the patient in doubt about the nature of the latter's emotional response to this situation, as well as to the specific details of the interaction that underlies this rather terse verbal summation of probably thousands of transactions between the couple. Only vivid reimaging of a specific encounter is likely to create a situational content that makes it possible for the patient to experience the emotions evoked by the specific event and also to communicate these emotions effectively to the therapist. In one of Woody Allen's movies, the protagonist complains that he does not understand what went wrong in his marriage, but in a flashback, we see his wife saying, "I can't stand you, and also I just don't dig you physically. It's nothing personal, however." Having seen this image on the screen, with the tremendous weight of humiliation it carries, we can understand very quickly that attempts to work on that marriage will be fraught with failure.

In effect, since we cannot carry videocameras around with us in all of our interpersonal transactions, we must be able to present vivid descriptions based on our memories to others if we are to communicate effectively the specificity of scenes. In the course of this reconstruction, we are necessarily "looking" at the images we conjure up and thus inevitably will respond with some affect. The therapist also is now "looking" at the scene and responds in part with his/her own spontaneous reaction and, in part, from the patient's point of view, which he/she has attempted to determine from the limited store of other scenes already received from this particular patient. In the somewhat absurd but not completely untrue-to-life example from the movie cited above, Woody Allen as a patient might have gone on to say to the therapist that he could not understand why he was feeling distressed and hurt since, after all, his wife really had not meant what she had said "personally." The therapist might have been able to bring the patient back in touch with his own feelings and denial tendencies through imagery, because it appears that there is no way that most people can avoid being humiliated by such remarks even when told that they are not meant "personally."

The ongoing stream of thought is connected to not only memory but also projections into a variety of possible futures (Singer, 1975a). Even though respondent thought, as Klinger calls it, may not have any immediate directed intention, it is likely that it serves, over the longer run, as a kind of preparation for many potential actions or as a kind of reorganization of self-representation. Recently, Bandura (in press) has placed increased emphasis upon the self-system and has pointed out the extent to which individuals constantly reshape and reorganize situational influences through a continuing process of self-observation, elaboration of private goals, and other forms of rehearsal.

Indeed, Bandura might have gone further in tying in this notion of self-monitoring and self-goal setting to a host of projected fantasies and playful elaborations of the future, which characterize ongoing thought (Singer, 1975a; Singer & Pope, 1978).

Bandura writes, "Self-generated influences cannot be excised from among the determinants of human behavior without sacrificing considerable explanatory and predictive power" (in press, pp. 351). What seems likely is that a kind of playful self-projection into a variety of "realistic" or even "absurd" imagined scenes may be an important element in ongoing thought that has significant motivational properties.

The continuing nature of such self-projection in the form of daydreaming, may account for the fact that certain types of behavior may be more amenable to psychotherapeutic modification through the use of imagery than others. Thus, Little and Curran (1978) have pointed out that covert-sensitization techniques seem more effective in dealing with the problems of sexual deviance than with problems of alcoholism, smoking, or obesity. Since the drinking, smoking, or eating conditions involve a strong effect of direct sensory experience, while sexual deviance is often reflected much more in an elaborate series of *fantasies* about human relationships, especially in sexual encounters, one can understand why the imagery modality might be more powerful in modifying sexually deviant behavior. Representation of self in relation to others with self-efficacy or self-monitoring and self-reinforcing images linked together in sexual settings may lead to overemphasis on particular types of sexual encounter. The heavy imagery component in the ongoing experience may also make this type of behavior more amenable to change through a comparable technique.

Similarly, self-efficacy imagery may be a critical component in a great many kinds of psychotherapy. Images of one's communication and association with the therapist, using a particular technique, may lead to the motivation to try new forms of behavior. In the past, such self-images of an ongoing sort were simply dismissed as placebo effects. It seems much more likely that the placebo effect, if it does occur in some form of therapeutic encounters, is itself a reflection of the powerful affective implications and motivational properties of self-reinforcing patterns.

Social-learning theorists have taken important steps in moving into fairly systematic examinations of the self-systems and in trying to operationalize it more precisely than earlier personality theorists from Freud to Rogers had done. They have not completely embedded the notion of self into a view that thought is continuous and closely tied to the arousal of emotion, an idea that was implied in the early theorizing of Tomkins and has been elaborated more recently by Singer (1974). The imagery systems represents a method for drawing on the natural patterning of ongoing thought which is, for most people, made up to a fairly high degree of continuing images as well as of some self-talking (Meichenbaum, 1978). If we keep this in mind, we can then look more systematically at what imagery can and cannot do for the therapist in the clinical situation.

REFERENCES

Bandura, A. Self-efficacy: Toward a unifying theory of behavioral change. *Psychological Review*, 1977, *84*, 191-215.
Bandura, A. Self-referent thought: The development of self-efficacy. In J. H. Flavell & L. D. Ross (Eds.), *Development of social cognition*, in press.
Cautela, J., & McCullough, L. Covert conditioning. In J. L. Singer & K. S. Pope (Eds.), *The power of human imagination*. New York: Plenum, 1978.
Dollard, J., & Miller, N. E. *Personality and psychotherapy*. New York: McGraw Hill, 1950.
Ekman, P., & Friesen, W. V. *Unmasking the face*. Englewood Cliffs, New Jersey: Prentice Hall, 1975.
Gazzaniga, M. D. *The bisected brain*. Appleton-Century-Crofts, New York, 1970.
Horowitz, M. J. Controls of visual imagery and therapist intervention. In J. L. Singer & K. S. Pope (Eds.), *The power of human imagination*. New York: Plenum, 1978.
Izard, C. *Human emotions*. New York: Plenum, 1977.
Izard, C. *Emotions in personality and psychopathology*. New York: Plenum, 1978.
Izard, C. E., & Tomkins, S. S. Affect and behavior: Anxiety as a negative affect. In C. Spielberger (Ed.), *Anxiety and behavior*. New York: Academic Press, 1966.
Janis, I. Stress and frustration. In I. Janis, G. Mahl, J. Kagan, & R. Holt, *Personality*. New York: Harcourt-Brace-World, 1969.
Klinger, E. The nature of fantasy and its clinical use. *Psychotherapy: Theory, Research and Practice*, 1977, *14*, 223-231.

Leuner, H. Basic principles and therapeutic efficacy of Guided Affective Imagery (GAI). In J. L. Singer & K. S. Pope (Eds.), *The power of human imagination.* New York: Plenum, 1978.

Little, L. M., & Curran, J. P. Covert sensitization: A clinical procedure in need of some explanations. *Psychological Bulletin,* 1978, *85,* 513-531.

McGuigan, P. J. Imagery and thinking: Covert functioning of the motor system. In G. E. Schwartz and D. Shapiro (Eds.), *Consciousness and self-regulation,* Vol. 2, New York: Plenum, 1978.

Meichenbaum, D. (Ed.), *Cognitive-behavior modification newsletter,* No. 3, 1977, University of Waterloo.

Meichenbaum, D. Why does using imagery in psychotherapy lead to change? In J. L. Singer & K. S. Pope (Eds.), *The power of human imagination.* New York: Plenum, 1978.

Neisser, U. *Cognitive psychology.* New York: Appleton-Century-Crofts, 1967.

Neisser, U. *Cognition and reality.* San Francisco: W. H. Freeman & Co., 1976.

Ornstein, R. E. *The psychology of consciousness.* Second Edition. New York: Harcourt, Brace, Jovanovich, 1977.

Paivio, A. *Imagery and verbal processes.* New York: Holt, Rinehart and Winston, 1971.

Piaget, J. *Play, dreams, and imitation in childhood.* New York: Norton, 1962.

Pope, K. S., & Singer, J. L. (Eds.), *The stream of consciousness.* New York: Plenum, 1978

Rapaport, D. The psychoanalytic theory of motivation. In M. R. Jones (Ed.), *Nebraska Symposium on Motivation.* Nebraska: University of Nebraska Press, 1960.

Reyher, J. Emergent uncovering therapy. In J. L. Singer & K. S. Pope (Eds.), *The power of human imagination.* New York: Plenum, 1978.

Schachtel, E. *Metamorphosis.* New York: Basic Books, 1959.

Schank, R. R., & Abelson, R. P. *Scripts, plans, goals, and understanding.* New York: Halsted, 1977.

Schultz, W. D. *Joy: Expanding human awareness.* New York: Grove Press, 1967.

Schwartz, G., Davidson, R. J., Maer, R., & Bromfield, E. Patterns of hemispheric dominance in musical, emotional, verbal and spatial tasks. *Paper read at Society for Psychophysiological Research* meetings, Galveston, Texas, 1973.

Schwartz, G. E., & Shapiro, D. *Consciousness and self-regulation: Advances in research,* Vol. 1. New York: Plenum, 1976.

Schwartz, G. E., & Shapiro, D., *Consciousness and self-regulation: Advances in research,* Vol. 2. New York: Plenum, 1978.

Seamon, J. Imagery codes and human information retrieval. *Journal of Experimental Psychology,* 1972, *96,* 468-470.

Shepard, R. N. The mental image. *American Psychologist,* 1978, *33,* 125-137.

Shontz, F. C. *Perceptual and cognitive aspects of body experience.* New York: Academic Press, 1969.

Singer, J. L. *Daydreaming.* New York: Random House, 1966.

Singer, J. L. *Imagery and daydream methods in psychotherapy and behavior modification.* New York: Academic Press, 1974.

Singer, J. L. *The inner world of daydreaming.* New York: Harper & Row, 1975. (a)

Singer, J. L. Navigating the stream of consciousness: Research in daydreaming and related inner experience. *American Psychologist,* 1975, *30,* 737-738.(b)

Singer, J. L., & Pope, K. S. (Eds.), *The power of human imagination.* New York: Plenum, 1978.

Tomkins, S. S. *Affect, imagery, and consciousness,* Vol. 1. New York: Springer, 1962.

Tomkins, S. S. *Affect, imagery, and consciousness,* Vol. 2. New York: Springer, 1963.

Tomkins, S. S. Script theory: Differential magnification of affects. *Nebraska Symposium on Motivation,* 1978.

4

Cerebral Asymmetries, Emotional Experience, and Imagery: Implications for Psychotherapy.[1]

ROBERT G. LEY

The behavioral manifestations of functional cerebral asymmetries in man embody a current psychological Zeitgeist, which dates from Sperry's (1968) seminal work on the effects of split-brain surgery for intractable epilepsy. By severing the corpus callosum and anterior commissure, a bundle of nerve fibers that joins the two halves of the brain, Sperry and his co-workers showed a dissociation of the experiences and capacities of the two hemispheres. His ingenious experiments provided a dramatic demonstration of the "left hand [or hemisphere] not knowing what the right hand [or hemisphere] doeth" (Matthew 6:3). The interest of both scientist and layman has been piqued by the possibility that "the mind is essentially dual" (Wigan, 1844).

Hemispheric differences in function have been marshalled to suggest explanations for a variety of behaviors, such as differences in clinical groups (Ley & Bryden, 1977) and personality styles (Day, 1968), as well as other behaviors as diverse as vocational choice (Bakan, 1971), classroom seating (Gur, Sackheim, &

[1] During the completion of this work, the author was supported by Canada Council Grant #452-783150. Portions of this paper were presented at the Second American Conference on the Fantasy and Imaging Process, Chicago, 1978. I would like to thank David Darvill, Richard Steffy, Donald Meichenbaum, and Philip Bryden for helpful comments on earlier drafts of this paper.

Robert G. Ley, Department of Psychology, University of Waterloo, Waterloo, Ontario, Canada.

Gur, 1976), tennis playing (Gallwey, 1974), and advertising strategies. Left and right hemispheric modes of cognitive style have also been used metaphorically, to elucidate differences in religious and political philosophies (Ornstein, 1972), and belief systems (Frank, 1977), the development of civilizations (Jaynes, 1976), and educational practice (McLuhan, 1977).

A variety of research strategies, involving dichotic listening and tachistoscopic paradigms, EEG alpha suppression and evoked potential, and reaction time differences have confirmed that the two cerebral hemispheres are specialized for different, cognitive functions. Typically, in right-handed people, language and arithmetic processes are primarily dependent on the left hemisphere, while the right hemisphere is specialized for spatial relations and some musical functions. However, it should be emphasized that what most characterizes each hemisphere is the way in which it works, rather than with what it works. It is not so much that each hemisphere is specialized to work with a different type of material — the left with words, the right with spatial relationships — but that each is specialized for a different cognitive style. The styles are more or less efficient in the processing of different types of material. For example, the left hemisphere has been described as a logical, analytic, and sequential processor for which words are most appropriate. The right hemisphere has been characterized as a holistic, gestalt, and diffuse processor for which spatial forms and music are most suited (Levy, Trevarthen, & Sperry, 1972; Nebes, 1971; Semmes, 1968). However, the plethora of research which has been carried out to investigate these brain and behavior correspondences has been one-sided, so to speak. The past emphasis has been largely on the cognitive side, and the emotional side of mind and man was ignored.

Recent, experimental work, however, has shown that cerebral differences in emotional experience also exist and that, in particular, the right hemisphere has a greater role than the left in processing emotional and imagic material (Ley & Bryden, 1979a; Schwartz, Davidson, & Maer, 1975). The right hemisphere also seems to predominate in a variety of states of consciousness, such as dreaming (day and night), hypnosis and meditation, as well as religious and drug-induced states, in which emotional and imagery components are salient.

In this chapter I shall review and integrate the experimental and theoretical work on hemispheric differences in affective and imagery experience, suggest that early childhood experiences are differentially coded and stored in the brain, and examine the implications of these assertions for psychotherapy.

Before proceeding, it is important that one is keenly aware of the differences between the empirical or descriptive, and metaphorical utility of hemispheric differences. The latter purpose is often intellectually enticing and sometimes results in a novel conceptualization of a problem. Unfortunately such extrapolations are often devoid of, or far removed from a data base. The recent popularity of the brain laterality domain has been fraught with considerable misinterpretation and overinterpretation of functional cerebral asymmetries, and a confusion of explanatory purposes. The litany of brain-behavior relationships in the opening para-graphs of this paper is a partial testimony to the variety of behaviors and concepts that have been related to lateral asymmetries. Social, cultural, philosophical, and psychological history abound with dichotomous formulations. However, it is most unreasonable to expect, or attempt to explain all such differences in light of cerebral hemispheric functions. Goleman (1977) has in fact, described this domain as psychology's most recent "fad" and has cautioned against the possibility that the concept of asymmetry may get out of hand. I am most mindful of such caveats. Although mediational processes in psychotherapy will be examined within a fra-mework of hemispheric information-processing "styles," the data which provide the foundation for this interpretation are reviewed and integrated. Nevertheless, the reader should be prepared for the case to be advanced here: it includes data ranging from human pathology, to the perception lab, to animal work. Some of the evidence may be viewed as circumstantial, and some of the evidence may be suspect experimentally. Methodological criticisms have been attenuated somewhat so that the presentation does not collapse in a heap of qualifications. These com-ments withstanding, the aggregate of this divergent evidence indicates a connec-tion between concepts of right hemispheric functioning, asymmetrical influences on emotions and imagery, and events in psychotherapy. It is believed that the case for this connection is both provocative and persuasive.

Hemispheric Differences in Emotional Behavior[2]

Several lines of evidence point to hemispheric mediation of, or specialization for emotionality. This evidence comes from research on clinical and normal groups.

Research on Clinical Groups

Clinical investigations of the emotional behavior of patients with unilateral brain lesions (Gainotti, 1969, 1972; Goldstein, 1939) and patients receiving sodium amobarbytal injections (Rossi & Rosadini, 1967; Terzian, 1964) have shown that a characteristic asymmetrical pattern of emotional responsivity follows unilateral hemispheric damage or intervention. Left-hemisphere lesioned patients were most likely to show "catastrophic" reactions, which included crying, swearing, anxiety reactions, and aggressive behaviors. Right-hemisphere lesioned patients were most likely to manifest "euphoric or indifferent" reactions, which included behaviors such as explicit indifference, denial, or unawareness of the disability, jokes and minimization.

---

[2] See Ley and Bryden (1979b) for an extensive review of this literature.

The descriptions of the emotional reactions of patients following hemispheric inactivation due to sodium amobarbytal injections are markedly similar (Terzian, 1964). These data suggest an asymmetry of emotional response typical of injury to either hemisphere. This conclusion is suspect however, given interpretive, methodological, and artifactual difficulties with the studies (cf. Ley & Bryden, 1977). For example, it is difficult to evaluate the extent to which premorbid personality factors account for the observed emotional behavior and whether the "catastrophic" reaction following left hemispheric inactivation is due to the loss or disruption of language. The case for a hemispheric asymmetry of emotional representation is not as well founded therefore, as the case demonstrating an overall right hemispheric superiority in representing emotionality and processing emotional stimuli.

Further clinical documentation implicates the tie between emotionality and right-hemisphere functioning. For example, study of split-brain patients has shown that the right hemisphere can independently (without verbal or linguistic mediation) generate an emotional response to an evocative stimulus (Gazzaniga, 1967). Additionally, the "mute" right hemisphere often employs emotional, gestural, or facial prompts to cue the "verbal" left hemisphere concerning the correctness or incorrectness of answers to item recognition tasks.

Research on hysterics also indicates a right hemispheric involvement. Three recent studies of hysterical conversion symptoms have demonstrated a 2:1 ratio of left-to right-sided symptoms (Galin, Diamond, & Braff, 1977; Ley, 1978; Stern, 1977). Given the crossing of the sensory and motor pathways (i.e. the left hemisphere controls the right side of the body and vice versa), the greater proportion of left-sided hysterical symptoms differentially implicates the right hemisphere. This seems to indicate that the right hemisphere may mediate the conversion of emotional experience to somatic representations. One can cautiously speculate that perhaps the right hemisphere also has a preponderant role in other "physical" complaints that are believed to have strong emotional components. The validity of such a generalization has been partially demonstrated by Kenyon's (1964) study of patients experiencing hypochondriacal states and Halliday's (1937) study of patients with nonarticular rheumatism. Both of these conditions, which have been described as psychosomatic, likewise have shown a prevalence of left-sided symptoms.

Sidedness differences are also apparent in anosognosia. Anosognosia, or "la belle indifference," is a condition in which a patient with a severe neurological deficit, such as a hemiplegia or hemianopia, is unaware of, indifferent to, or simply denies the disability. Anosognosia is most frequently found with left- rather than right-side paralysis, and Hecaen (1962) indicates that the right hemisphere is affected seven times more frequently than the left. The emotional presentation of indifference and denial, which often characterize the hysteric, are also apparent in the anosognosic.

Prosopagnosics are a relatively rare, clinical group, who as a result of cerebral disease or injury, have difficulty recognizing familiar faces. At their most extreme, prosopagnosics may not be able to differentiate faces of men, women, adults, or children, and may be unable to identify themselves in photographs or mirrors (Beyn & Knyazeva, 1962; Cole & Perez-Cruet, 1964). What is most germane to the present argument is that first, prosopagnosia typically involves damage to the right hemisphere (Hecaen & Angelergues, 1962), and second, prosopagnosics often have difficulty recognizing or comprehending emotional expressions (i.e. anger), although they are able to give a physical description of the facial or expressive features (i.e. brow furrowed, eyes narrowed, mouth drawn tight, etc.).

The final thread of clinical evidence supporting the notion of the predominant role of the right hemisphere in emotional experience can be drawn from research on the therapeutic efficacy of electroconvulsive shock treatment (ECT). It now seems to be accepted that unilateral, nondominant (right-hemisphere) ECT is more effective in remitting pathological depressions than the more traditional, bilateral, or unilateral, dominant (left-hemisphere) ECT (Galin, 1974; Robertson & Inglis, 1977). Such differential outcomes would seem to indicate differential hemispheric involvement in depression.

Deglin (1973) also investigated the effects of ECT on emotion recognition and expression. He found that patients had greater difficulty recognizing vocal intonations representing emotional expressions of happiness, sadness, or anger after electric shock administered to the right, as opposed to the left hemisphere.

The clinical literature thus suggests a predominant, right hemispheric involvement in emotional reactivity. However, one must be wary of making conclusions about normal brain functions based on observations of clinical populations. Clinical populations may exhibit multiple pathology with disparate etiology. Experimental approaches exist, however, which permit the assessment of hemispheric-laterality effects in individuals with intact nervous systems. Dichotic listening and tachistoscopic paradigms are two such techniques.

Research on Normal Subjects

Employing different methodologies and working with normal subjects, several researchers have shown right hemispheric mediation of emotional material.[3] King and Kimura (1971) showed a slight, left-ear advantage (LEA) for recognizing dichotically presented nonverbal, human sounds, such as laughing. The dichotic

---

[3] Recent experimental work has demonstrated a possible asymmetry of emotional representation in normal subjects as well (Tucker, 1977, 1978). Most of this research has utilized conjugate, lateral eye movements as a dependent variable; but its utility has been criticized by Ehrlichman and Weinberger (1978). Although it is perhaps too early to evaluate the substantiveness of such an association, Ley and Bryden (1979b) have offered potential explanations for these results.

listening procedure permits a discrete presentation of material to the left and right hemisphere. As a result, observed, lateral differences in say, response time or accuracy, are indicants of the differential involvement of each hemisphere in processing the stimulus information. For example, a LEA in recognition accuracy indicates that the right hemisphere has greater "facility" in processing the stimuli presented. A slight LEA was also reported by Haggard and Parkinson (1971) for the recognition of the emotional tone of a dichotically presented sentence. Carmon and Nachson (1973) dichotically presented nonverbal sounds, the cries, shrieks, and laughter of a child, of an adult female and of an adult male, and found a slight, LEA or right hemispheric advantage.

Safer and Leventhal (1977) had subjects listen to taped, monaural passages which had three affective levels of content (positive, neutral, and negative) and which were read in three tones of voice (positive, neutral, and negative). Subjects who listened with the left ear predominantly (right hemisphere) used the tone of voice cues to rate the passages. Again the results demonstrate a right hemispheric superiority for processing emotional information.

Suberi and McKeever (1977) tachistoscopically presented faces to the left and right visual fields, and recorded faster manual reaction times for right hemispheric memory of emotional faces. Another tachistoscopic study (Ley & Bryden, 1979a) showed significant left visual-field (right-hemisphere) superiorities for both face and emotional-expression recognition and also demonstrated the independence of these effects. It is interesting to note that the left visual-field superiority for emotional judgments in the Ley and Bryden (1979a) study was related to the degree of affective expression in the stimuli, especially to the extremely negative expressions. Dimond and Farrington (1977) also found greater, negative, affective judgment with right-hemisphere presentation of motion picture material. They obtained judgments of emotional content of films presented to each hemisphere. Significantly more ratings of "unpleasant" and "horrific" were made when the picture was viewed in the left visual field.

In summary, a substantial number of clinical and experimental observations indicate that the right hemisphere has a greater role than the left, in recognizing and processing emotional stimuli, as well as perhaps in mediating emotional experiences more generally. This asymmetry for emotion recognition can be interpreted as an expression of the right hemisphere's integrative and synthetic characteristics, and of its holistic and gestalt mode of processing information (cf. Ley & Bryden, 1979b). As indicated in the following sections, a third possible reason for this superiority may be a tripartite association between the right hemisphere, affect, and imagery.

The Right Hemisphere and Imagery

While the association between the right hemisphere and emotional stimuli has been investigated, the association between the right hemisphere and imagery has been relatively ignored. The existing basis of this latter relationship is not empirically or logically sound. It is largely inferential. For example, research has shown that hypnosis appears to be related to right hemispheric functions (Bakan, 1969). Therefore, it is assumed that, because hypnosis involves imagery, imagery should have something to do with the right hemisphere. Similar associations can be made for the right hemisphere, daydreaming or night dreaming and imagery, the right hemisphere, meditation, and imagery, and a variety of other altered states. Although the reasoning is specious, the relationship may not be. For example, it is difficult to design a study in which one can confidently separate emotion and imagery effects in a lateralized stimulus. Given sufficient, affective potency, stimulus salience, and the vast and elusive individual differences in imaging ability and cognitive styles (i.e. "picture" thinkers versus "word" thinkers), imagic and emotional stimulus components may be inextricable in practice. In short, it may be reasonable to assume a realtionship between imagery, emotionality, and the right hemisphere.[4]

A few studies have affirmed this relationship. In an EEG study, Robbins and McAdam (1974) measured interhemispheric alpha activity while subjects were engaged in covertly imaging familiar, pictorial material, in this case picture postcards. Subjects were asked to image the material in terms of the shapes and colours in the stimuli (to "form a picture in their minds"), or in terms of words (to "subvocally describe the scene"), or in terms of a combination of the two. They found suppression of alpha activity in the hemisphere engaged in the cognitive mode employed by the subject. Alpha suppression indicates the primary involvement of a hemisphere in processing information (Galin & Ornstein, 1972). Thus, when subjects were imaging the scenes in visual-spatial terms, alpha suppression was greatest over the right hemisphere. Alpha suppression over the left hemisphere during imaging in linguistic terms was also demonstrated. The Robbins and McAdam study implicates the association between the right hemisphere and visual imagery. Likewise Morgan, McDonald, and MacDonald (1971) demonstrated an EEG alpha asymmetry over the right hemisphere during questions that

---

[4] Implicitly, the association seems indisputable, if one assumes that imagery is a subset or component of visual-spatial skills. Visual-spatial abilities have been firmly linked to the right hemisphere (Galin & Ellis, 1975; Galin & Ornstein, 1972). Explicitly, the term "imagery" is notable by its absence from laterality studies of visual-spatial abilities. The inferential leap is left to the reader. In short, the association between the right hemisphere and imagery is a reasonable one, if we assume that it is closely related to visualizing or "spatializing" abilities. The association seems gratuitous, except in the case of imaging in verbal modes (Day, 1977; Robbins & McAdam, 1974).

required visualizing of various scenes. Another study in a different domain also supports the imagery and right-hemisphere association. Cohen, Berent, and Silverman (1973) have shown that right-hemisphere, unilateral ECT produces memory decrement in a nonverbal recall task involving visual imagery. But what of emotionality?

Davidson and Schwartz (1976) designed an ingenious study which varied mode of imagery and affect. They recorded EEG activity while subjects self-induced covert affective and nonaffective states using either verbal or visual strategies. During the emotional trials, subjects were asked to "relive the feelings" of angry and relaxing scenes from their past which they had previously selected and rated as very intense. The visual imagery terms required writing of a letter to a friend describing the situation. Nonemotional trials involved imaging the activities of a particular day. They found that the self-generation of affective imagery was associated with significantly greater, relative right-hemisphere activation than was the self-generation of nonaffective imaging.

Failure of a modality condition in the Davidson and Schwartz study also is intriguing. A nonsignificant difference was found between the verbal- and visual-imagery modes, although, as hypothesized, the effect was in the direction of the right hemisphere. A possible reason for this failure is the inextricability of affect and image, as mentioned above. Seventy per cent of the subjects spontaneously mentioned that it was extremely difficult to perform the verbal-emotional trials in the absence of visual imagery. This outcome supports a contention that these modes may be separable (i.e. left- and right-hemisphere effects), if the task is relatively benign or emotionally uninvolving. This was the case in the Robbins and McAdam (1974) study, which employed visual and verbal imaging of picture postcards. If however, the stimulus is potent and arousing, such as the intensely negative, personal experiences of the Davidson and Schwartz study, the right hemisphere is primarily engaged. Simply put, the imagic and affective components of the stimulus "overwhelm" the verbal or cognitive components, and the predicted separation of effects is mitigated. This line of argument also suggests that in those studies reviewed above investigating the right hemisphere and emotional stimuli, a significant proportion of the difference may be accounted for by the covariation of imagery and affect. Although in most of these studies the stimuli were perhaps too benign to evoke any imagery, one can speculate that more lifelike stimuli such as screams, laughter, gruesome faces, or horrifying emotional scenes could induce the subjects' imaging. This possibility is exemplified in a study by Schwartz, Davidson, and Maer (1975).

Schwartz et al. recorded subjects' conjugate lateral eye movements (LEMS) to emotional or neutral questions and also varied the verbal and spatial dimensons of the questions. They found significantly greater left LEMS to emotional than to nonemotional questions. Again remembering the contralateral innervation of the human body, this result is presumed to represent a greater activation of the right hemisphere in responding to emotional questions. Tucker, Roth, Arneson, and Buckingham (1977) replicated this finding and additionally found that left, lateral eye movements increased under a stress condition, which suggests perhaps that stress, or emotional arousal, increases the likelihood of right hemispheric activation. Although both the Schwartz et al. and Tucker et al. results offer support for the notion of the association between the right hemisphere and emotionality, it is difficult to assess the extent to which imaging accompanied affective questions. Given the nature of the imagery questions (i.e. "visualize your father's face"), it is probably safe to conclude that such instructions "pull" for both imagery and affective responses.

Research on lateral eye movements offers further, but tentative, support for the idea of an association between imagery and the right hemisphere. It had been observed that when people are asked a question requiring momentary reflection, they will typically avert their gaze before answering: they tend to look briefly to either the left or right (Bakan, 1971; Day, 1968). This lateral directionality of eye movement has been related to the asymmetry of the human brain. Since activation of each hemisphere produces orientation to the contralateral side of the body, left lateral eye movements presumably represent the primary engagement of the right hemisphere, and right, lateral eye movements represent left hemispheric activation. Individuals also seem to differ in the extent to which they tend to look in one direction or the other, and consequently can be classified as either "left or right lookers." A few studies in this area are relevant here. Bakan (1969) found that in comparison to right-looking men, left-looking men were likely to show a greater use of imagery and tended to rate their visual imagery as clearer. Harnad (1972) found that left-looking mathematicians tended to utilize imagery to a greater degree than right movers in solving problems. Meskin and Singer (1974) reported left lookers to be more "inner attentive" than right lookers, as measured by the Singer-Antrobus Imaginal Processes Inventory, and to experience greater vividness of imagery

Other studies, however, have failed to corroborate the association between imagery and the right hemisphere. Hiscock (1977) found no differences between left and right movers on the Paivio Individual Differences Questionnaire, which serves to evaluate the extent to which a person thinks in words or pictures (verbally or imaginally). In another study, it was reported that left and right movers did not differ in mental imagery on the Betts Questionnaire (Wolf-Dorlester, 1976).

Generally, it is difficult to evaluate the validity of the eye movement research. In a recent review (Ehrlichman & Weinberger, 1978), exception is taken to the three main premises of this literature: that the hemispheric model accounts for the occurrence of an eye movement following a question, that the model of hemispheric asymmetry is grounded in a neurophysiological context, and that left/right differences in ocular response indicate asymmetrical, hemispheric activation. These authors conclude that "there is at present insufficient evidence for accepting the model (the hemispheric asymmetry model of LEMs), and hence little justification for using LEMs as a method for studying hemispheric function" (p. 1098). They also note that the data in regard to LEMs and visual imagery are "discouraging." They point out however that the research on LEMs and emotionality is perhaps the most unequivocal in a research domain that is suspect because of poor methodology and conjectural theoretical grounding.

Mindful of Ehrlichman and Weinberger's caveats however, there still seems to be enough evidence for assuming the existence of a relationship between visual imagery and the right hemisphere, particulary if the purview is widened to include the wealth of studies demonstrating a strong, right hemispheric superiority for visual-spatial tasks (Galin & Ellis, 1975; Galin & Ornstein, 1972).

Evidence for a Right Hemisphere Coding and Storage of Early-Childhood Experiences

To this point, data has been reviewed which demonstrate that the right hemisphere has a greater role than the left, in mediating emotional experience and perhaps visual imagery. Before discussing the implications of this relationship for psychotherapy, it is necessary to digress and consider why this right hemispheric advantage may exist. The argument will be restricted to the ontogenic case, rather than the phylogenic. Jaynes (1976) presents a provocative case for the phylogenic development of cerebral asymmetries.

William James described the infant's world as a "booming and buzzing" confusion. The present contention is that these "booms and buzzes" are coded and stored primarily by the right hemisphere. The reason for this assertion is that evidence has shown that the right hemisphere of the brain develops more rapidly than the left, until about 18-24 months, when left hemispheric differentiation for language begins (Giannitrapani, 1967; Lenneberg, 1967). Because of these cerebral, maturational differences, it is assumed that the right hemisphere possibly has a greater involvement in processing and storing the young child's experience. Much of the prelinguistic child's world consists of visual-spatial relations, patterns, environmental sounds and rhythms. These are also the very same functions which are better established and processed in the right hemisphere. It is further argued that the emotional experiences of the infant — the sounds, pictures, images, and "feelings" which constitute much of an infant's early experiences — are disproportionately processed and stored by the right hemisphere during the formative stages of the brain. The rudimentary predominance of the right hemisphere eventually yields to the dominance of the left hemisphere as the child's cognitive-linguistic apparatus develops and outstrips the processing capacity of the right hemisphere

Nevertheless, the right hemisphere has been relatively specialized for visual-spatial tasks, emotional stimuli, and imagic functions during this period. The research reviewed previously showing a right hemispheric bias for these processes is supportive of this assertion.

One reason why the right hemisphere may be specialized for visual-spatial and emotional tasks is that it predominates at a period when these functions are most salient. It may have been necessary for the right hemisphere to develop these abilities and once developed, they remain. The left hemisphere, however, develops more slowly up to a point where language is becoming or has become most salient.

This argument is assailable on two counts however. First, it is dangerous to argue for childhood developmental differences on the basis of adult data, particularly between subjects. Second, it is a weak position to assert anatomical or biological differences based on indirect, behavioral observations. The quintessential study has not yet been carried out. Such a study would assess an individual's performance on a variety of visual-spatial and cognitive, lateralized tasks, at different, developmental periods from infancy to adulthood. It is easy to see why such a within-subject, longitudinal study has not yet been performed, as even a cross-sectional study is experimentally "expensive" and fraught with interpretive difficulties.

Although a dearth of direct evidence exists, it is possible to adduce other evidence, the accretion of which, supports a hypothesis of differential storage of childhood emotional experiences. The evidence is diverse and varies greatly in experimental rigor.

The first realm to be considered is research on eidetic imagery. Eidetic ability is the ability to "hold" a perception of a stimulus for several minutes following the removal of the stimulus. The eidetic image is much more enduring than an afterimage (and also does not require a fixed gaze), and the image can continue to be viewed as naturally and in as much detail as if the stimulus were still present (Jaensch, 1930; Haber & Haber, 1964). Some eidetic images seem indistinguishable from perceptions, even by objective criteria. In cases of exceptional eidetic ability, images can be held, superimposed, and recalled, hours, days, and even years later (Luria, 1960; Stromeyer & Psotka, 1970). What is most germane to the present argument is that eidetic imagery is negatively related to age. In other words, there is a greater incidence of eidetic imagery among young children (Morsh & Abbott, 1945; Teasdale, 1934) For example, Teasdale reported that 12.5% of his sample had eidetic imagery in their 10th year, while only 2% of the 14-year-olds could be classified as "eidetikers." The most reasonable explanation for the loss of this ability as the child approaches puberty, is that eidetic imagery is a component of a more general mode of concrete functioning which gives way to the more economical and adaptive, cognitive, abstract mode of thought and language.

Piaget has also hypothesized that a child shifts from *concrete* to *formal* cognitive operations around the age of 11 or 12 (Flavell, 1963). Prior to the acquisition of formal operations, the child tends to operate in a manner strikingly reminiscent of the ways of the eidetic child. The child's orientation is towards the concrete in organizing and structuring activities. Concrete operations are not concerned with the future or with what is possible, much as an eidetic image or ability cannot deal with the future. In contrast, formal operations *are* symbolizing and future oriented; hence, they would be incompatible with a continued use of eidetic images which involve present and past events. This developmental, cognitive shift also is supported by Lenneberg's (1967) report that left hemispheric lateralization of language is stabilized around the age of 12. Recent dichotic listening studies are also consistent with a "lateralization-by-puberty" hypothesis (Bryden, 1973; Bryden & Allard, 1978). With respect to eidetic imagery specifically, and cognitive functions more generally, it seems that words supercede images. Richardson (1969) explains the disappearance of this capacity as follows:

During the preadolescent period of physical and cerebral maturation the increased capacity for abstract thought is stimulated and encouraged in most school subjects. In accord with this trend, linguistic skills in oral and written expression take precedence over the inexpressible image. Though some personally experienced events may continue to be registered with something of their original sensory-affective quality, such events are also categorized in more abstract terms. Language is used more and more to compress, to represent and to express our experience. It is typically of more practical use for me to recall *that* I went to the post office yesterday and left a book on the counter when buying half a dozen four-cent stamps, than it is to recall *what* the sensory-affective experience of being in the post office was actually like. To re-see re-hear and re-feel the experience is uneconomical. Under these conditions it is perhaps not so surprising that the ability to use eidetic imagery in those who once possessed it begins to wither away from lack of use. Once lost it is not usually regained (p. 40).

It is being proposed that eidetic imagery is a function and vestige of the right hemisphere's storage of sensory-affective experience, and is a mode of operating characteristic of the young child. Consistent with this interpretation and the above information on eidetic imagery is Khatena's (1976) report of a decline in imagery in preadolescents. Khatena reported that this drop correlates with the more general fourth-grade decrease of creativity as suggested by Torrance (1970). Gowan (1978) has recently implied that these findings reflect "a transfer from the right-hemisphere processing of images to the left-hemisphere processing of verbal material" (p. 222).

It is interesting to note that the incidence of eidetic imagery is greater in those non-Western cultures in which life places greater demands on visual-spatial abilities. For example, two nonliterate societies in Africa, the Tiv of Central Kenya and the Ibo of Eastern Nigeria, have an incidence of eidetic imagery double that which occurs in our society (Doob, 1964, 1965). It has also been argued that such cultures are right-hemisphere cultures, while Western society is prototypically left hemisphere (Ornstein, 1972).

Dreaming shows a similar relationship to age as does eidetic imagery. Although the relationship is complicated and far from the unitary one initially hypothesized (Aserinsky & Kleitman, 1953), dreaming is assumed to be in rough correspondence with rapid eye movements or REM activity. REM periods, like eidetic imagery, are negatively related to age (Roffwarg, Muzio, & Dement, 1966). REM sleep constitutes about 20% of a sleep period in human adults. In neonates however, the proportionate amount of REM sleep is about 50%, and this ratio is halved by the time the child reaches age 3. By early adolescence REM periods are present for only 18% of the sleep cycle.

Data are now converging which seem to indicate that dreaming is primarily a function of the right hemisphere (Bakan, 1976, 1978). Research from EEG (Goldstein, Stoltzfus, & Gardocki, 1972), lateral eye movement (Bakan, 1976), and split-brain studies (Bogen, 1969) also suggests this association. For example, Goldstein et al. (1972) found a shift towards greater EEG activity in the right hemisphere immediately before the sleeper entered a REM period. Humphrey and Zangwill (1951) reported that patients with right hemispheric brain injury had lost the ability to dream and had, more generally, lost the capacity for visual imagery. Bogen (1969) noted that split-brain patients reported the absence of dreams following surgery. If indeed a relationship between the right hemisphere and dreaming does exist, and the relative diminution of dreaming with age does occur, the hypothesis that the right hemisphere may have an accelerated development and preponderant influence in the young child is supported. But this evidence is not pristine, as REM periods are greater still in the premature infant and fetus and also present in lower animals. Many of us would doubt the presence of "real" dreams in rats and bats and unborn children. This finding does not however invalidate the implication of the predominance of the right hemisphere in first, REM periods and second, the infant's life, especially when one considers that the world of lower animals and intrauterine children is almost exclusively a sensory-perceptual and not a cognitive-linguistic one.

A recent study of the asymmetrical, hemispheric distribution of early experiences would offer strong, confirmatory evidence for an association between the right hemisphere, emotionality, and infantile experience, were the subjects studied Purdue undergraduates rather than Purdue-Wistar laboratory rats. Denenberg, Garbanti, Sherman, Yutzey, and Kaplan, (1978) after reviewing similar literature to the above which demonstrated hemispheric differences in processing emotional stimuli, were likewise intrigued by the question of how these differences arise. Denenberg, an eminent "rat psychologist," turned to his preferred methodology and subject pool.

Evidence of brain asymmetry had been reported in rats (Zimmerberg, Glick, & Jerussi, 1974); and the effects of infantile experience on adult-rat behaviors, including exploratory activity and emotionality, had also been reported (Denenberg, 1969). The relationship between early experiences, laterality effects, and adult behaviors had not been studied however. The first, experimental variable in the Denenberg study was handling, since previous research had demonstrated that handling reduced emotionality and increased exploratory behavior. Emotionality in the case of the rat is defined as the degree of exploration in an open-field activity test. For example, an animal which huddles in the corner of the field and refuses to explore, would be operationally defined as more emotional, than one which moves freely about the field. Emotionality and exploratory activity are inversely related in this case. The second, experimental variable was rearing in enriched versus non-enriched environments, as an enriched environment has also been found to reduce emotionality and increase exploration (Denenberg & Morton, 1962). Finally, the rats underwent one of four surgical procedures: either a left or right neocortical ablation, a sham operation, or no surgery. One result of this ingenious study is most provocative with respect to the hypothesis presently being advanced. Denenberg et al. found significant activity differences amongst rats which were handled in infancy and which received left or right hemispheric ablations. The removal of the right brains caused extreme scores: handled rats without enriched environments were the most active (i.e. the least "emotional"), and handled rats exposed to the enriched environments were the least active. Denenberg concludes:

The results show lateralization of a behavioral function in lower mammals and confirm the hypothesis that the effects of early experience are asymmetrically distributed in the brain. The right brain is the repository for the interactive effects of handling and environment enrichment, at least as far as open-field activity is concerned (p. 1151).

Although the generalizability of such findings is suspect, studies of learned helplessness (Seligman, 1973), population density (Calhoun, 1962), and even cigarette smoking (Perard, 1967) have shown the extrapolation from mouse to man to be instructive in some instances. The important point to be taken from the Denenberg study is that the lateralization of affective and visual-spatial functions is likely phylogenetically older than lateralization of cognitive processes. If for a moment, one juxtaposes the Denenberg results and the generally discredited notion that "ontogeny recapitulates phylogeny", more evidence accrues for the notion of the preponderant influence of the right hemisphere in the infant and the disproportionate "loading" of experiences especially of a sensory-affective kind. The implications of the Denenberg study for child rearing and for expectations of cross-cultural laterality differences are also compelling, but they are beyond the purview of this chapter.

Finally, there is one last line of evidence which argues that early experiences exert a strong force upon later emotional behavior, and hints at the possibility that they may be differentially stored. The genetic principle of dynamic psychology embodies such a belief. Psychoanalytic theory explicitly states that early-childhood experiences influence adult emotional behavior. In a prescient paper, Galin (1974) suggests the possibility that the right hemisphere controls the unconscious processes that influence normal behavior. The incommensurability of the prearticulate, affective experience of the right hemisphere and the verbal, cognitive experience of the left hemisphere has also been described by Galin. The commonalities between clinical, dissociative experiences, such as hysterical-conversion symptoms, and the behavior of split-brain patients, and the real and proposed brain mechanisms for these conditions have been presented above.

A New Formulation of Infantile Amnesia

At this point, a reinterpretation of the analytic construct of infantile amnesia has utility for the implications of the brain laterality, emotionality, and imagery association for psychotherapy. Freud asserted that individuals were amnestic for those childhood experiences which occurred before the age of about 6 years. Freud (1938) formulated the problem thus:

"I refer to the peculiar amnesia which veils from most people (not from all) the first years of their childhood, usually the first six or eight years. So far, it has not occurred to us that this amnesia should surprise us, though we have good reasons for few incomprehensible memory fragments, we have vividly reacted to impressions that we have manifested human pain and pleasure and that we have expressed love, jealousy and other passions as they then affected us. Still we know nothing of all this when we become older. Why does our memory lag behind all our other psychic activities? We really have reason to believe that at no time of life are we more capable of impressions and reproductions than during the years of childhood" (p. 581).

Freud integrated this type of forgetting with his theory of infantile sexuality; as a result, emotional experiences generally and traumatic experiences specifically, may be repressed ("forgotten") because of their unacceptable and anxiety-arousing nature. Adults have difficulty under normal conditions recollecting events that occurred before the age of 5 or 6. Confabulated memories, prompted by pictures or accounts for instance, often pass for genuine memories. Veridical and unfettered memories are much rarer. Although empirical investigations of infantile amnesia are scant, an informal survey of friends or one's own personal reminiscences will support the contention. Although in agreement with the principle, the mechanism can be reinterpreted in the following way. Because of the relatively greater development and influence of the right hemisphere during this developmental period, early childhood experiences are primarily processed, coded, and stored in the right hemisphere. This *coding* is most likely to be of a nonverbal, imagic, or sensory-affective kind. As a result, these experiences are difficult to *decode* or "remember" by a verbal, linguistic, or cognitive means, which is the most typical recollective strategy employed by adults. Developmentally, these experiences are processed and stored when right hemispheric, conscious modes predominate (before the age of 3 or 4), and the retrieval attempts are occurring while left hemispheric modes of thought predominate (postadolescence). Simply put, one cannot use a left hemispheric key to open a right hemispheric lock. David McClelland (1960) articulates the above in the following passage from his classic textbook:

A child experiences a great many things during the first eighteen to twenty-four months of his life before he has symbol systems developed to the point where they can adequately represent what he has experienced. We have discussed how important language is in shaping mental content. What about all those experiences which occur before language or "consciousness" develops? One can either assume that they are of relatively little importance in determining subsequent behavior because they have not been symbolized, or that they go on influencing behavior but in a way which is relatively independent of the symbol systems developed in connection with later experiences. The latter assumption, which certainly seems more reasonable, is essentially the one the psychoanalysts have made in arguing for the importance of the "unconscious." If we read for "unconscious" some such term as "unverbalized" or "unsymbolized," it is easy to see on theoretical grounds why early experiences might continue to exert a disproportionate influence on subsequent behavior because they are not under symbolic control. In short, early experiences may assume such great importance in personality because they are not represented by the kinds of symbols, particularly verbal, which facilitate subsequent discrimination, assimilation, extinction, and control (p. 343).

One can easily reconstrue this passage within the framework of left and right hemispheric modes of experience and "communication." The left hemispheric symbol system is contraindicated for retrieving or "remembering" the unsymbolized, early experiences of the right.

To this point, experiments have been reviewed and a case has been made for a functional relationship between emotional experience, imagery, and the right hemisphere of the brain. Additionally, it has been argued that early-childhood experiences are differentially coded and stored by the right hemisphere and that they are not easily accessible to left hemispheric cognitive strategies. How then is this important for psychotherapy and therapeutic change?

Implications of An Association of Imagery, Emotional Experience, and the Right Hemisphere for Psychotherapy

The working assumption is that most therapeutic strategies, whether psychoanalytic, gestalt-experiential, semantic, or behavioral, are attempts at "communicating" with the right hemisphere. Therapies differ in the extent to which they attempt to gain access to a right hemispheric repository of experience, such as insight or cathartic therapies, or the extent to which they employ right hemispheric modes of thought to "operate" in the present or future. These latter strategies are likely to be more cognitive or behavioral in orientation. A diversity of psychotherapies can be construed as attempts at creating an environment that is congenial to right hemispheric mentation and facilitative of such a mode of experience. There are three primary features of therapy that contribute to the creation of a right hemispheric environment. These are, the therapeutic setting, the therapeutic "words," and the therapeutic "task." The latter two desgnations may seem to be an odd choice of words, but they will hopefully be clarified with elaboration.

The Therapeutic Setting

The setting employed in classical psychoanalysis might be considered prototypical of one type that would encourage right hemispheric mentation. The patient is reclining, staring at a continous, undifferentiated ceiling, and receiving relatively minimal tactile and verbal stimulation. It is not unlike sensory-deprivation conditions which have a tendency to facilitate right hemispheric experiences, such as illogical, prearticulate, hallucinatory, or heavily imagic associations (Brownfield, 1972). Other therapeutic settings, especially experiential, meditative, or reflective ones (such as those utilized in relaxation training) can also be viewed as facilitating a right hemispheric state.

The client's physical position within the therapeutic setting might also differentially engage the right hemisphere; for, research has shown that posture has a demonstrable effect on the nature and "flow" of thought processes (Pope & Singer, 1978). In fact there seem to be qualitative differences in thought in vertical and horizontal body positions (Pope, 1978). Beigel (1952) found that a reclining position has a tendency to remove reality constraints from mental processes. Similarly, Kroth (1970) has reported that people free-associate with greater ease and spontaneity in a reclining position. Most significant for the hypothesis associating the right hemisphere, imagery, and childhood experiences are reports that vivid imagery increased in a sensory-deprivation study when the subjects were reclining (Morgan & Bakan, 1965), and that more and earlier memories were evoked when subjects were reclining rather than sitting (Berdach & Bakan, 1967). After studying the relationship between thought processes and body positions, G. S. Klein (1976) concluded that one of Freud's most intuitive insights was the recognition of the importance of the couch in the association process of a psychoanalytic therapy hour.

The nature of the cognitive processes described in the above research seems similar to that of right hemispheric productions. Numerous therapeutic settings feature the client in a reclining or prone position: two examples are systematic desensitization and psychoanalysis. This position may be considered to activate right hemispheric material, such as imagic, sensory-kinesthetic, and emotional experiences. Alternatively, few psychotherapies require the client to stand or sit "bolt upright," other than particular variants of in vivo desensitization procedures, such as those that might be used for crowd or public-speaking phobics. Although a direct test of a correlation between body position and functional, hemispheric asymmetries has yet to be made, extant evidence would seem to favor such a hypothesis.

The Therapeutic "Words"

The fact that words and the left hemisphere are strongly associated, would seem to invalidate a claim that psychotherapy or "talk therapies" are a right hemispheric experience. Naturally, we are culturally bound to linguistic communication. However, the words which are used in psychotherapy and the way in which they are used set "talk therapies" clearly apart from normal discourse. When imagery-laden or emotionally evocative words are used, especially in a creative, nonlinear, nonsyntactic fashion, the right hemisphere is primed. Research has demonstrated an association between the right hemisphere and imagic, emotional words (Day, 1977).

Psychotherapists seem to employ words in this manner. The basic rule of psychoanalysis, in which the patient is asked to relax and to say everything that occurs to him/her, reporting whatever thoughts, feelings, and impulses come to mind, is an examplar of such word use. Free association techniques primarily tap right hemispheric productions, which are nevertheless mediated by words. The variety of inductive techniques employed in hypnosis are further examples of using figurative, dreamlike, imagery-laden words to gain access to the right hemisphere. In short, the difference between right hemispheric and left hemispheric language is like the difference between the language of poetry and of economics.

Free associative language also seems closely allied with primary-process thinking. Fenichel (1945) has stated that primary-process thinking is "carried out more through pictorial, concrete images, whereas the secondary process is based more on words . . . [primary process thinking] is remote from any logic. But it is thinking nevertheless because it consists of imaginations according to which later actions are performed" (p. 47). Fenichel (1945) stressed that "such pictorial thinking . . . is less fitted for objective judgment because . . . [it is] relatively unorganized, primitive, magical, undifferentiated, based on common motor reactions, ruled by emotions, full of wishful fearful misconceptions, archaic, vague, regressive, primal . . . [lacking] in intellectual interest . . . and [typified] by emotional fantasy" (p. 47). The parallels with right hemispheric processes are apparent. An association between the right hemisphere, primary process thinking, and unconscious process has also been elaborated by Galin (1974).

Horowitz (1972) has proposed a model of defensive mechanisms founded on modes of ideational representation. Two of these modes are designated as "imagic" and "lexical" or verbal modes. These can be broadly construed as relating to right and left hemispheric styles. Horowitz argues that many patients' experiences are more vividly, intensely represented and finely articulated in an image than in a lexical mode. Furthermore, lexical representations are more likely to be constrained by conscious censoring processes, and he notes efforts by Freud and Jung to circumvent patients' avoidances of threatening material by having them think in images rather than words. However, these experiences must nevertheless be communicated linguistically, and the words chosen by the patient must necessarily be of the same ilk as the experience and/or gradually approximate it.

Watzlawick (1978) has suggested that it is the bizarre language of the unconscious which is the domain of therapeutic change. Rather than engage the patient in the "translation" phase of psychotherapy in which the patient is "given" the jargon of a particular psychotherapeutic theory (Frank, 1974; Meichenbaum, 1977), the therapist should learn the patient's language and thereby facilitate the recollection and description of inarticulate experiences. In short, Watzlawick argues for patient and therapist communication in what has been described above as the language of the right hemisphere.

Watzlawick discusses a number of features of language patterns that he believes characterize right hemispheric language. These aspects of right hemispheric communication are (a) condensation, which includes such things as neologisms and slips of the tongue, (b) figurative language, (c) *pars pro toto,* or the manner in which constituent parts can substitute or evoke complex wholes: a classic example occurs in Proust's *Swann's Way* when the protagonist bites into a tea-soaked cake and is instantly overtaken by a stream of childhood memories, (d) aphorisms, in which two thoughts or concepts are related in an unusual or striking way, such as the slogan of the National Rifle Association: "If guns are outlawed, only outlaws will have guns" (Watzlawick, p. 77), and (e) ambiguities, puns, and allusions.

Watzlawick has proposed that these features of language use are most conducive to right hemispheric communication, and therapists should invoke such linguistic techniques.

Watzlawick also suggests another means of gaining access to the right hemisphere, namely to block or skirt the logical, analytical processes of the left hemisphere. He describes a number of techniques, such as "confusion," koans, paradoxical intent, symptom displacement, doublebinding, reframing, and illusions of alternatives which "circumvent the left hemisphere ... thereby permitting the right to become dominant" (p. 91.) Most of these methods are drawn from the unique and ingenious hypnotherapeutic strategies of Milton Erickson. Although Watzlawick's "neurologizing" is suspect, his linguistic prescriptions of therapeutic communication are reasonable and consistent with left and right hemispheric cognitive modes.

The Therapeutic "Task"

Finally, the various *tasks* imposed on the patient in psychotherapy differentially involve the right hemisphere. Clearly, the common denominator of Watzlawick's techniques for "blocking" the left hemisphere is that they are mostly direct prescriptions for certain behaviors. For example, in Erickson's (1964) "confusion" technique, direct therapeutic suggestions are embedded in a stream of obtuse, complicated inanities. Bateson's (1972) double binding and Frankl's (1960) paradoxical intention techniques involve a symptom prescription which prohibits the attempted solution and, as a result, the symptom. Bandler and Grinder (1975) describe such an instance: a patient whose symptom was an inability to say "no" was ordered by the therapist to say "no" to every member of the group. The paradox or "bind" is apparent.

The implicit association in Watzlawick's thesis between specific linguistic techniques and the right hemisphere is not empirically as well grounded as an association between imagery and the right hemisphere however.

It is most likely that explicit imagery techniques in psychotherapy activate the right hemisphere, as demonstrated by studies reviewed above. Numerous and varied imagery techniques exist; over 20 specific imagery strategies could be cited (Meichenbaum, 1978; Sheikh & Panagiotou, 1975; Singer, 1974). Wolpe's (1958) systematic desensitization, Cautela's (1977) covert conditioning, Lazarus' (1976) BASIC ID technique, Ahsen's[5] (1968) eidetic psychotherapy, Leuner's (1977) guided affective imagery, and Morrison and Cometa's (1977) emotive-reconstructive psychotherapy all involve specific imagery techniques and affective invocations, as do many other behavioral and psychodynamic approaches to varying degrees.

Other specific interventions, such as Carl Whittaker's (1976) and John Rosen's (1953) use of a baby bottle to feed patients, can be considered as likely to evoke right hemispheric memories and processes. The strongly regressive aspects of primal therapy (Janov, 1970), in which the client lies on a mat, may cuddle a plush toy or "security" blanket, or may be gently rocked or held by a therapist, may invoke similar processes. Therapies which involve considerable touching, holding, massaging, sensory awareness, or sensitivity training (i.e. the so-called "touchy-feelies") may also induce right hemispheric recollections of times when such physical involvements were primary and potent, such as infancy and childhood.

The search for commonalities among psychotherapies and common therapeutic - change mechanisms (Frank, 1974; Meichenbaum, 1977) has largely overlooked the possibility that a variety of therapeutic techniques may engage right hemispheric experiences and mentation. For example, a relationship between imagery tasks and the right hemisphere may be one reason such a host of therapeutic strategies, borne of diverse theoretical predispositions, enjoy similar success. Similarly, more cathartic or "depth" approaches strive for greater insight and elicitation of affect. In so doing, these strategies may also primarily engage right hemispheric processes. Finally, therapeutic interventions that aim for patient experiential regression (primal therapy), transpositions (psychodrama), or role play-

[5] Ahsen (1977) has recently written on the hemispheric structural method. This diagnostic and therapeutic technique focuses on the subject's eidetic images of his/her parents, the left-right localization in space, horizontal-vertical distances, displacement, and the perceptual pull of the images. The effects on perception, displacement, and emotional memories are studied.

ing (gestalt or behavioral techniques) also may differentially "turn on" the right hemisphere or gain access to its repository of experiences and memories.

In summary, a case has been presented for considering the right hemisphere as the primary mediator of a variety of therapeutic experiences and techniques. In elaborating this speculation, hemispheric modes have been used in a more metaphoric sense, in order to offer a novel conceptualization as to a possible mediational mechanism in the therapeutic process. However, this assumption is grounded in the research on emotional and imagic asymmetries reviewed previously.

In the above, the therapeutic setting, "words," and "tasks" have been separated for expository purposes. It was not intended that these be regarded as separate, or even separable, effects. The interactive nature of these features embodies the gestalt principle, "that the whole is more than the sum of the parts." The reciprocal and combinative influence of setting, "words," and "task" engender what Theodore Reik (1948) has called the "therapeutic atmosphere." It has been argued that the atmosphere and language necessary for psychotherapeutic change are right hemispheric and that a variety of psychotherapeutic techniques can create such an environment and mode of communication.

REFERENCES

Ahsen, A. *Basic concepts in eidetic psychotherapy.* New York: Brandon House, 1968.

Ahsen, A. Eidetics: An overview. *Journal of Mental Imagery,* 1977, *1*, 5-38.

Aserinsky, E., & Kleitman, N. Regularly occurring periods of eye motility and concommitant phenomena during sleep. *Science,* 1953, *118*, 273.

Bakan, P. Hypnotizability, laterality of eye movement, and functional brain asymmetry. *Perceptual and Motor Skills,* 1969, *28*, 927-932.

Bakan, P. The eyes have it. *Psychology Today,* 1971, *4*, (Apr.), 65-67.

Bakan, P. The right brain is the dreamer. *Psychology Today,* 1976, *11*, (Nov.), 66-68.

Bakan, P. Dreaming, REM sleep, and the right hemisphere: A theoretical integration. *Journal of Altered States of Consciousness,* 1978, *3*, 285-307.

Bandler, R., & Grinder, J. *The structure of magic, I.* Palo Alto: Science & Behavior Books, 1975.

Bateson, G. *Steps to an ecology of mind.* New York: Ballantine Books, 1972.

Beigel, H. G. The influence of body position on mental processes. *Journal of Clinical Psychology,* 1952, *8*, 193-199.

Berdach, E., & Bakan, P. Body position and free recall of early memories. *Psychotherapy: Theory, Research, and Practice,* 1967, *4*, 101-102.

Beyn, E. S., & Knyazeva, G. R. The problem of prosopagnosia. *Journal of Neurology, Neurosurgery, and Psychiatry,* 1962, *25*, 154-158.

Bogen, J. The other side of the brain: An oppositional mind. *Bulletin of the Los Angeles Neurological Society,* 1969, *34*, 135-162.

Brownfield, C. *The brain benders: A study of the effects of isolation.* New York: Exposition Press, 1972.

Bryden, M. P. Perceptual asymmetry in vision: Relation to handedness, eyedness, and speech lateralization. *Cortex,* 1973, *9*, 418-432.

Bryden, M. P., & Allard, F. Dichotic listening and the development of linguistic processes. In M. Kinsbourne (Ed.), *Hemispheric asymmetry of function.* London: Cambridge University Press, 1978.

Calhoun, J. B. Population density and social pathology. *Scientific American*, 1962, *206*, 139-150.

Carmon, A., & Nachson, I. Ear asymmetry in perception of non-verbal stimuli. *Acta Psychologica*, 1973, *37*, 351-357.

Cautela, J. Covert conditioning: Assumptions and procedures. *Journal of Mental Imagery*, 1977, *1*, 53-64.

Cohen, B., Berent, S., & Silverman, A. J. Field dependence and lateralization of function in the human brain. *Archives of General Psychiatry*, 1973, *28*, 165-167.

Cole, M., & Perez-Cruet, J. Prosopagnosia. *Neuropsychologia*, 1964, *2*, 237-246.

Davidson, R., & Schwartz, G. Patterns of cerebral lateralization during cardiac biofeedback versus the self-regulation of emotion: Sex Differences. *Psychophysiology*, 1976, *13*, 62-74.

Day, J. H. Right hemisphere language processing in normal right handers. *Journal of Experimental Psychology: Human Perception and Performance*, 1977, *3*, 518-528.

Day, M. E. Attention, anxiety and psychotherapy. *Psychotherapy: Theory, Research, and Practice*, 1968, *78*, 189-195.

Deglin, V. L. Clinical-experimental studies of unilateral electroconvulsive shock. *Journal of Neuropathology and Psychiatry*, 1973, *11*, 1609-1621.

Denenberg, V. H. In E. Hafez (Ed.), *The behavior of domestic animals*. London: Balliere, Tindall & Cassell, 1969.

Denenberg, V. H., Garbanti, J., Sherman, G., Yutzey, D., & Kaplan, R. Infantile stimulation induces brain lateralization in rats. *Science*, 1978, *201*, 1150-1151.

Denenberg, V. H., & Morton, J. C. Effects of environmental complexity and social groupings upon modification of emotional behavior. *Journal of Comparitive and Physiological Psychology*, 1962, *55*, 242-246.

Dimond, S. J., & Farrington, L. Emotional response to films shown to the right or left hemisphere of the brain measured by heart rate. *Acta Psychologica*, 1977, *41*, 255-260.

Doob, L. W. Eidetic images about the Ibo. *Ethnology*, 1964, *3*, 357-363.

Doob, L. W. Exploring eidetic imagery among the Kamba of Central Kenya. *Journal of Social Psychology*, 1965, *67*, 3-22.

Ehrlichman, H., & Weinberger, A. Lateral eye movements and hemispheric asymmetry: A critical review. *Psychological Bulletin*, 1978, *85*, 1080-1101.

Erickson, M. H. The confusion technique in hypnosis. *American Journal of Clinical Hypnosis*, 1964, *6*, 183-207.

Fenichel, O. *The psychoanalytic theory of neurosis*. New York: Norton, 1945.

Flavell, J. H. *The developmental psychology of Jean Piaget*. Princeton, N.J.: Van Nostrand, 1963.

Frank, J. D. *Persuasion and healing*. New York: Schocken, 1974.

Frank, J. D. Nature and functions of belief systems: Humanism and transcendental religion. *American Psychologist*, 1977, *32*, 555-559.

Frankl, V. E. Paradoxical intention. *American Journal of Psychotherapy*, 1960, *14*, 520-535.

Freud, S. Three contributions to the theory of sexuality. In A. Brill (Ed.), *The basic writings of Sigmund Freud*. New York: Modern Libraries, 1938.

Gainotti, G. Reactions "catastrophiques" et manifestations l'indifference au cours des atteintes cerebrales. *Neuropsychologia*, 1969, *7*, 195-204.

Gainotti, G. Emotional behavior and hemispheric side of the lesion. *Cortex*, 1972, *8*, 41-55.

Galin, D. Implications for psychiatry of left and right cerebral specialization. *Archives of General Psychiatry*, 1974, *31*, 572-583.

Galin, D., Diamond, R., & Braff, D. Lateralization of conversion symptoms: More frequent on the left. *American Journal of Psychiatry*, 1977, *134*, 578-580.

Galin, D., & Ellis, R. Asymmetry in evoked potentials and an index of lateralized cognitive processes. *Neuropsychologia*, 1975, *13*, 45-50.

Galin, D., & Ornstein, R. Lateral specialization of cognitive mode: An EEG study. *Psychophysiology*, 1972, *9*, 412-418.

Gallwey, W. T. *The inner game*. New York: Random House, 1974.

Gazzaniga, M. S. The split brain in man. *Scientific American*, 1967, *217*, 24-29.

Giannitrapani, D. Developing concepts of lateralization of cerebral functions. *Cortex*, 1967, *3*, 353-370.

Goldstein, K. *The organism: A holistic approach to biology derived from pathological data in man.* New York: American Books, 1939.

Goldstein L., Stoltzfus, N., & Gardocki, J. Changes in interhemispheric amplitude relationships in the EEG during sleep. *Physiology and Behavior,* 1972, *8,* 811-815.

Goleman, D. Split-brain psychology: Fad of the year. *Psychology Today,* 1977, *11,* (Nov.), 89-90.

Gowan, J. C. The role of imagination in the development of the creative individual. *Humanitas,* 1978, *14,* 209-225.

Gur, R. C., Sackheim, H. S., & Gur, R. E. Classroom seating and psychopathology: Some initial data. *Journal of Abnormal Psychology,* 1976, *85,* 122-124.

Haber, R. N., & Haber, R. B. Eidetic imagery: Frequency. *Perceptual and Motor Skills,* 1964, *19,* 131-138.

Haggard, M. P., & Parkinson, A. M. Stimulus and task factors as determinants of ear advantages. *Quarterly Journal of Experimental Psychology,* 1971, *23,* 168-177.

Halliday, J. Psychological factors in rheumatism. *British Medical Journal,* 1937, *1,* 264-269.

Harnad, S. R. Creativity. Lateral saccades and the nondominant hemisphere. *Perceptual and Motor Skills,* 1972, *34,* 653-654.

Hecaen H. Clinical symptomatology in right and left hemispheric lesions, In V. B. Mountcastle, (Ed.), *Interhemispheric relations and cerebral dominance.* Baltimore: Johns Hopkins Press, 1962.

Hecaen, H., & Angelergues, R. Agnosia for faces (prosopagnosia). *Archives of Neurology,* 1962, *7,* 92-100.

Hiscock, M. Eye movement asymmetry and hemispheric function: An examination of individual differences. *Journal of Psychology,* 1977, *97,* 49-52.

Horowitz, M. J. Image Formation: Clinical observations and a cognitive model. In P. Sheehan (Ed.), *The function and nature of imagery.* New York: Academic Press, 1972.

Humphrey, M. E., & Zangwill, O. L. Cessation of dreaming after brain injury. *Journal of Neurological, Neurosurgical, Psychiatry,* 1951, *14,* 322-325.

Jaensch, E. *Eidetic imagery and typological methods of investigation.* New York: Harcourt, Brace, 1930.

Janov, A. *The primal scream: Primal therapy.* New York: Putnam, 1970.

Jaynes, J. *The origins of consciousness in the breakdown of the bicameral mind.* Boston: Houghton Mifflin, 1976.

Kenyon F. E. Hyponcondriasis: A clinical study. *British Journal of Psychiatry,* 1964, *110,* 478-488.

Khatena, J. Creative imagination imagery: Where is it going? *Journal of Creative Behavior,* 1976, *10,* 189-192.

King, F., & Kimura, D. Left ear superiority in dichotic perception of vocal nonverbal sounds. Research Bulletin 188, Dept. of Psychology, University of Western Ontario, 1971.

Klein, G. S. *Psychoanalytic theory: An exploration of essentials.* New York: International Universities Press, 1976.

Kroth, J. A. The analytic couch and response to free association. *Psychotherapy: Theory, Research and Practice,* 1970, *7,* 206-208.

Lazarus, A. *Multimodal behavior therapy.* New York: Springer, 1976.

Lenneberg, E. *Biological foundations of language.* New York: Wiley, 1967.

Leuner, H. Guided affective imagery: An account of its development. *Journal of Mental Imagery,* 1977, *1,* 73-92.

Levy, J., Trevarthen, C., & Sperry, R. W. Perception of bilateral chimeric figures following hemispheric deconnexion. *Brain,* 1972, *95,* 61-78.

Ley, R. G. Asymmetry of hysterical conversion symptoms. Paper presented at the annual meeting of the Canadian Psychological Association, Ottawa, Ontario, 1978.

Ley, R. G., & Bryden, M. P. The right hemisphere and emotion. University of Waterloo Research Report #51, Waterloo, Ontario, 1977.

Ley, R. G., & Bryden, M. P. Hemispheric differences in recognizing faces and emotions. *Brain and Language,* 1979, *7,* 127-138. (a)

Ley, R. G., & Bryden, M. P. Consciousness, emotion and the right hemisphere. In R. Stevens & G. Underwood (Eds.), *Aspects of consciousness.* New York: Academic Press, in press, 1979. (b)

Luria, A. R. Memory and structure of mental processes. *Problems of Psychology,* 1960, *1,* 81-93.

McClelland, D. C. *Personality.* New York: Holt, Rinehart & Winston, 1960.

McLuhan, H. M. *City as classroom: Understanding language and media.* Agincourt, Ontario: Book Society of Canada, 1977.

Meichenbaum, D. *Cognitive-behavior modification.* New York: Plenum, 1977.

Meichenbaum, D. Why does using imagery in psychotherapy lead to change? In J. L. Singer, & K. Pope (Eds.), *The power of human imagination.* New York: Plenum, 1978.

Meskin, B., & Singer, J. L. Daydreaming, reflective thought, and laterality of eye movements. *Journal of Personality and Social Psychology,* 1974, *30,* 64-71.

Morgan, A., McDonald, P., & MacDonald, H. Differences in bilateral alpha activity as a function of experimental task with a note on lateral eye movements and hypnotizability. *Neuropsychologia,* 1971, *9,* 459-469.

Morgan, R. F., & Bakan, P. Sensory deprivation, hallucinations and other sleep behavior as a function of positions, method or report, and anxiety. *Perceptual and Motor Skills,* 1965, *20,* 19-25.

Morrison, J., & Cometa, M. Emotive-reconstructive psychotherapy: A short term cognitive approach. *American Journal of Psychotherapy,* 1977, *33,* 294-301.

Morsh, J. E., & Abbott, H. D. An investigation of after-images. *Journal of Comparitive Psychology,* 1945, *38,* 47-63.

Nebes, R. Superiority of the minor hemisphere in commissurotomized man for perception of part-whole relations. *Cortex,* 1971, *7,* 333-349.

Ornstein, R. *The psychology of consciousness.* San Francisco: Freeman, 1972.

Perard, A. Effect of tobacco and frustration of tobacco on some aspects of a white rat's behavior. *Psychologie Francaise,* 1967, *12,* 53-57.

Pope, K. S. Gender, solitude, and position. In K. Pope, & J. L. Singer (Eds.), *The stream of consciousness.* New York: Plenum, 1978.

Pope, K. S., & Singer, J. L. (Eds.), *The stream of consciousness.* New York: Plenum, 1978.

Reik, T. Listening with the third ear. New York: Farrar, Straus, 1948.

Richardson, A. *Mental imagery.* New York: Springer, 1969.

Robbins, K., & McAdam, D. Interhemispheric alpha asymmetry and imagery mode. *Brain and Language,* 1974, *1,* 189-193.

Robertson, A. D., & Inglis, J. The effects of electroconvulsive therapy on human learning and memory. *Canadian Psychological Review,* 1977, *18,* 285-307.

Roffwarg, H., Muzio, J., & Dement, W. Ontogenetic development of the human sleep-dream cycle. *Science,* 1966, *152,* 604-618.

Rosen, J. *Direct analysis.* New York: Grune & Stratton, 1953.

Rossi, G. F., & Rosadini, G. R. Experimental analysis of cerebral dominance in man. In D. H. Millikan (Ed.), *Brain mechanisms underlying speech and language.* New York: Grune & Stratton, 1967.

Safer, M., & Leventhal, H. Ear differences in evaluating emotional tones of voice and verbal content. *Journal of Experimental Psychology: Human Perception and Performance,* 1977, *3,* 1, 75-82.

Schwartz, G., Davidson, R., & Maer, F. Right hemispheric lateralization for emotion in the human brain: Interactions with cognition. *Science*, 1975, *190*, 286-288.

Seligman, M. E. P. Fall into helplessness. *Psychology Today*, 1973, *7*, (July), 43-48.

Semmes, J. Hemispheric specialization, a possible clue to mechanism. *Neuropsychologia*, 1968, *6*, 11-26.

Sheikh, A. A., & Panagiotou, N. C. Use of mental imagery in psychotherapy: A critical review, *Perceptual and Motor Skills*, 1975, *41*, 555-585.

Singer, J. L. *Imagery and daydream methods in psychotherapy and behavior modification.* New York: Academic Press, 1974.

Sperry, R. W. Hemispheric disconnection and unity in conscious awareness. *American Psychologist, 1968, 23*, 723-733.

Stern, D. Handedness and the lateral distribution of conversion reactions. *Journal of Nervous and Mental Disease*, 1977, *164*, 122-128.

Stromeyer, C. F., & Psotka, J. The detailed texture of eidetic images. *Nature*, 1970, *225*, 346-349.

Suberi, M., & McKeever, W. Differential right hemispheric memory storage of emotional and non-emotional faces. *Neuropsychologia*, 1977, *15*, 757-768.

Teasdale, H. H. A. quantitative study of eidetic imagery. *British Journal of Educational Psychology*, 1934, *4*, 56-74.

Terzian, H. Behavioral and EEG effects of intracarotid sodium amytal injections. *Acta Neurochirugia*, 1964, *12*, 230-240.

Torrance, E. P. *Encouraging creativity in the classroom.* Dubuque, Iowa: W. C. Brown, 1970.

Tucker, D. M. Dialectical processes in emotion and hemispheric function. Paper presented to the International Neuropsychological Society, 1978.

Tucker, D. M., Roth, R. S., Arneson, B. A., & Buckingham, V. Right Hemisphere activation during stress. *Neuropsychologia*, 1977, *15*, 697-700.

Watzlawick, P. *The language of change.* New York: Basic Books, 1978.

Whittaker, C. The learning tree. In S. B. Kopp (Ed.), *The naked therapist.* San Diego: Edits, 1976.

Wigan, A. L. *The duality of the mind.* London: Longman, 1844.

Wolf-Dorlester, B. Creativity, adaptive regression, reflective eye movements, and the Holzman movement response. *Dissertation Abstracts International*, 1976, *36*, 6458-6459B.

Wolpe, J. *Psychotherapy by reciprocal inhibition.* California: Stanford University Press, 1958.

Zimmerberg, B., Glick, S., & Jerussi, T. Neurochemical correlates of a spatial preference in rats. *Science*, 1974, *623*, 623-625.

5

Guided Imagining and Hypnosis: Theoretical and Empirical Overlap and Convergence in a New Creative Imagination Scale

THEODORE X. BARBER
SHERYL C. WILSON

The term *hypnosis* refers to the effects produced by a wide variety of suggestions; for instance, it refers to the effects of (a) suggestions to enter an altered state of consciousness ("You are becoming relaxed . . . drowsy . . . entering a hypnotic state."), (b) direct suggestions that certain effects are occurring or will occur ("Your arm is becoming rigid . . . You cannot bend it."), and (c) suggestions that ask the subject to imagine a specific target effect ("Imagine a heavy weight in the palm of the left hand . . . The [imagined] weight is becoming heavier and heavier and the arm is moving down and down.").

When subjects are given the latter kinds of suggestions, which ask them to imagine, it is obvious that hypnosis and imagining have something in common. However, even when the suggestions do not directly ask the subjects to imagine, there is nevertheless a marked degree of overlap between the procedures and cognitive processes that are labeled as *hypnosis* and those that are subsumed under such terms as *directed fantasy* (Cordner, 1978), *fantasy-imaging process* (Bosdell, 1978;

Theodore X. Barber and Sheryl C. Wilson, Proseminar Institute, Research Division, Cushing Hospital, Framingham, Mass. 01701. Writing of this paper was supported in part by a grant from the Proseminar Institute.

May, 1978; Rosner, 1978), *guided fantasy* (Damashek, 1978; Sommer, 1978), and *guided imagery* (Don, 1978; Hershey & Kearn, 1978).

In this paper, we shall focus on an important aspect of hypnosis, namely, that aspect which is closely related to imagining. Let us first briefly specify five overlapping features between these two sets of concepts:

1. The overlap between hypnosis and imagining was noted at the very beginning of the history of hypnotism. The formal or "official" history began about 200 years ago in France when Mesmer mistakenly thought he was manipulating an invisible fluid ("animal magnetism") when he was producing his dramatic cures. Typically, Mesmer would touch his patients with an iron wand or would make "passes" over the patients; as a result of this kind of stimulation, some of the patients would undergo a convulsive crisis and, after recovery from the crisis, would report that they were cured of their ailments. To determine what factors were involved in Mesmer's cures, the king of France appointed an investigative commission which included distinguished individuals such as Benjamin Franklin who at that time was the American ambassador to France, the great chemist Lavoisier, and the famous astronomer Bailley. After a careful investigation, which included several controlled experiments, the commissioners concluded that Mesmer's cures were due, not to the supposed fluid ("animal magnetism"), but primarily to the *imagination* of the patients and also to "imitation" and "contact". Their concluding statements were worded as follows:

> The commissioners have ascertained that the animal magnetic fluid is not perceptible by any of the senses; that it has no action, either on themselves or on the patients subjected to it. They are convinced that pressure and contact . . . affect the imagination. Finally, they have demonstrated by decisive experiments that imagination apart from magnetism, produces convulsions, and that magnetism without imagination produces nothing . . . the . . . effects observed in patients under public treatment are due to contact, to the excitement of the imagination, and to the mechanical imitation which involuntarily impels us to repeat that which strikes our senses (Binet & Féré, 1888, pp. 16-17).

Thus, from the very beginning of the "official" history of hypnosis, qualified observers concluded that the effects attributed to a fluid that was controlled by the mesmerist or hypnotist were actually due primarily to the patients' own mental processes which they labeled as "the excitement of the imagination."

2. Today, as in Mesmer's day, knowledgeable observers and researchers agree that the phenomena attributed to hypnosis are closely dependent on the subjects' own imaginative-cognitive processes. This consensus among investigators has been documented in a recent paper (Spanos & Barber, 1974). After reviewing the theoretical formulations of the major researchers in the area, Spanos and Barber concluded that "theorists appear to be converging on the conclusion that responsiveness to hypnotic suggestions involves a shift in set or orientation away from the pragmatic one that governs our everyday transactions to one that involves imagining. This shift in orientation appears to involve at least two interrelated

components: (a) a tendency to carry out and also to elaborate imaginings consistent with the suggestions that are administered, together with (b) a tendency to simultaneously ignore or reinterpret information that contradicts the imaginings." This conclusion summarizes an important aspect of the empirical data and theories proffered by such major investigators as Arnold, Shor, Hilgard, Gill, Sarbin, and Barber. For instance, some years back, Magda Arnold (1946) concluded from her research that "hypnosis essentially consists in concentrating and therefore intensifying the subject's imaginative processes. Directed toward one focus, the situation described by the experimenter, the subject will be able to imagine this situation much more intensely than he is able to do ordinarily, without the usual internal and external distractions" (p. 116). Along similar lines, Ernest R. Hilgard (1965) and Josephine R. Hilgard (1970) concluded from their empirical research that the responsive hypnotic subject is especially capable of creating and becoming involved in an imaginative or fantasy production that is initiated by an external source such as by music, a motion picture, a novel, or by the suggestions of the hypnotist. Another line of research carried out by Barber, Spanos, and Chaves (1974) led to a similar conclusion: good hypnotic subjects become involved in thinking and imagining those things that are suggested. Also, Sarbin and Coe (1972) concluded from a separate series of investigations that subjects who are said to be hypnotized are indistinguishable from individuals who are fully utilizing their abilities to imagine and fantasize.

3. The aforementioned consensus among researchers — that hypnosis is closely related to imagining — is not surprising when we note a salient fact: a substantial proportion of the suggestions used in both experimental and clinical hypnotic settings clearly ask the subject to imagine or fantasize. For instance, in experimental settings, hypnotic subjects are typically exposed to one of the Stanford Hypnotic Susceptibility Scales and are asked, for example (a) to imagine that they are holding something heavy in a hand and the hand and arm feel heavy, as if the weight were pressing down, or (b) to imagine that they have something sweet tasting in their mouth and as they think about this sweet taste they can actually begin to experience it, or (c) to imagine a force acting on their hands pushing them apart, as though one hand were repelling the other, etc. (Weitzenhoffer & Hilgard, 1962, pp. 17-19).

Similarly, in clinical settings, the clinician-hypnotist often asks the client to vividly imagine the effects that are desired. For instance, in four recent clinical studies in which women were able to increase the size of their breasts by utilizing hypnotic and self-hypnotic procedures, the women were asked to imagine vividly that there were swelling sensations and feelings of pulsation in the breasts, or tightness of the skin and slight tenderness in the breasts, or that either a heat lamp or wet, warm towels had been placed on the breasts (Honiotes, 1977; Staib & Logan, 1977; Willard, 1977; Williams, 1974).

4. Over a period of many years, researchers have been attempting to find personality characteristics that are related to hypnotic responsiveness. The investigations in this area, summarized by Barber (1964) and Hilgard (1965), yielded inconsistent and contradictory results; none of the earlier studies indicating that hypnotic responsiveness is correlated with a specific personality characteristic (e.g., extraversion, ego-strength, or need for affiliation) could be replicated in later research. However, during recent years, one consistent and replicable finding has been obtained in a series of investigations which used semistructured interviews or self-report questionnaires to assess to what degree subjects felt they become immersed or absorbed in activities involving imagining, such as watching a movie, reading a novel, daydreaming, dramatic acting, etc. Studies in this area revealed significant positive correlations between hypnotic responsiveness and ability to become involved in activities utilizing imagining (Andersen, 1963; As, 1962; As, O'Hara, & Munger, 1962; Atkinson, 1971; Barber & Glass, 1962; Coe, 1964; Coe & Sarbin, 1966; Davis, Dawson, & Seay, 1978; Diamond & Taft, 1975; J. R. Hilgard, 1970; Lee-Teng, 1965; Sarbin & Lim, 1963; Sheehan, 1972; Shor, Orne, & O'Connell, 1962; Spanos & McPeake, 1975; Sutcliffe, Perry, & Sheehan, 1970; Tellegen & Atkinson, 1974).

5. A number of investigators have proffered very similar analogies, involving imagining and fantasy, to clarify what good hypnotic subjects do when they are responding to suggestions for age regression, hand anesthesia, visual or auditory hallucinations, etc. For instance, Shor (1970) specified how responding to hypnotic suggestions is similar to becoming involved in imagining while reading a novel. He noted that both the responsive hypnotic subject and the individual who is absorbed in a novel utilize information from an external source to generate and elaborate imaginings that temporarily become the main focus of attention. When reading a novel, some individuals "think the thoughts in the story and they feel the emotions"; in an analogous way, good hypnotic subjects let their thoughts, imaginings, and emotions be guided by the suggestions they are given.

A similar analogy was offered by Barber (1970) who compared the responsive hypnotic subject to the individual who is immersed in watching a movie. Some individuals who are observing a motion picture think and imagine with the communications they are receiving; they imagine, fantasize, feel, and experience in line with the intentions of the writer of the screenplay — they may feel happy or sad and may empathize, laugh, cry, experience fear, etc. In a similar way, when a person is responding to suggestions in a hypnotic situation, he is thinking and imagining with the communications that he is receiving and is experiencing the feelings and emotions that are suggested. Barber (1970) noted that:

The messages or communications from the actors are intended to elicit certain types of thoughts, feelings, and emotions — to empathize, to feel happy or sad, to laugh or to weep, to feel excited or shocked — whereas the messages or communications (test suggestions) from the [hypnotist] are intended to elicit somewhat different types of thoughts, feelings, or emotions — to experience an arm as heavy, to experience oneself as a child, to forget preceding events, and so forth. From this viewpoint, the member of the audience and the subject who is responding to test suggestions are having different experiences, *not because they are in different "states" but because they are receiving different communications.*

Sarbin (1976) has compared the responsive hypnotic subject to the child who is involved in imaginative play. In dramatic or symbolic play, the child can be fully immersed, for example, in talking to a "person" on a toy telephone. Also, as Sarbin notes, when absorbed in imaginative play, "a stick can be a horse, a fairy's wand, a conductor's baton, a magical instrument, or just a stick." Also, "with practice, the child can get along even without sticks and can construct any number of magical worlds." Similarly, the responsive hypnotic subject can become immersed in talking to a person who is visualized but who is not actually present, can respond to an object, such as a stick in a variety of imaginative ways, and can construct any number of "magical worlds."

Convergence of Imagining and Hypnosis: The Creative Imagination Scale

During recent years, a major portion of the work in our laboratory has focused on the overlap between guided imagining and hypnosis. We began this research endeavor by first constructing an instrument that could measure equally well those aspects of human functioning that have been labeled as *guided imagining* and those labeled as *responding to hypnotic suggestions.* Specifically, we constructed an instrument in which subjects are given suggestions to imagine over a period of time and are guided to experience the objective consequences of their imagining; for example, subjects are asked to actively imagine the sun shining on the back of their hand and to feel the hand becoming hot in the same way as it would if the sun were actually shining on the hand.

The instrument that we constructed to measure the effects of suggestions to imagine, which we labeled as the Creative Imagination Scale (Wilson, 1976; Wilson & Barber, 1978), is presented verbatim in Appendix A. The scale is comprised of 10 standardized suggestions which ask subjects to utilize various sensory modalities to think and imagine the following:

1. *Arm Heaviness.* Suggestions are given to guide the subjects to imagine that heavy dictionaries are being placed on the outstretched palm of the hand, causing the arm to feel very heavy.

2. *Hand Levitation.* Suggestions are given to guide the subjects to imagine that a strong stream of water from a garden hose is pushing against the palm of the outstretched hand, pushing the hand up.

3. *Finger Anesthesia.* Suggestions are given to guide subjects to imagine that novocain has been injected into the side of the hand, causing two fingers to feel numb.

4. *Water "Hallucination."* Suggestions are given to subjects to imagine that they are very thirsty and then to imagine quenching their thirst by drinking cool mountain water.

5. *Olfactory-Gustatory "Hallucination."* Suggestions are given to guide the subjects to imagine that they are smelling and tasting an orange.

6. *Music "Hallucination."* Suggestions are given to guide the subjects to re-experience "hearing" wonderful music that they had heard previously.

7. *Temperature "Hallucination."* Suggestions are given to guide the subjects to imagine that the sun is shining on the top of the right hand, causing it to feel hot.

8. *Time Distortion.* Suggestions are given to guide the subjects to imagine that time is slowing down.

9. *Age Regression.* Suggestions are given to guide the subjects to recreate the feelings they had experienced when they were children in elementary school.

10. *Mind-Body Relaxation.* Suggestions are given to guide the subjects to imagine that they are lying under the sun on a beach and becoming very relaxed.[1]

The 10 suggestions on the Creative Imagination Scale (CIS) provide detailed descriptions to guide the subjects to use their own creative imagining in order to experience the suggested effects. For example, to create the experience of arm heaviness, the CIS includes statements such as the following: "By letting your thoughts go along with these instructions you can make your hand and arm feel heavy . . . Now imagine that a very heavy dictionary is being placed on the palm of your left hand. Let yourself feel the heaviness . . . You create the feeling of heaviness . . . by thinking of a large, heavy dictionary . . . Push up . . . as you imagine the weight; notice how your arm feels heavier and heavier" (Wilson & Barber, 1978). Similarly, the CIS includes descriptive statements which guide the subjects to use their own thinking and imagining to experience the smell and taste of an orange; for example "By using your imagination creatively, you can experience the smell and taste of an orange. Picture yourself picking up an orange and imagine that you're peeling it. As you create the image of the orange, feel yourself peeling it and let yourself see and feel the orange skin on the outside and the soft white pulp on the inside of the skin . . . let yourself smell it and touch it and feel the juiciness of

[1] Administration of the Creative Imagination Scale requires 18 minutes, and subjects' self-scoring of their experiences usually requires less than 5 minutes. The scale can be presented either in spoken form by the examiner or by a tape-recording of the examiner's voice. Subjects are asked to keep their eyes closed during administration of the scale. The Creative Imagination Scale can be administered as easily to a group as to an individual, either (a) without special preliminaries, for example, after the subjects or clients are told simply that they are to receive a test of imagination, (b) after special preliminary instructions such as task motivational instructions (Barber, 1969, p. 46), human potential instructions (Barber, Spanos, & Chaves, 1974, pp. 119 ff.), or think-with instructions (Barber & Wilson, 1977), and (c) after a traditional hypnotic induction procedures.

it . . . Experience how juicy, luscious and flavorful it is as you imagine taking a deep, deep bite . . . Feel the juice and feel the pulp" (Wilson & Barber, 1978).

In scoring the CIS, the subjects are asked to compare the experience produced by their imagination to the actual experience as it occurs in reality (see Appendix B). The subjects rate each item on a five point scale ranging from "not at all the same" as the real thing (score of 0) to "almost exactly the same" as the real thing (score of 4). For example, Item 1 (Arm Heaviness) is scored as follows:

"In the first test you were asked to imagine that one, two, and then three dictionaries were being piled on the palm of your hand. Compared to what you would have experienced if three dictionaries were actually on your hand, what you experienced was:

0	1	2	3	4
0%	25%	50%	75%	90+%
Not at all the same	A little the same	Between a little and much the same	Much the same	Almost exactly the same

The CIS has been shown to possess satisfactory test-retest reliability ($N = 22$; $r = .82$; $p < .01$), split-half reliability ($N = 217$; $r = .89$; $p < .001$), and factorial validity ($N = 217$; all 10 test-suggestions load on the first and only factor) (Wilson & Barber, 1978). Norms for the CIS as well as detailed reliability and validity data are presented by Wilson and Barber (1978).

Correlations of CIS with Other Measures of Imagery, Imagining, and Hypnosis

As stated above, each of the 10 items on the CIS asks subjects to imagine things which are similar to some of the things subjects are asked to imagine in situations labeled as *hypnosis*. Since the scale can be used to measure responsiveness in a guided imagining situation as well as in a situation labeled as hypnosis, we might expect that scores on the scale will correlate significantly with scores on tests of imagining and also with scores on hypnotic scales. In fact, studies have generally found significant correlations with tests in both areas. Two studies (Kiddoo, 1978; McConkey, Sheehan, Law, & White, 1977) revealed scores on the CIS to be significantly correlated with both (a) scores on instruments that aim to measure either imagery or absorption in imagining, and (b) responsiveness on hypnotic susceptibility or suggestibility scales. Kiddoo (1978) found scores on the CIS to be significantly correlated with scores on (a) the Tellegen Absorption Scale (Tellegen & Atkinson, 1974) that measures ability to become immersed in imagining, (b) the Betts Test of Mental Imagery (Sheehan, 1967), (c) the imagery portion of the Individual Differences Questionnaire (Paivio, 1971), and (d) the Barber Suggestibility Scale (Barber, 1969). McConkey et al. (1977) obtained a significant correlation between scores on the CIS and scores on (a) the Betts Test of Mental Imagery, and (b) the Harvard Group Scale of Hypnotic Susceptibility: Form A (Shor & Orne, 1962). For females but not for males, the latter investigators also found scores on the CIS to be significantly correlated with scores on (a) the Tellegen Absorption Scale, and (b) the Gordon Test of Imagery Control (Richardson, 1969).

The Imagination Inventory as a Predictor of Response to the CIS

We recently conducted a study to investigate the relationship between involvement in active ongoing imaginings generated by verbal suggestions as measured by the CIS and the following three sets of variables: self-predicted ability to imagine vividly; childhood play history; and history of imaginative involvements. To measure these three variables, we constructed a paper and pencil questionnaire that we labeled as the *Imagination Inventory.* This instrument, which is presented verbatim in Appendix C, has three subscales as follows:

The first subscale is labeled as *Predicted Imagining.* The five items on this subscale ask subjects questions along the following lines: "If you tried to imagine a specific thing, such as hearing a siren, how vivid would the imagined siren be compared to a real siren?"

The second subscale refers to *Play History.* This subscale derives from observations by Sarbin (1976) that the behavior of a subject who is involved in suggested imaginings or hypnotic suggestions is very much like that of a child involved in make-believe play; for example, a child who is absorbed in talking on a toy telephone to an imagined or hallucinated friend is engaged in magical thinking, is accepting logical inconsistencies, etc. The items on this subscale assess whether a subject as a young child preferred realistic skill-oriented play or make-believe, imaginative play and also the degree of imaginative involvement while playing.

The third subscale is labeled *History of Involvements.* This subscale derives from Josephine Hilgard's (1970) research which indicated that subjects' degree of involvement in various nonhypnotic activities (e.g., reading a novel, watching a movie, or experiencing nature) was related to their responsiveness to the test-suggestions of the Stanford Hypnotic Susceptibility Scale. J. Hilgard interviewed her subjects to obtain the information pertaining to involvements. The basic findings from these interviews were utilized in the eight items that composed our third subscale on History of Involvements; that is, the items on this subscale ask subjects to rate the extent of their involvements in the nonhypnotic activities which were found, by J. Hilgard, to correlate significantly with responsiveness to test-suggestions.

One hundred seventeen male and female introductory psychology students at two colleges participated in a study which we carried out to determine to what extent scores on the Imagination Inventory are related to responsiveness on the CIS[2]. The students completed the Imagination Inventory first and then were tested later on the CIS[3].

Total scores on the Imagination Inventory were significantly correlated ($r = .45$, $p < .001$) with total scores on the CIS. Significant correlations were also obtained between scores on the CIS and scores on each of the three subscales of the Imagination Inventory: Predicted Imagining ($r = .39$, $p < .001$); Play History ($r = .23$, $p < .01$); and History of Involvements ($r = .19$, $p < .05$).

Table 1
Correlations of Items on
Imagination Inventory with Total Scores on CIS

Predicted Imagining		*Play History*		*History of Involvements*	
1. leg heavy	.26 **	6. preferred make-		8. watching movie,	
2. ice cream	.39 ***	believe play	.24 **	TV	-.02
3. siren	.30 ***	7. involvement in		9. imaginery	
4. ice water	.40 ***	make-believe		companion	.15
		play	.10	10. reading	
5. speeding car	.32 ***			involvement	-.02
				11. "physical	
				memories"	.25**
				12. eager for new	
				experiences	.04
				13. involvement in	
				nature	-.05
				14. physical	
				adventures	.12
				15. reading to	
				stimulate	
				imagination	.21*

Note: *** $p < .001$
   ** $p < .005$
   * $p < .01$

---

[2] In the same study with the 117 students, the split-half reliability (odd items vs. even items) of the Imagination Inventory was found to be satisfactory ($r = .76$, $p < .001$). We are indebted to Kimberley P. Kiddoo, Ph.D., for testing the subjects at Boston University and to Beverly L. Ryder for testing the subjects at the University of Massachusetts in Boston.

[3] At one college, the students ($N = 79$) completed the Imagination Inventory the first semester and then were tested on the CIS several months later during the second semester. At the other college, the students ($N = 38$) completed the inventory and were tested on the CIS during the same semester with a minimum of 1 week between the two assessments. In both colleges, the CIS was administered by a tape recording after subjects were told simply that they were to be given a test of imagination.

Separate correlation coefficients were also computed between total scores on the CIS and scores for each of the 15 items on the Imagination Inventory. These correlations are presented in Table 1. As this table shows, all five items on the first subscale — Predicted Imagining — correlated significantly with total scores on the CIS. The item on the second subscale — Play History — which correlated significantly pertains to childhood preference for make-believe games. On the third subscale — History of Involvements — two items correlated significantly: ability to re-experience in one's imagination physical memories such as the feeling of a soft breeze or warm sand, and reading in order to stimulate one's imagination.

In summary, scores on the CIS are significantly correlated with total scores on the Imagination Inventory and also with the total scores and individual items on each of the three subscales. An abbreviated version of the Imagination Inventory, which includes only the eight items which correlate significantly with the CIS, should prove useful in future studies as a quick and simple way to predict which subjects are most likely to perform well on tests of guided imagining and tests of hypnotizability.

Usefulness of the Creative Imagination Scale

The CIS can be utilized in at least two distinct ways. When it is preceded by a hypnotic induction procedure, it can be used as a measure of "hypnotizability"; that is, it can measure responsiveness to suggestions of the type given in hypnotic situations — suggestions of hand levitation, anesthesia, hallucinations, time distortion, age regression, etc. When used in this way, the CIS differs from other measures of "hypnotizability" — for example, the Stanford Hypnotic Susceptibility Scales (Weitzenhoffer & Hilgard, 1959, 1962), the Harvard Group Scale of Hypnotic Susceptibility (Shor & Orne, 1962), and the Barber Suggestibility Scale (Barber & Glass, 1962) — in that it does not include either "challenge" suggestions which tell the subjects that they cannot carry out a common behavior (e.g., "Try to say your name, you can't.") or "command" suggestions which tell the subjects that they will carry out a behavior simply because they are commanded to do so (e.g., "When this experiment is over, every time I click, you'll cough automatically."). In brief, when preceded by a hypnotic induction procedure, the CIS measures an important aspect of hypnosis — the aspect which involves imagining; other hypnosis scales, such as the Stanford scales, the Harvard Group scale, and the Barber scale, include some suggestions which ask the subject to imagine but they also include "challenge" suggestions and "command" suggestions.[4]

---

[4] It should be noted, however, that no extant scale of "hypnotizability" measures all of the many aspects of hypnosis. For example, no scale measures responsiveness to the types of suggestions that are at times used in stage hypnosis, such as suggestions to behave in a "silly" manner or to carry out the human-plank feat (Meeker & Barber, 1971), and no scale measures responsiveness to the types of suggestions commonly used in clinical hypnosis settings such as suggestions to stop smoking or to lose weight.

When the CIS is not preceded by a hypnotic induction procedure, it can be used in a second way — to measure guided imagining. When utilized in this way, the subjects are simply asked to close their eyes and to imagine that three large dictionaries are being placed on the palm of their outstretched hand, making the arm feel heavy, that novocain is moving into two fingers, making the fingers insensitive, etc. To the best of our knowledge, the CIS is the only standardized instrument that was designed to measure active, guided imagining which continues for a significant period of time and which guides the subjects to actually experience objective consequences of their imagining; for example, to experience a hand rising involuntarily when they are imagining a strong stream of water from a garden hose pushing against the palm of the hand. All other available tests of imagery or imagining — per example, the Betts Test of Mental Imagery (Sheehan, 1967), the Gordon Test of Imagery Control (Richardson, 1969), the imagery portion of the Individual Differences Questionnaire (Paivio, 1971), and the Vividness of Visual Imagery Questionnaire (Marks, 1973) — ask the subjects simply to image, imagine, or visualize for a brief period of a few seconds (White, Sheehan, & Ashton, 1977). Instead of simply asking the subjects briefly to image or to visualize, say, the sun, as would be the procedure used in the tests listed above, the CIS asks the subjects to visualize the sun, to feel its warmth penetrating into the right hand, and to continue feeling the heat increasing for a significant period of time while the right hand itself actually becomes pleasantly hot. Norms for the CIS, as well as reliability and validity data, have been obtained when the CIS was used in this way as a standardized test of guided imagining (Wilson & Barber, 1978).

The CIS is equally useful in either an experimental or a clinical setting. In fact, permission can be relatively easily obtained to use the scale in a wide variety of settings, such as elementary schools, churches, social clubs, prisons, etc., especially since it is permissive and nonthreatening — each of the 10 items is presented in terms of the examiner helping the subjects use their own mental abilities. It has been observed in studies using the CIS that subjects enjoyed responding to the items on the scale and generally found it to be a personally valuable experience (Barber & Wilson, 1978/1979).

The CIS has been translated into Spanish (de Alvarez, 1977) and Polish (Siuta, 1978) and has been used recently in one clinical investigation (Straus, 1978) and in eleven experimental studies pertaining to hypnosis (Barber & Wilson, 1977; Barber, Wilson, & Scott, in press; Canale, 1976; Crawford & Katz, 1978; DeStefano, 1977; Katz & Crawford, 1978; Kiddoo, 1978; McConkey et al., 1977; Ryder, 1978; Straus, 1978; Wilson, 1976). We expect the CIS will also prove useful in both clinical and experimental work in the areas of imagery and guided imagining. For instance, the CIS can be used in a clinical setting as a nonthreatening, permissive method of measuring the clients' ability to actively imagine over an extended period of time and to actually experience the effects of their imagining. The CIS can also be used to provide clients with practice in responding to interesting and worthwhile suggestions.

REFERENCES

Andersen, M. L. Correlates of hypnotic performance: An historical and role-theoretical analysis. Unpublished doctoral dissertation, University of California, Berkeley, 1963.

Arnold, M. B. On the mechanism of suggestion and hypnosis. *Journal of Abnormal and Social Psychology*, 1946, *41*, 107-128.

As, A. Non-hypnotic experiences related to hypnotizability in male and female college students. *Scandinavian Journal of Psychology*, 1962, *3*, 112-121.

As, A., O'Hara, J. W., & Munger, M. P. The measurement of subjective experiences presumably related to hypnotic susceptibility. *Scandinavian Journal of Psychology*, 1962, *3*, 47-64.

Atkinson, G. A. Personality and hypnotic cognition. Unpublished doctoral dissertation, University of Minnesota, 1971.

Barber, T. X. Hypnotizability, suggestibility, and personality: V. A critical review of research findings. *Psychological Reports*, 1964, *14*, 299-320.

Barber, T. X. *Hypnosis: A Scientific Approach.* New York: Van Nostrand Reinhold, 1969. (Reprinted in 1976 by Psychological Dimensions, 10 W. 66 St., New York, 10023.)

Barber, T. X. Suggested ("hypnotic") behavior: The trance paradigm versus an alternative paradigm. (Medfield Foundation Report 103) Medfield, Mass.: Medfield Foundation, 1970.

Barber, T. X., and Glass, L. B. Significant factors in hypnotic behavior. *Journal of Abnormal and Social Psychology*, 1962, *64*, 222-228. ·

Barber, T. X., Spanos, N. P., & Chaves, J. F. *Hypnosis, imagination, and human potentialities.* Elmsford, N.Y.: Pergamon Press, 1974.

Barber, T. X., and Wilson, S. C. Hypnosis, suggestions, and altered states of consciousness: Experimental evaluation of the new cognitive-behavioral theory and the traditional trance-state theory of "hypnosis". *Annals of the New York Academy of Sciences*, 1977, *296*, 34-47.

Barber, T. X. & Wilson, S. C. The Barber Suggestibility Scale and the Creative Imagination Scale: Experimental and Clinical Applications. *American Journal of Clinical Hypnosis*, 1978/1979, *21*, 84-108.

Barber, T. X., Wilson, S. C., & Scott, D. S. Effects of a traditional trance induction on response to 'hypnotist-centered' versus 'subject-centered' test-suggestions. *International Journal of Clinical and Experimental Hypnosis*, in press.

Binet, A., & Féré, C. *Animal magnetism.* New York: Appleton, 1888.

Bosdell, B. Training counselors in the fantasy imaging process. Paper presented at Second American Conference on the Fantasy and Imaging Process, Chicago, November 3-5, 1978.

Canale, J. A. The effect of situational controlled suggestibility on Jungian personality types. Doctoral dissertation, Boston University, 1976.

Coe, W. C. The heuristic value of role theory and hypnosis. Unpublished doctoral dissertation, University of California, Berkeley, 1964.

Coe, W. C., & Sarbin, T. R. An experimental demonstration of hypnosis as role enactment. *Journal of Abnormal Psychology*, 1966, *71*, 400-405.

Cordner, G. M. Directed fantasy and religious symbols. Paper presented at Second American Conference on the Fantasy and Imaging Process, Chicago, November 3-5, 1978.

Crawford, V. L., & Katz, N. W. Comparison of induction techniques under plateau conditions. Albuquerque, N.M.: Department of Psychology, University of New Mexico, 1978.

Damashek, R. Personal mythology through guided fantasy. Paper presented at Second American Conference on the Fantasy and Imaging Process, Chicago, November 3-5, 1978.

Davis, S., Dawson, J. G., & Seay, B. Prediction of hypnotic susceptibility from imaginative involvement. *American Journal of Clinical Hypnosis*, 1978, *20*, 194-198.

De Alvarez, B. M. *Escala de Imaginacion Creativa*. Chihuahua, Chih., Mexico: Instituto Interamericano de Estudios Psicologicos Y Socioles, 1977.

De Stefano, R. The "inoculation" effect in Think-With Instructions for "hypnotic-like" experiences. Doctoral dissertation, Temple University, 1977.

Diamond, M. J., & Taft, R. The role played by ego permissiveness and imagery in hypnotic responsivity. *International Journal of Clinical and Experimental Hypnosis*, 1975, *23*, 130-138.

Don, N. S. Research in the altered states of consciousness with special emphasis on guided imagery. Paper presented at Second American Conference on the Fantasy and Imaging Process, Chicago, November 3-5, 1978.

Hershey, M., & Kearn, P. The effect of relaxation and guided imagery exercises on creative thinking ability. Paper presented at Second American Conference on the Fantasy and Imaging Process, Chicago, November 3-5, 1978.

Hilgard, E. R. *Hypnotic susceptibility*. New York: Harcourt, Brace & World, 1965.

Hilgard, J. R. *Personality and hypnosis*. Chicago: University of Chicago Press, 1970.

Honiotes, G. J. Hypnosis and breast enlargement — a pilot study. *Journal of the International Society for Professional Hypnosis*, December 1977, *6*, No. 4, 8-12.

Katz, N. W., & Crawford, V. L. A little trance and a little skill: Interaction between models of hypnosis and type of hypnotic induction. Albuquerque, N.M.: Department of Psychology, University of New Mexico, 1978.

Kiddoo, K. P. A factor analytic study of imagining and theoretically related cognitive and personality variables. Doctoral dissertation, University of Missouri, 1978.

Lee-Teng, E. Trance-susceptibility, induction-susceptibility, and acquiescence as factors in hypnotic performance. *Journal of Abnormal Psychology*, 1965, *70*, 383-389.

Marks, D. F. Visual imagery differences in the recall of pictures. *British Journal of Psychology*, 1973, *14*, 407-412.

May, D. The fantasy-imaging process used with the aging. Paper presented at Second American Conference on the Fantasy and Imaging Process, Chicago, November 3-5, 1978.

McConkey, K. M., Sheehan, P. W., Law, H. G., and White, K. D. Structural analysis of the Creative Imagination Scale. St. Lucia, Queensland, Australia: Department of Psychology, University of Queensland, 1977.

Meeker, W. B., & Barber, T. X. Toward an explanation of stage hypnosis. *Journal of Abnormal Psychology*, 1971, *77*, 61-70.

Paivio, A. *Imagery and Verbal Processes*. New York: Holt, Rinehart and Winston, 1971.

Richardson, A. *Mental Imagery*. New York: Springer Publishing Company, 1969.

Rosner, C. Gestalt use of the fantasy-imaging process. Paper presented at Second American Conference on the Fantasy and Imaging Process, Chicago, November 3-5, 1978.

Ryder, B. L. The relationship of empathy to the imaginative aspect of hypnosis. Senior Honors Thesis, Department of Psychology, University of Massachusetts/ Boston, 1978.

Sarbin, T. R. The quixotic principle: Believed-in imaginings. Santa Cruz, California: Department of Psychology, Stevenson College, University of California, 1976.

Sarbin, T. R., & Coe, W. C. *Hypnosis: A social psychological analysis of influence communication.* New York: Holt, Rinehart & Winston, 1972.

Sarbin, T. R., & Lim, D. T. Some evidence in support of the role-taking hypothesis in hypnosis. *International Journal of Clinical and Experimental Hypnosis*, 1963, *11*, 98-103.

Sheehan, P. W. A shortened form of Betts Questionnaire upon Mental Imagery, *Journal of Clinical Psychology*, 1967, *23*, 386-389.

Sheehan, P. W. Hypnosis and the manifestations of "imagination". In E. Fromm & R. E. Shor (Eds.) *Hypnosis: Research developments and perspectives*. Chicago: Aldine-Atherton, 1972. Pp. 293-319.

Shor, R. E. The three factor theory of hypnosis as applied to the book reading fantasy and to the concept of suggestion. *International Journal of Clinical and Experimental Hypnosis*, 1970, *18*, 89-98.

Shor, R. E., & Orne, E. C. *The Harvard group scale of hypnotic susceptibility, Form A*. Palo Alto, Calif.: Consulting Psychologists Press, 1962.

Shor, R. E., Orne, M. T., & O'Connell, D. N. Validation and cross-validation of a scale of self-reported personal experiences which predicts hypnotizability. *Journal of Psychology*, 1962, *53*, 55-75.

Siuta, J. [Polish translation of Creative Imagination Scale.] Krakow, Poland: Instytut Psychologii, Uniwersytet Jagiellonski, 1978.

Sommer, C. Use of gestalt in guided fantasy. Paper presented at Second American Conference on the Fantasy and Imaging Process, Chicago, November 3-5, 1978.

Spanos, N. P., & Barber, T. X. Toward a convergence in hypnosis research. *American Psychologist*, 1974, *29*, 500-511.

Spanos, N. P., & McPeake, J. D. The effects of involvement in everyday imaginative activities and attitudes toward hypnosis on hypnotic suggestibility. *Journal of Personality and Social Psychology*, 1975, *31*, 594-598.

Staib, A. R., & Logan, D. R. Hypnotic stimulation of breast growth. *American Journal of Clinical Hypnosis*, 1977, *19*, 201-208.

Straus, R. A. Experimentation in a clinical setting: Effects of hypnotic induction upon Creative Imagination Scale performance. Sacramento, Calif.: 3400 Cottage Way, Stress and Habit Control Centre, 1978.

Sutcliffe, J. P., Perry, C. W., & Sheehan, P. W. Relation of some aspects of imagery and fantasy to hypnotic susceptibility. *Journal of Abnormal Psychology*, 1970, *76*, 279-287.

Tellegen, A., & Atkinson, G. Openness to absorbing and self-altering experiences ("absorption") a trait related to hypnotic susceptibility. *Journal of Abnormal Psychology*, 1974, *83*, 268-277.

Weitzenhoffer, A. M., & Hilgard, E. R. *Stanford hypnotic susceptibility scale, Forms A and B*. Palo Alto, Calif.: Consulting Psychologists Press, 1959.

Weitzenhoffer, A. M., & Hilgard, E. R. *Stanford hypnotic susceptibility scale, Form C*. Palo Alto, Calif.: Consulting Psychologists Press, 1962.

White, K., Sheehan, P. W., & Ashton, R. Imagery assessment: A survey of self-report measures. *Journal of Mental Imagery*, 1977, *1*, 145-170.

Willard, R. D. Breast enlargement through visual imagery and hypnosis. *American Journal of Clinical Hypnosis*, 1977, *19*, 195-200.

Williams, J. E. Stimulation of breast growth by hypnosis. *Journal of Sex Research*, 1974, *10*, 316-326.

Wilson, S. C. An experimental investigation evaluating a Creative Imagination Scale and its relationship to "hypnotic-like" experiences. Doctoral dissertation, Heed Universtiy, Hollywood, Florida, 1976.

Wilson, S. C., & Barber, T. X. The Creative Imagination Scale as a measure of hypnotic responsiveness: applications to experimental and clinical hypnosis. *American Journal of Clinical Hypnosis*, 1978, *20*, 235-249.

APPENDIX A

Creative Imagination Scale

1. *Arm Heaviness.* By letting your thoughts go along with these instructions, you can make your hand and arm feel heavy. Please close your eyes, and place your left arm straight out in front of you at shoulder height with the palm facing up.

[Begin timing.] Now imagine that a very heavy dictionary is being placed on the palm of your left hand. Let yourself feel the heaviness. Your thoughts make it feel as if there is a heavy dictionary on your hand. You create the feeling of heaviness in your hand by thinking of a large, heavy dictionary. Now think of a second large, heavy dictionary being placed on top of the first heavy dictionary. Feel how very heavy your arm begins to feel as you push up on the dictionaries. Push up on the heavy dictionaries as you imagine the weight; notice how your arm feels heavier and heavier as you push up on them. Now tell yourself that a third big, heavy dictionary is being piled on top of the other two heavy dictionaries in your hand and your arm is very, very heavy. Let yourself feel as if there are three heavy dictionaries on the palm of your hand and your arm is getting heavier and heavier and heavier. Feel your arm getting heavier and heavier and heavier, very, very, very heavy, getting heavier and heavier and heavier ... very heavy. [End of timing: about 1'20'']

Now tell yourself that your hand and arm feel perfectly normal again and just let your hand and arm come back down and relax.

2. *Hand Levitation.* By directing your thoughts, you can make your hand feel as if it is rising easily, without effort. Keep your eyes closed, and place your right arm straight out in front of you at shoulder height with the palm facing down.

[Begin timing.] Now, picture a garden hose with a strong stream of water pushing against the palm of your right hand, pushing up against the palm of your hand. Think of a strong stream of water pushing your hand up. Let yourself feel the strong stream of water pushing up against the palm of your hand, pushing it up. Feel the force of the water, pushing your hand up. Feel it pushing against the palm of your hand. Tell yourself that the force of the water is very strong and, as you think about it, let your hand begin to rise. Feel your hand rising as you imagine a strong stream of water pushing it up, and up, and up, higher and higher. Tell yourself that a strong stream of water is pushing your hand up and up, raising your arm and hand higher and higher as the strong stream of water just pushes it up, just rises and pushes and just pushes it up, higher and higher. [End of timing: about 1'10'']

Now tell yourself its all in your own mind and just let your hand and arm come back down and relax.

3. *Finger Anesthesia.* By focusing your thinking, you can make your fingers feel numb. Please place your left hand in your lap with the palm facing up. Keep your eyes closed so you can focus fully on all the sensations in the fingers of your left hand.

[Begin timing.] Now, try to imagine and feel as if novocain has just been injected into the side of your left hand next to the little finger so that your little finger will begin to feel like it does when it 'falls asleep'. Focus on the little finger. Become aware of every sensation and the slight little changes as you think of the novocain slowly beginning to move into your little finger, just slowly moving in. Notice the slight little changes as the little finger begins to get just a little numb and a little dull. The little finger is becoming numb as you think of the novocain moving in slowly.

Now think of the novocain moving into the second finger next to the little finger. Tell yourself that the second finger is getting duller and duller, more and more numb as you think of how the novacain is beginning to take effect.

Tell yourself that these two fingers are beginning to feel kind of rubbery and are losing feelings and sensations. As you think of the novocain moving in faster, the fingers feel duller and duller . . . more and more numb . . . dull, numb, and insensitive. As you think of the novocain taking effect, the two fingers feel duller and duller . . . more and more numb . . . dull . . . numb . . . insensitive.

Keep thinking that the two fingers are dull, numb, and insensitive as you touch the two fingers with your thumb. As you touch the two fingers with your thumb notice how they feel duller and duller, more and more numb, more and more insensitive . . . dull, numb, rubbery, and insensitive. [End of timing: about 1'50"]

Now tell yourself its all in your own mind and you're going to bring the feeling back; bring the feeling back into the two fingers.

4. *Water "Hallucination."* Keep your eyes closed. By using your imagination constructively, you can experience the feeling of drinking cool, refreshing water.

[Begin timing.] First, imagine you've been out in the hot sun for hours and you're very, very thirsty and your lips are dry and you're so thirsty. Now, picture yourself on a mountain where the snow is melting, forming a stream of cool, clear water. Imagine yourself dipping a cup into this mountain stream so you can have a cool, refreshing drink of water. As you think of sipping the water, tell yourself it's absolutely delicious as you feel it going down your throat . . . cold and beautiful and delicious. Feel the coolness and beauty of the water as you take a sip. Now, think of taking another sip of water and feel it going over your lips and tongue, going down your throat, down into your stomach. Feel how cool, refreshing, delicious, and beautiful it is as you take another sip . . . so cool . . . cold . . . sweet . . . beautiful . . . delicious and refreshing. Think of taking another sip now, and feel the cool water going into your mouth, around your tongue, down your throat and down into your stomach . . . so beautiful and cool and wonderful . . . absolutely delicious . . . absolute pleasure. [End of timing: about 1'30"]

5. *Olfactory-Gustatory "Hallucination."* Keep your eyes closed. By using your imagination creatively, you can experience the smell and taste of an orange.

[Begin timing.] Picture yourself picking up an orange, and imagine that you're peeling it. As you create the image of the orange, feel yourself peeling it and let yourself see and feel the orange skin on the outside and the soft white pulp on the inside of the skin. As you continue peeling the orange, notice how beautiful and luscious it is, and let yourself smell it and touch it and feel the juiciness of it. Now think of pulling out one or two of the orange sections with your fingers. Pull out part of the orange, and bite into it. Experience how juicy, luscious, and flavorful it is as you imagine taking a deep, deep bite. Let yourself smell and taste the orange, and notice that it's absolutely delicious. Let yourself feel how delicious, beautiful, and luscious it is. Just the most beautiful, juicy orange . . . absolutely juicy and wonderful. Let yourself taste and smell the juicy orange clearly now as you think of taking another large bite of the delicious, juicy orange. [End of timing: about 1'30"]

6. *Music "Hallucination."* Keep your eyes closed.

[Begin timing.] Now, think back to a time when you heard some wonderful, vibrant music; it could have been anywhere, and by thinking back you can hear it even more exquisitely in your own mind. You make it yourself, and you can experience it as intensely as real music. The music can be absolutely powerful . . . strong . . . exquisite . . . vibrating through every pore of your body . . . going deep into every pore . . . penetrating through every fiber of your being. The most beautiful, complete, exquisite, overwhelming music you ever heard. Listen to it now as you create it in your own mind. [End of timing: about 45"]

[15-second pause] You may stop thinking of the music now.

7. *Temperature "Hallucination."* Keep your eyes closed, and place your hands in your lap with the palms facing down and resting comfortably on your lap. By focusing your think-

ing, you can make your right hand feel hot.

[Begin timing.] Picture the sun shining on your right hand, and let yourself feel the heat. As you think of the sun shining brightly, let yourself feel the heat increasing. Feel the sun getting hotter, and feel the heat penetrating your skin and going deep into your hand. Think of it getting really hot now . . . getting very hot. Feel the heat increasing. Think of the sun getting very, very hot as it penetrates into your hand . . . getting very hot. Tell yourself, 'The rays are increasing . . . the heat is increasing . . . getting hotter and hotter.' Feel the heat penetrating through your skin. Feel the heat going deeper into your skin as you think of the rays of the sun increasing and becoming more and more concentrated . . . getting hotter and hotter. Feel your hand getting hot from the heat of the sun. It's a good feeling of heat as it penetrates deep into your hand . . . hot, pleasantly hot, penetrating your hand now. It's a pleasantly hot feeling, pleasantly hot. [End of timing: about 1'15"]

Now tell yourself it's all in your own mind, and make your hand feel perfectly normal again.

8. *Time Distortion.* Keep your eyes closed. By controlling your thinking, you can make time seem to slow down.

[The following is to be read progressively more and more slowly, with each word drawn out and with long, i.e., 2- to 6-second pauses between statements.] [Begin timing.] Tell yourself that there's lots of time, lots of time between each second. Time is stretching out, and there's lots of time . . . more and more time between each second. Every second is stretching far, far out . . . stretching out more and more . . . lots of time. There's so much time . . . lots of time. Every second is stretching out. There's lots of time between each second . . . lots of time. You do it yourself, you slow time down. [End of timing: about 1'40"]

[The following is to be read at a normal rate.] And now tell yourself that time is speeding back up to its normal rate again as you bring time back to normal.

9. *Age Regression.* Keep your eyes closed. By directing your thinking, you can bring back the feelings that you experienced when you were in elementary school — in first, second, third, fourth, or fifth grade.

[Begin timing.] Think of time going back, going back to elementary school, and feel yourself becoming smaller and smaller. Let yourself feel your hands, small and tiny, and your legs and your body, small and tiny. As you go back in time, feel yourself sitting in a big desk. Notice the floor beneath you. Feel the top of the desk. You may feel some marks on the desk top, or maybe it's a smooth, cool surface. There may be a pencil slot and perhaps a large yellow pencil. Feel the under side of the desk, and you may feel some chewing gum. Observe the other children around you, and the teacher, the bulletin board, the chalkboard, the cloakroom, and the windows. Smell the eraser dust or the paste. You may hear the children and the teacher speaking. Now just observe, and see what happens around you. [End of timing: about 1'20"]

[15-second pause] Now tell yourself its all in your own mind, and bring yourself back to the present.

10. *Mind-Body Relaxation.* Keep your eyes closed. By letting your thoughts go along with these instructions, you can make your mind and body feel very relaxed.

[The following is to be read slowly.] [Begin timing.] Picture yourself on a beautiful, warm summer day lying under the sun on a beach of an ocean or lake. Feel yourself lying on the soft, soft sand or on a beach towel that is soft and comfortable. Let yourself feel the sun pleasantly warm and feel the gentle breeze touching your neck and face. Picture the beautiful, clear, blue sky with fluffy, little, white clouds drifting lazily by. Let yourself feel the soothing, penetrating warmth of the sun, and tell yourself that your mind and body feel completely relaxed and perfectly at ease . . . peaceful, relaxed, comfortable, calm, so at ease, at peace with the universe . . . completely relaxed . . . relaxed, peaceful, lazy, tranquil . . . calm . . .

comfortable. Your mind and body are completely relaxed ... completely relaxed ... calm, peaceful, tranquil, flowing with the universe. [End of timing: about 2'05"]

Now as you open your eyes let yourself continue to feel relaxed and yet perfectly alert ... peaceful, alert, and normal again. Open your eyes.

APPENDIX B

Scoring of the Creative Imagination Scale

Please answer each item as honestly as possible. There are no right or wrong answers.

Read the statements below describing the possible responses for each item. Then, circle the number (0, 1, 2, 3, or 4) which corresponds to the statement that most nearly matches your experience.

1. In the first test, you were asked to imagine that one, two, and then three dictionaries were being piled on the palm of your hand. Compared to what you would have experienced if three dictionaries were actually on your hand, what you experienced was:

0	1	2	3	4
0% Not at all the same	25% A little the same	50% Between a little and much the same	75% Much the same	90+% Almost exact- ly the same

2. In the second test, you were asked to think of a strong stream of water from a garden hose pushing up against the palm of your hand. Compared to what you would have experienced if a strong stream of water were actually pushing up against your palm, what you experienced was:

0	1	2	3	4
0% Not at all the same	25% A little the same	50% Between a little and much the same	75% Much the same	90+% Almost exact- ly the same

3. In the third test, you were asked to imagine that novocain had been injected into your hand, and it made two fingers feel numb. Compared to what you would have experienced if novocain had actually made the two fingers feel numb, what you experienced was:

0	1	2	3	4
0% Not at all the same	25% A little the same	50% Between a little and much the same	75% Much the same	90+% Almost exact- ly the same

4. In the fourth test, you were asked to think of drinking a cup of cool mountain water. Compared to what you would have experienced if you were actually drinking cool mountain water, what you experienced was:

0	1	2	3	4
0% Not at all the same	25% A little the same	50% Between a little and much the same	75% Much the same	90+% Almost exact- ly the same

5. In the fifth test, you were asked to imagine smelling and tasting an orange. Compared to what you would have experienced if you were actually smelling and tasting an orange, what you experienced was:

0	1	2	3	4
0%	25%	50%	75%	90+%
Not at all the same	A little the same	Between a little and much the same	Much the same	Almost exactly the same

6. In the sixth test, you were asked to think back to a time when you heard some wonderful music and to re-experience hearing it. Compared to what you would have experienced if you were actually hearing the music, what you experienced was:

0	1	2	3	4
0%	25%	50%	75%	90+%
Not at all the same	A little the same	Between a little and much the same	Much the same	Almost exactly the same

7. In the seventh test, you were asked to picture the sun shining on your hand, making it feel hot. Compared to what you would have experienced if the sun were actually shining on your hand, what you experienced was:

0	1	2	3	4
0%	25%	50%	75%	90+%
Not at all the same	A little the same	Between a little and much the same	Much the same	Almost exactly the same

8. In the eighth test, you were asked to imagine time slowing down. Compared to what you would have experienced if time actually slowed down, what you experienced was:

0	1	2	3	4
0%	25%	50%	75%	90+%
Not at all the same	A little the same	Between a little and much the same	Much the same	Almost exactly the same

9. In the ninth test, you were asked to think back to a time when you were in elementary school. Compared to the feelings you would have experienced if you were actually in elementary school, the feelings you experienced were:

0	1	2	3	4
0%	25%	50%	75%	90+%
Not at all the same	A little the same	Between a little and much the same	Much the same	Almost exactly the same

10. In the tenth test, you were asked to picture yourself lying under the sun on a beach and becoming very relaxed. Compared to what you would have experienced if you were actually relaxing on a beach, what you experienced was:

0	1	2	3	4
0%	25%	50%	75%	90+%
Not at all the same	A little the same	Between a little and much the same	Much the same	Almost exactly the same

APPENDIX C

Imagination Inventory

Predicted Imagining

Please place a check mark (√) in front of the answer which best applies to you. (There are no right or wrong answers.)

1. If I tried to imagine that my leg was so heavy that I could not move it, my leg would feel (check only one):

_____ so heavy that I couldn't move it

_____ very heavy

_____ slightly heavy

_____ not at all heavy

2. If I tried to imagine that I was eating an ice cream cone, I would feel the cold and the taste of the ice cream in my mouth (check only one):

_____ in the same way as when I actually eat ice cream

_____ much the same as when I actually eat ice cream

_____ a little the same as when I actually eat ice cream

_____ not at all the same as when I actually eat ice cream; that is, I would not at all feel the cold and the taste of the ice cream in my mouth

3. If I tried to imagine that I was hearing a siren on an ambulance or a fire truck, I would hear the siren (check only one):

_____ as clearly as a real siren

_____ much the same as a real siren

_____ a little the same as a real siren

_____ not at all the same as a real siren

4. If I tried to imagine that my foot was in ice water, my foot would feel (check only one):

_____ about as cold as it would feel if it were actually in ice water

_____ cold

_____ slightly cold

_____ not at all cold

5. If I closed my eyes and tried to imagine that I was riding in the passenger seat of a car which was going very fast, about 120 miles per hour, down a fairly crowded highway, I would experience (check only one):

_____ the same anxiety and fright that I would feel if I actually were in the car

_____ much of the same anxiety and fright that I would feel if I actually were in the car

_____ a little anxiety and fright

_____ no anxiety or fright

Play History

6. Some children (below age 12) prefer to play make-believe games which require imagining or pretending such as pirates, cowboys, school, house, etc. Other children prefer to play realistic games which require skills such as hopscotch, jump rope, marbles, checkers, building things, ball games, etc. Check the response which most nearly describes you when you were a child.

_____ I preferred to play make-believe games

_____ I preferred to play realistic games

7. When I was playing as a child, I would often imagine so vividly that what I pretended became real. For instance, I would either carry on a lively conversation on a toy telephone, or my stuffed animals or dolls really seemed to be alive, or I felt as if I were driving a real car, tractor, truck, or train rather than a toy one, or I really felt as if I were a cowboy, a teacher, a doctor, a nurse, a mother, a father, etc. This describes me (check only one):

_____ exactly
_____ somewhat
_____ slightly
_____ not at all

History of Involvements

8. While watching a good movie, stage play, or T.V. show, I become so involved that I experience the story as if it were real, and I may be moved to anger, tears, and laughter. This describes me (check only one):

_____ exactly
_____ somewhat
_____ slightly
_____ not at all

9. When I was a child, I had an imaginary companion (or companions) which I can remember vividly. This describes me (check only one):

_____ exactly
_____ somewhat
_____ slightly
_____ not at all

10. When I am reading a good book (e.g., novel, biography, mystery, adventure, science fiction, etc.), I become deeply involved in the action and feel the emotions of the story such as sadness, fear, or joy. This describes me (check only one):

_____ exactly
_____ somewhat
_____ slightly
_____ not at all

11. I often have "physical memories"; that is, I can re-experience in my imagination such things as: the feeling of a soft breeze, warm sand under bare feet, the softness of fur, cool grass, the warmth of the sun, and the smell of freshly cut grass. This describes me (check only one):

_____ exactly
_____ somewhat
_____ slightly
_____ not at all

12. Compared to others of my sex and age, I am more eager to have new and unusual experiences. This describes me (check only one):

_____ exactly
_____ somewhat
_____ slightly
_____ not at all

13. I can become deeply immersed in nature; that is, I can become deeply involved in look-ing at such things as a sunset or wild flowers or an expanse of multicolored fields. This de-scribes me (check only one):

_____ exactly

_____ somewhat

_____ slightly

_____ not at all

14. Some people engage in activities such as mountain climbing, sky diving, skiing, airplane flying, etc., in order to improve or perfect skills, to compete with others or with "the ele-ments," and to gain a sense of achievement. Other people engage in activites such as those listed above in order to escape from ordinary everyday life and to enjoy the feelings of the moment (e.g., feelings of excitement, power, exhilaration, or freedom from restraint, etc.) Check the response which most nearly describes you.

_____ I do not engage in any activities such as mountain climbing, sky diving, skiing, airplane flying, etc.

_____ I engage in these or similar activities for the sense of achievement, the competi-tion, and to perfect my skills.

_____ I engage in these or similar activities in order to escape from ordinary life and to enjoy the feelings of excitement, power, freedom from restraint, etc.

15. Some people read material such as science fiction, metaphysics, parapsychology (ESP, reincarnation, etc.), Eastern philosophy, etc., to satisfy their intellectual curiosity or to decide what is possible and what is entirely impossible, etc. Other people read material such as that listed above in order to stimulate their imagination or to learn to release their inner potential, etc. Check the response which most nearly describes you.

_____ I do not read material such as science fiction, metaphysics, parapsychology, Eastern philosophy, etc.

_____ I read such material for intellectual reasons or to determine what is possible and impossible, etc.

_____ I read such material to stimulate my imagination or to learn to release my inner potential, etc.

6

Imagery Processes and Hypnosis: An Experiential Analysis of Phenomena

PETER W. SHEEHAN

Since the days of J. B. Watson, imagery has undergone a massive resurgence of interest. The study of imagery and fantasy phenomena burgeoned once psychology admitted to the genuineness of imagery and the meaningfulness of investigating it, and the respectability of studying imagery phenomena is no longer contested. That resurgence of interest appeared to reach its peak in the late 1960's and early 1970's and was heralded when Robert Holt (1964) made his plea to researchers to "come on in — the water's fine." The indications now are that psychology in general is returning to a nonbehavioristic view of man, one framed in terms of consciousness for its definition and description of its field of inquiry. In personality theorizing, the impetus is captured by the movement called "interactionism" which recognizes explicitly the influence of the person in context and looks to the individual as an intentional, active agent who interprets situations and assigns cognitive meaning to them (Endler & Magnusson, 1974). According to this viewpoint, individuals are not influenced mechanistically by the contexts or situations in which they are placed, but are shaped and modify in turn their environment in an effortful, active, cognitive way. As Ekehammar (1974) indicates, psychology has turned to re-assess the significance of what was said long ago. Angyal's (1941) biosphere conception, Sullivan's (1953) interpersonal theory, and Lewin's (1951) field theory are only a sample of the frameworks of thinking that basically recognize interactionist assumptions.

Peter W. Sheehan, Department of Psychology, University of Queensland, St. Lucia, Australia, 4067.

Imagery and fantasy as thought processes become an important part of the cognitive modes of operation of the thinking, apprehending person, and as phenomena relevant to this change in the Zeitgeist, they have acquired a new significance that has not really yet been appreciated in the experimental literature. If human beings are to be acknowledged as sentient, cognizing, and apprehending persons, then the active nature of their imagery becomes an important part of their functioning for psychology to explore. Many salient features of that activity fail to be captured by much of the experimentation one reads about in the current literature. Part of the problem, of course, is that imagery is a difficult process to index. As Bugelski (1971) notes, we tell people to image something, and they inform us that they have done so. Investigators inevitably fall back on using their instructions as operational definitions of imaging when all they have at hand is the person's personal description of what he/she is doing. The problematic nature of verbal reports represents a major difficulty, and their disadvantages have been sharply debated elsewhere (Nisbett & Wilson, 1977).

Part of the problem with changes of emphasis in our discipline is the difficulty of isolating particular techniques of assessment that flow directly from new theoretical assumptions. Choice of appropriate assessment methods is necessary, however, if knowledge about the validity and accuracy of our frameworks of thinking are to advance. Just as Sullivan's interpersonal theory may be appropriately implicated by structural analysis of a 2-person interview situation, Freudian theory by the method of free association, and aspects of dynamic theorizing by projective testing, so too the interactionist view of man requires its own assessment model to enable us to explore the model's validity in appropriate fashion. It certainly must mean something different from self-report measurement of traits and stimulus analysis of impinging events.

The link between revealing the nature of things and the way we assess is equally relevant to the study of imagery. Work over the last 10 years has consolidated the study of imagery as the analysis of a phenomenon which is functionally related to perception. Functional correspondences between imagery and perception, for example, are studied in ways that reflect the regularity of association between external stimulus events, events manipulated by the experimenter that are assumed to involve the process of imaging, and the behavior of subjects. Data indicate, for instance, that there is a strong positive relationship between the imageability of stimuli and accuracy of recall in a number of distinct learning test situations (Paivio, 1971), that visual imagery interferes with the detection of visual signals while auditory imagery interferes with the' detection of auditory signals (Segal & Fusella, 1970), and that imagined rotations have a distinct component that is shared with processes occurring when the same individual is actually perceiving an external rotation of the stimulus (Cooper & Shepard, 1973). In all of this research imagery is isolated as part-process of a total functioning organism, and the relationship of imagery is examined within a single process framework linked to either perception or memory. In the search for uniform and consistent effects, researchers have come to by-pass the potential advantages of analyzing individual differences in styles of imagery or modes of cognitive representation. The study of these differences still remains largely the province of the clinician, but due to the shift in Zeitgeist, these differences are now emphasized much more for others as well.

Motivation and Imagery Phenomena

Consider the relevance of the process of motivation to imagery and fantasy phenomena. In the experimental literature (see Paivio, 1971), the relevance of motivation is discounted by argument, quite legitimate in its own right, that motivation or interest cannot reasonably explain the differential effects of imaginal and verbal mediators. The fact that persons unexpectedly recalling events show strong imagery effects as compared to learning situations where recall is expected makes the hypothesis a difficult one to hold in the way it has been studied. In the literature where depth psychology or dynamic orientations to the study of human beings is emphasized, much more than this is said, however, about the relevance of motivation. Holt, (1972), for instance, argues that at all times, presentation-forming programs of the mind have to be under the control of motive systems of a particular kind, "and there is good reason to suppose that in many if not all people, unconscious motive systems over which there is little if any voluntary control are forming and processing sensory presentations a great deal of the time, possibly always" (p. 29). The same trend in theorizing is manifest in the work on unbidden images where imagery may flood into consciousness when stress and anxiety are present (Horowitz, 1970).

The area which most explicitly recognizes the functional role imagery has to play in relation to the motivations of persons, however, is clearly the field of therapy. Ahsen (1977), for example, views the troubled individual as someone who must be retrained to experience his/her imagery in threatened areas. Therapy that focuses on eidetic imagery aims, for example, specifically to explore the patient's eidetics following the general principle of elucidating the picture, feeling, and meaning aspects of this mode of representation. Such an approach focuses distinctively on the interplay between attitudes, emotions, and motivations in shaping the influence of the imagery response in the *total* functioning person. In a framework of this kind, the interactive aspects of personality and imagery are emphasized and are said to be critical in the process of recovery. Other theorists than Ahsen (e.g., Assagioli, 1965; Fretigny & Virel, 1968; Leuner, 1977) argue equally cogently for utilizing the processes of imagination directly in therapeutic treatment. Collectively, these various viewpoints draw their validity from the clinician's assumption that pictorial representations can be enlivened with affect and meaning in ways that conceptual representations cannot, and recovery can result from the process (Sheehan, 1971; see also, Sheikh & Panagiotou, 1975 for review of the relevant evidence). Understanding the role of affect and conscious and unconscious motivations importantly relates to the extent to which we apprehend the processes of recovery and the relevance of imagery to facilitating cure.

At the moment there seems to be little point of contact between the laboratory researcher who excludes motivation as relevant to the function of imagery and the clinician who incorporates the interactive aspects of imagery and motivation within his/her theoretical frame of reference. Further, close scrutiny of the differences in orientation reveals that the former approach segmentalizes processes where the latter does not. Motivation for the task is studied in the first instance, whereas intrapsychic events that are not necessarily task-oriented tend to be analyzed in the second. In the first also, memory imagery seems often to be at issue, whereas the latter frequently focuses on so-called imagination imagery. Certainly, the role of affect and motivation is heralded differently in the two orientations depending on the type of imagery processes being discussed. It is thus necessary at this point to analyze some of the points of definition frequently debated in the literature concerning the various processes of imagination to which we refer.

Definitions of Terms

Fantasy and imagery are clearly related and argument can be made that it is spurious to separate the terms too closely. Ullman (1959), for example, blurs the distinction by identifying one of the major formal aspects of dream consciousness as the employment of concrete means of presentation, mostly in the form of visual imagery. Fantasy, however, tends to be traditionally considered as a form of creative imagination where the images or trains of imagery are controlled and directed by a person's motivations in a clearly evident way. Fantasy for many suggests an active, effortful, constructive organization of past experience which is subject to the special influence of motivational and emotional states, and, like imagery, may be outer or inner directed. Fantasy has been argued to be more of a reproductive synthesis than imagery, largely motivational in origin, and representing more of a totality of past experiences. Imagery, on the other hand, tends to define a situation where the subject reports "seeing" or "picturing" something when there is no actual object present to the senses as in perception; the object of recall has a clearly evident "thing-quality" which is distinguished from hallucination, for example, by the absence of conviction that the object being imaged does, in fact, exist. Finally, the label "imagine" usually denotes the general term implying one or more of these processes in action; persons who are imagining, for example, may be involving themselves in either imagery or fantasy activities.

Differences of these kinds do relatively little justice to the richness and variety of clinically evident psychological experience. Part of the problem, however, is that the techniques we adopt to study imagination processes maintain such conceptual distinctions; rarely, if ever, for example, does the laboratory analysis of memory imagery acknowledge the impact of motivation and the interactive aspects of cognition in relation to affect and needs; only work on eidetic imagery within the laboratory setting has tended to capture this emphasis (Gray & Gummerman, 1975). For the most part, in study of memory imagery subjects have been presented with tasks requiring accurate solution. The function of imagery is then frequently judged by the extent to which the imaging subject reproduces the response that the investigator thinks is appropriate. In this way, test situations elicit data that probably reflect more about the techniques of assessment themselves and the investigator's preconceived notions about imagery, than about the phenomena at issue.

Some discussion of the situational demands on the persons we study serves to illustrate the point. Imaginative activity may clearly be free in form and relatively unconstrained by physical reality. Asking a subject to imagine himself/herself in a setting he/she finds particularly pleasant places relatively few demands on the kind of setting that is imagined, how it is defined, its detailed structure, or the exact nature of his/her specific relationship to it. Ask someone to imagine a picture he/she has just seen, or something that a string of concrete words represents, however, and you begin to far more heavily constrain the person to imagine events in a literal, reproductive manner; the cues are that the situation should be reproduced in a fashion that is accurate, at least in part. How much, then, do we limit analysis of phenomena and the possible functions of imagery by asking subjects to repeat words or other stimuli that they have just seen in a controlled and systematic presentation of previous events? If assessment procedures for measuring imagery serve themselves to place considerable pressure on subjects to experience events in a literal fashion, then the functional ties with perception that current work has isolated may underestimate the constructive, synthesizing function we normally attribute to fantasy, dreaming, and other manifestations of imagination at work.

My argument here is that data which support the relationship of imaginal events to original perceptual experience serve to emphasize relatively close functional ties with perception, yet the demand characteristics, or cues apparent in the assessment situations that are employed, indicate quite clearly that standards of reality and accuracy are the ones to be used to evaluate the appropriateness of performance. In this sense, the nature and specificity of the instructions which the investigator gives may be an important factor in determining the extent to which subjects' reports will be literal, or embellished in a more constructive fashion. The exact wording of instructions and the type of imaginative activity being requested can set quite strict limits on just how literal the subject is in conforming to the investigator's requests. Instructions to dream, for example, permit, or legitimize, constructions and embellishment that are normally not countenanced by instructions to "picture what you have just seen now, in your mind's eye." The terms "fantasy" and "imagery", then, may well serve to reinforce constraints built in by our chosen modes of assessment. Such task constraints may draw attention away from relevant processes reflecting the involvement of different mental subsystems that depict the active, constructive interplay of cognitions, affect, and need states.

The Relevance of Hypnosis

Hypnosis has a special relevance in elucidating some of the issues I am attempting to highlight. It guarantees a situation where the investigator requests that the subject engage in imagery and fantasy and poses a variety of specific tasks in which subjects are motivated to experience as cooperatively, as they can. Hypnotic situations normally offer a range of imaginative experiences from imaging that one's hand is heavy, to dreaming about what hypnosis means, to going back to being a small child, and finally to experiencing events as forgotten or attempting to see or hear events that physically are not present. In hypnosis the naturalness of the subject's response is emphasized, albeit within a framework of cooperation. Hypnotic tasks also usefully differ in the extent to which they place specific constraints on the subject to reproduce events in a literal fashion. One can well observe, then, the functions of imagery and fantasy without necessarily excluding, by the mode of assessment chosen, study of the interactive features of motivation and cognition.

A common conceptualization for considering hypnosis is that it involves the fading of everyday reality orientation into the background of awareness with the consequence that ongoing experiences become relatively isolated from their normal frame of reference. The structure of this reality orientation as Shor (1959, 1962) defines it, permits what is called secondary process thinking. Viewed in this way, the capacity to temporarily relinquish reality in hypnosis corresponds to a regression to the kind of functioning that may facilitate the flow of prelogical ideational processes; vigilance, for example, can be reduced in a comparable way through sleep. With the loss of this orientation, the distinction between reality and imagination fades, and primary process modes of thought such as imagery and fantasy are allowed to flow more easily into awareness. The new orientation that is created by the flow of primary process material can be expected to show some of the qualities of the dream state; hypnosis, then, may involve a greater concern than usual with internal mental processes than does the waking state, and, as a result, vivid imagery, hallucinations, fantasies, and dreamlike phenomena may more easily occur. Argument on the data concerning this issue is made elsewhere (Barber, 1978; Sheehan, in press, a).

This display of imagery and fantasy implicates special skills and aptitudes on the part of the hypnotizable person as well as illustrates the fact that ideational processing is legitimized and encouraged by the context in which this person is placed. Yet what makes the hypnotic situation so useful for studying the functions of imagination is that while ideational processing is facilitated, the evidence clearly indicates that the hypnotic subject accurately registers reality. The hypnotic person's verbal reports reflect fantasied events but may also acknowledge denial of the same fantasy. Hilgard's (1977) research on divided consciousness and the hidden observer phenomenon — where subjects both assert and deny pain following anaesthesia suggestions at one and the same time — indexes the complex nature of the cognitive processing that characterizes the hypnotizable person.

Hypnosis, then, provides cogent theoretical reasons why imagination processes will be operative and reduces some of the constraints of standard test situations that tie the subject to preconceived notions of appropriate, "literal" response. Active imagination is permitted by the hypnotist who attempts to create the most favorable situation possible for the display of the subject's capacities and cognitive talents, and reality and fantasy coexist to potentially influence the subject in how he/she chooses to behave. It is also a situation where the processes of motivation are explicitly indicated. The hypnotized subject appears especially willing to cooperate with the hypnotist, and evidence exists to indicate that in certain ways, some hypnotized subjects are particularly willing to do what the hypnotist requests (Dolby & Sheehan, 1977; Sheehan & Dolby, 1975). Provided with good motivational reasons for responding otherwise, for example, some susceptible subjects will lay those reasons aside and resolve their conflict to favor the hypnotist's intent. In this way, the "motivated cognitive commitment" (Sheehan, in press, b) of these subjects is clearly evident. Overall, the hypnotic situation seems particularly well suited to analyzing the interactions of motives and cognitions as illustrated through the processes of imagination.

Case Illustration

The following case of Subject "O" illustrates complex ideational processing at work and highlights the importance of measuring imagination in a way that least inhibits the initiative or constructive efforts of the subject. The subject was a highly motivated and susceptible person and sophisticated in the skills of introspection. The subject spontaneously reported the experiences which followed many months after being hypnotized, and the text reported here gives her verbatim record of those events. The record represents for me one of the most fascinating accounts of imaginative involvement in hypnosis in my research experience, and it demonstrates in a highly relevant fashion the processes that I have previously outlined.

My first experience with hypnosis was when I read a notice in the Psychology Department: "Subjects Wanted for Hypnosis Experiments." My curiosity was aroused, and I decided to go along to see what it was all about. However, I arrived late and missed the introductory remarks of the HGSHS: A tape, and consequently I wasn't at all sure whether to cooperate or to resist the suggestions. Having misconceptions about hypnosis, I decided to resist. That was not so easy, however. Every now and then I found myself listening to the voice, and I experienced considerable difficulty in resisting. It was as if part of me was drawn in by the voice and wanted to let go and do as he said, and I had to remind myself constantly that I wasn't going to be hypnotized, that I was going to resist. At the end of the session, I was confused. Had I been hypnotized or not? How could I tell? I decided that I couldn't have been because I hadn't felt all that different, and I certainly had not been asleep as the voice suggested, quite the contrary! To my surprise I was later told that I had scored 9 out of 12.

My next experience was nearly 4 years later, when I was asked unexpectedly to be a subject for the demonstration of hypnosis at a hypnosis workshop. This time I was willing to cooperate and decided to just let things happen. It was similar to that first experience in that I was drawn in by the voice but instead of resisting I seemed to repeat the hypnotist's words in my mind. He took me to a beach where 20 steps led down to the water and as we counted I went down. I could see that scene so vividly, it was as if I was really there. I enjoyed being there, it was warm and peaceful, but I didn't mind when he took me away from there and back to my school days. Going back to childhood was funny, it was like watching a film that is running too fast, the years flashed past so quickly I couldn't really see anything but stopped whenever he stopped them.

The hypnotist then told me that he was going to talk to the audience but it wouldn't disturb me, and that's just how it was. I was aware that he was talking to them about me, yet I felt so detached from it all, it didn't disturb me in the least.

I felt very relaxed and enjoyed it all very much that I was disappointed when he said that he was going to count and bring me back. I didn't really want to.

I remember thinking, "That isn't fair, he said it would take about 30 minutes and now he is going to stop it already after only a few minutes." Then he simply counted and that didn't feel at all right. Everything inside me was calling out to him, "No — you can't do that — you have to take me back to the beach," and as he counted I became more and more anxious, I wanted to come up the stairs again. I kept thinking, "Why doesn't he take me back to the beach and up the stairs?" I was all churned up inside, yet seeing the video some time later, I was absolutely amazed that I didn't show any outward signs of this inner struggle. I saw myself sitting there quite calmly, not moving or giving any indication of what was going on.

For some weeks after the session and for no apparent reason an image of the beach would flash into my mind, and I would have a strong desire to go back up those stairs. This feeling and the image would last for a split second only, but it was quite strong. Even to this day, approximately 14 months later, I still get the feeling that I would like to come back up the stairs. It does not occur as frequently now or as strongly, and I can dismiss it more rationally, but nevertheless it is still with me. I have even tried to visualize myself going up the stairs, and I can do this very successfully, but the next time the image occurs, I am always back at the bottom of the stairs!

Some 8 months later I took part in a workshop in hypnosis where members in small groups practiced pain reduction techniques. After a baseline measure, a brief induction and introduction of a specific technique, the person's arm was again placed in a bucket of ice water and the person rated himself from 1 - 10 for pain and suffering.

The member hypnotizing me used a brief relaxation induction and suggestions of analgesia. I didn't feel nearly as detached as I did at the previous workshop, however, but was very much aware of everything. In fact, I remember thinking, "I won't be able to stand that ice water again, that really hurt." Then my arm began to feel quite numb, with every stroke it really became more and more numb, I could hardly feel his hand touch my arm. When he placed my arm into the water I thought, "Oh, oh, here it goes! I won't be able to stand this." But to my surprise it didn't even worry me, then, after a while my hand began to hurt a little, but my arm didn't hurt at all, I simply couldn't feel it. Then, as far as I remember, the hypnotist simply told me to wake up. I was somewhat bewildered, I knew I was awake, yet something didn't seem right, and my arm felt very numb. I recall saying, "What have you done to my arm, it's numb!" After a brief group discussion, it was decided that he put me "under" again and remove the suggestion. The hypnotist told me to relax, that I was hypnotized again, and that upon opening my eyes my arm would feel normal.

Well, first of all, I didn't feel hypnotized the second time, it was much too quick, I felt, and secondly he did not touch my arm again. He simply *said* it would feel normal again. Yet, when he induced the numbness he did it by *stroking,* saying that *with every stroke* my arm would become more and more numb. Whatever the reason, when I opened my eyes, my arm still felt numb, not as much, but still quite numb. Not wanting to make a fuss and thinking that it was perhaps the ice water anyway that made it feel numb, I decided not to say anything more. For the rest of the seminar, however, I kept rubbing my arm, thinking, "How much longer is it going to take? Surely the effects of the ice water should be wearing off by now."

The following day it was much better but still numb enough to annoy me. It was as if something inside me reminded me that my arm felt numb and it did. My arm still felt numb 36 hours later, and I was beginning to get really annoyed and tried hard to be rational, saying things to myself like, "You are being silly, your arm doesn't feel numb, and you know it, be sensible. How can it be numb when all he did was stroke it, nothing else? How can that possibly make your arm numb? You are just imagining it, it's all in your head."

The funny thing was that I agreed with all this, I could see and understand the logic of it and yet — my arm felt numb! It was as if that part of me that was responsible for the numb feeling either didn't take any notice of my reasoning or it couldn't even hear me.

When, after 48 hours, I was still battling with myself, and it interfered even with my driving — I had to rest my arm on the car window because it felt too heavy and numb to hold the steering wheel — I decided that I had had enough. Imagination or reality, I wasn't going to put up with it any longer. I didn't want to look foolish, however, and contact the chairman of the workshop, so I confided in a colleague who agreed to remove the suggestion. After an induction, he took me back to the day of the workshop and suggested that there were two buckets. The ice bucket and another containing warm, soothing water. He then told me to take my numb arm out of the ice water and to place it in the other bucket, and as I did, the warm water would bring the feeling back, that my arm would feel warm and comfortable just the way it normally felt. This experience was very real, I could see the room and the people, feel the warm water and the numbness leaving my arm. When I took my arm out of the bucket it felt good and no longer numb. The hypnotist then counted backwards and told me to wake up. That's when an extraordinary thing happened. I "saw" the room and the people in it superimposed on the wall. I couldn't believe my eyes and blinked a few times but the image remained. I could see the white tiled wall very clearly, I knew where I was, I was awake, but I saw the workshop room and the people in it right there on the wall.

It was as if I or at least some part of me was still there in that room. It was most peculiar. When I mentioned it to the hypnotist he reintroduced hypnosis and told me that I was leaving the workshop room, that I was coming back to the present, that it was Monday and I was back in my room. When I opened my eyes, everything was back to normal, the image had disappeared, there was only a white wall.

I was glad that everything had ended well, yet something odd has remained with me since that day. When *I think back* to that workshop *I know* that there was only one bucket — the ice bucket — I know exactly what transpired, yet when *I visualize* that day, I can *"see"* two buckets, the ice bucket and the warm-water bucket. On one level I know what really happened, on another I don't. A part of me has been fooled, and I have a feeling that I can't reach that part, the two just can't seem to get together."

This case is important in a number of ways. First, it demonstrates the cognitive initiative of a subject who was sophisticated about hypnosis and obviously had her own personal expectations of appropriate response. When images and fantasies were aroused that were not matched by the instructions of the hypnotist, internal tensions were created which then needed to be resolved. The processes of imagination she evidenced could not be predicted by the text of the instruction. Her transparency report, for example, was spontaneous and illustrates a rarely observed feature of hypnosis that is normally distinctive of highly susceptible subjects. The interaction between her imagery, affect, and positive motivation to cooperate was clearly evident, and special imaginative skills were displayed that led to the emergence of phenomena which were not suggested at all by the hypnotist or his test procedures.

Traditional methods of inquiry in hypnosis do not necessarily facilitate such reports and are not especially geared to the isolation of experiential phenomena of these kinds. What is needed is an assessment procedure, sensitively attuned to the isolation of imagery phenomena, that reflects the interaction between motives, expectancies, cognitions, and need states, yet at the same time, places minimal constraints on the subject by virtue of task demands and directive cuing as to appropriate response. We turn now to consider one such technique that has been developed by myself and my co-workers very recently (Sheehan, McConkey, & Cross, 1978). Specifically, it aims to facilitate the readiness of subjects to express their imagery and fantasy in an individual and personally meaningful way. In systematic fashion, the technique canvasses experientially the capacities of subjects to re-experience imagined events so as to allow interpretive comment on past processes in action.

Experientially Based Assessment

Our technique is an adaptation of the Interpersonal Process Recall method which was developed originally for use in the counselling setting (Kagan, 1975). Basically, the method consists of the use of videotape playback of the counselling situation so as to stimulate recall of the underlying dynamics involved in the interaction between counselor and client. In its traditional format, the counsellor leaves the scene and the client interacts with another person normally referred to as the inquirer. The inquirer stimulates the client to relate new and additional thoughts and feelings which are activated directly by viewing the videotape of preceding events. The client stops the playback as often as he/she wants to discuss his/her feelings or elaborate on the meaning of his/her experiences. The absence of any constraint on the initiative of the subject to report his/her imaginative experience has several clear advantages. Imaginative events, for instance, are explored or studied in order of importance to the subject rather than the investigator, and the subject is in direct control of the recall of his/her own experiences. The motivational implications of the interaction between subject and investigator can also be studied intensely, as also the emotional expressiveness of the imaging subject.

In its application to the hypnosis setting (Sheehan et al., 1978), subjects were shown a videotaped version of their hypnotic session, in the presence of an independent inquirer whose task it was to foster subjects' spontaneous comments on their hypnotic experiences as relived in video playback. Both quantitative aspects of recall (e.g., length of verbal report, number of times subjects stopped the tape to comment) and qualitative features of experience (e.g., level of fantasy involvement, indications of need states, and style of cognition) were measured. The inquirer probed during the inquiry so as to allow subjects to comment as fully as possible on their ideation and experience. Areas of inquiry included the nature of the cognitive activity ("What were you thinking at the time?"), imagery and imagination ("Were you having any images or fantasy going through your mind then?"), expectancy of events ("What were you expecting to happen next?"), image presentation ("How did you want the hypnotist to see you at that point?"), perception of events ("What were you thinking the hypnotist was wanting at that stage?"), associations of events ("Did this remind you of anything else you have experienced?"), and sundry feeling states ("How were you feeling about your involvement at that point?").

The technique had immediacy and was enjoyed by subjects who considered that it provided them with an opportunity to relive events in a lively and concrete fashion. The data revealed considerable evidence of what we have termed elsewhere (Sheehan et al., 1978) "individuation of response;" subjects responded in an individual or personally idiosyncratic way which bore directly on the nature of their experience. Experiences for some subjects obviously occurred in a highly motivated context. As one subject reported, "I feel as if I can't do anything unless he says . . . the hypnotist asks you to do . . . I just couldn't do anything unless he wanted it . . . by pleasing him, I would be pleasing myself, in a way." The important aspect of the data which needs emphasis in this paper is that quite distinct modes of cognition were implicated. Three such modes emerged, and they were labelled by us "concentrative-cooperative," "cognitive-independent," and "cognitive-constructive." No support is being claimed for types of subjects, but rather for the operation of distinct modes of cognition or imaginative involvement that may well interact with task complexity in response to the suggestions or instructions which subjects received. The first style (concentrative-cooperative) emphasized subjects' well motivated desire to cooperate in their imagery by thinking hard and concentrating on what was happening. The second style (cognitive-independent) emphasized the naturalness of personal responsiveness and illustrated the absence of any compulsion to concentrate on and adhere to what the investigator was literally suggesting. The third style (cognitive-constructive) is one that requires special emphasis because it relates to distinctions outlined earlier between the processes of imagery and fantasy. For some subjects, the degree of the idiosyncratic nature of their responses suggested the need to formulate a specific tendency to synthesize. Some persons consistently reacted in a decidedly more effortfully cognitive fashion than others. These subjects planned cognitively, as it were, to interpret the difficult task in an ideational manner which permitted them to comfortably respond in a positive way. One subject, for instance, when asked to see numbers on the TV screen actually in front of her, reported imagining the numbers rather than seeing them. She proceeded to report that the TV set was not switched on, and therefore she considered that imagining was far more appropriate to her than seeing, or hallucinating.

One of the major inferences drawn from application of this technique was that many of the persons studied could not be simply categorized as passive recipients of their instruction, and their imagination reports were virtually never in literal accord with the communications they were given. These subjects not only actively interpreted the instructions that they received, but imbedded them into their own preferred fantasies, and while hypnotized were often aware of conflicting ideas. Reports further demonstrated the influence of expectancies and positive need states on the nature of the ideation that was expressed. In this sense, the mode of assessment explicitly recognized the *total* functioning person.

Conclusion

As Sheikh and Panagiotou (1975) have indicated, "Imagery is multiple in determination and function, and the methodology applied to images is among the determinants of their function" (p. 579), and imagery does not function uniformly but has characteristics which allow it to be used in various ways. Application of the assessment procedure outlined above demonstrates that mental information can be integrated in a fashion that moves beyond the obvious constraints of standard imaging tasks. The experience of many subjects, when assessed in different ways, emphasizes the constructive or synthesizing aspects of their ideation. The link between the processes of imagery and the processes of construction has been made in other contexts many times previously. Neisser (1972) argued, for instance, that considering the relatedness of perception and imagery was important to recognizing that both were instances of active construction rather than passive registration and recall. Segal (1972) also drew attention in her work on cognitive assimilation to the relevance of construction to image formation. Research relating to the effects of need and expectancy states on perceptual reports has further come to emphasize the major importance of the cognitive activity of the perceiver. In the work on imagery, particularly in the standard laboratory context, however, the activity of the imaging subject as motivated by expectancy and need states has tended to be underemphasized. The interaction between ideation and motivation tends to be lost in the specificity and cue characteristics of the routine tasks that are used to direct subjects' experience reports. The notion that subjects schematically integrate their imagery so as to reflect their attitudes and motivations has long been recognized in the clinical and therapeutic literature, but in the set for functional efficiency and accuracy, as cued by standard tasks and test procedures, the isolation and interpretation of imagery phenomena have been affected as a result. Emphasis upon the activity of the processes by which observers construct their imagery out of past experiences and memories and use concurrent sensory input to "flesh it out" (Segal, 1972, p. 229) serves usefully to highlight the essential arbitrariness of differentiating imagery and fantasy by reserving the influence of motivation and the processes of synthesis for the latter rather than the former type of imaginative experience. When assessed in particular ways, imagery may illustrate far less of a replay of past experiences than a reintegration of experience to suit current needs and motives.

The focus on distinct modes of cognition and individual differences in the kind of imagery that may be manifest leads inevitably to a reassessment of past research on imagery function. Past work of my own, for instance, has argued that vivid imagers perceive literally while poor imagers use coding devices to organize their perceptions, and that differences in the retentive behavior of good and poor imagers are related to individual differences in the organizing of visual information at perception (Sheehan, 1967). In confirmation of that hypothesis, data showed that subjects with poor (i.e., not vivid) imagery had less difficulty in reconstructing obviously patterned visual displays than they had with unpatterned displays; and this difference was relatively unimportant for subjects with vivid imagery. Data of that kind indicate that the organizational properties of stimuli are relevant to how well visual imagers can recall, but the notion rather mistakenly implies that vivid imagers are tied to the immediacy of their experience in a way that poor imagers are not and that they will show less evidence of complex coding. Styles of perception are obviously important, but emphasis should also be placed on styles of cognition in recall. Differences in the behavior of persons imaging will reflect differences in the styles of cognitive representation; some persons will show, for example, greater capacity for schematic restructuring than others, and vividness of imagery may well overlap with this capacity, in the sense that accuracy of recall will depend not only on the vividness or richness of the imagery involved but also on the tendency of subjects to embellish or reintegrate past experiences in an individual attempt to personalize their experience. Such an expression of the relationships between style of cognition and quality of imagery provides a clearer conceptual framework for understanding the constructive nature of much of our ideation, while acknowledging the adaptive utility of imagery and the potential influence of expectancy and need states on imagery experience.

Singer and Antrobus (1972) made the claim some years ago that future research on imagery or ongoing fantasy must take into account differing styles of mentation. Their analysis of day-dreaming, for instance, highlighted manifestations of daydreaming which reflected varying dimensions of cognitive experience. This paper serves to re-emphasize that point in another way and draws attention to imagery as a multidimensional process requiring test procedures that are optimally geared to reveal its full potential. An experientially based technique like the EAT highlights phenomena, reveals important issues regarding the function and nature of imagery and aims to recognize the possible influence of motives and cognitions in interaction. The adaptiveness of imagery should not simply be judged in terms of imagery aiding the solution of problems in a structured fashion. Imagery is a rich and creative process that serves the needs of the organism in many different ways and frequently by synthesizing past experiences in a manner that is both appropriate to the situation and personally meaningful. To study that synthesis systematically and in detail requires the development of assessment techniques that are theoretically attuned to subsystems of the organism in interaction rather than in isolation and that utilize tasks that facilitate rather than inhibit the spontaneous occurrence of imagery phenomena. My hope is that this paper contributes a little toward that end.

REFERENCES

Ahsen, A. *Psycheye: Self-analytic consciousness.* New York: Brandon House, 1977.
Angyal, A. *Foundations for a science of personality.* Cambridge: Harvard University Press, 1941.
Assagioli, R. *Psychosynthesis: A collection of basic writings.* New York: Viking, 1965.
Barber, T. X. *Imagination and hypnosis.* Paper presented at the Second American Conference on the Fantasy and Imaging Process, Chicago, November, 1978.
Bugelski, B. R. The definition of the image. In S. Segal (Ed.), *Imagery: Current cognitive approaches.* New York: Academic Press, 1971.
Cooper, L. A., & Shepard, R. N. Chronometric studies of the rotation of mental images. In W. G. Chase (Ed.), *Visual information processing.* New York: Academic Press, 1973.
Dolby, R. M., & Sheehan, P. W. Cognitive processing and expectancy behavior in hypnosis. *Journal of Abnormal Psychology,* 1977, *36,* 334-345.
Endler, N. S., & Magnusson, D. *Interactionism, trait psychology, psychodynamics, and situationism.* Report from the Psychological Laboratories, University of Stockholm, 1974.
Ekehammar, B. Interactionism in modern personality from a historical perspective. *Psychological Bulletin,* 1974, *81,* 1026-1048.
Fretigny, R., & Virel, A. *L'imagerie mentale.* Geneva: Mont-Blanc, 1968.
Gray, C. R., & Gummerman, K. The enigmatic eidetic image: A critical examination of methods, data, and theories. *Psychological Bulletin,* 1975, *82,* 383-407.
Hilgard, E. R. *Divided consciousness.* New York: Wiley, 1977.
Holt, R. R. The return of the ostracized. *American Psychologist,* 1964, *19,* 254-264.
Holt, R. R. On the nature and generality of mental imagery. In P. W. Sheehan (Ed.), *The function and nature of imagery.* New York: Academic Press, 1972.
Horowitz, M. J. *Image formation and cognition.* New York: Appleton-Century Crofts, 1970.

Kagan, N. I. *Interpersonal process recall: A method of influencing human interaction.* Michigan: Michigan State University, 1975.

Leuner, H. Guided affective imagery: An account of its development. *Journal of Mental Imagery,* 1977, *1,* 73-92.

Lewin, K. *Field theory in social science: Selected theoretical papers.* New York: Harper, 1951.

Neisser, U. Changing conceptions of imagery. In P. W. Sheehan (Ed.), *The function and nature of imagery.* New York: Academic Press, 1972.

Nisbett, R. E., & Wilson, T. D. Telling more than we can know: Verbal reports on mental processes. *Psychological Review,* 1977, *84,* 231-259.

Paivio, A. *Imagery and verbal processes.* New York: Holt, Rinehart & Winston, 1971.

Segal, S. J. Assimilation of a stimulus in the construction of an image: The Perky effect revisited. In P. W. Sheehan (Ed.), *The function and nature of imagery.* New York: Academic Press, 1972.

Segal, S. J., & Fusella, V. Influence of imaged pictures and sounds on detection of visual and auditory signals. *Journal of Experimental Psychology,* 1970, *83,* 458-464.

Sheehan, P. W. Visual imagery and the organizational properties of perceived stimuli. *British Journal of Psychology,* 1967, *58,* 247-252.

Sheehan, P. W. Quelques réflexions sur la nature de l'imagerie visuelle: Le problème de l'affect. *Psychothérapies,* 1971, *2,* 10-13.

Sheehan, P. W. Hypnosis and the processes of imagination. In E. Fromm and R. E. Shor (Eds.), *Hypnosis: Research developments and perspectives* (Revised Edition). Chicago: Aldine-Atherton, in press (a).

Sheehan, P. W. Expectancy behavior in hypnosis. In R. H. Woody (Ed.), *Encyclopedia of clinical assessment.* New York: Jossey-Bass, in press (b).

Sheehan, P. W., & Dolby, R. M. Hypnosis and the influence of most recently perceived events. *Journal of Abnormal Psychology,* 1975, *84,* 331-345.

Sheehan, P. W., McConkey, K. M., & Cross, D. Experiential analysis of hypnosis: Some new observations on hypnotic phenomena. *Journal of Abnormal Psychology,* 1978, *87,* 570-573.

Sheikh, A. A., & Panagiotou, N. C. Use of mental imagery in psychotherapy: A critical review. *Perceptual and Motor Skills,* 1975, *41,* 555-585.

Shor, R. E. Hypnosis and the concept of the generalized reality-orientation. *American Journal of Psychotherapy,* 1959, *13,* 572-602.

Shor, R. E. Three dimensions of hypnotic depth. *International Journal of Clinical and Experimental Hypnosis,* 1962, *10,* 23-38.

Singer, J. L., & Antrobus, J. S. Daydreaming, imaginal processes, and personality: A normative study. In P. W. Sheehan (Ed.), *The function and nature of imagery.* New York: Academic Press, 1972.

Sullivan, H. S. *The interpersonal theory of psychiatry.* New York: Norton, 1953.

Ullman, M. The adaptive significance of the dream. *Journal of Nervous and Mental Disease,* 1959, *129,* 144-149.

7

Psychosomatics and Mental Imagery: A Brief Review

ANEES A. SHEIKH
PHYLLIS RICHARDSON
L. MARTIN MOLESKI

The history of medical science appears to be divided into two distinct periods: the pre-Cartesian era and the post-Cartesian one. In the earlier, invariably psychosomatic or holistic era, no mind-body problem existed: mental and physical events were unified by a common substrate, a biological soul, which had both cognitive and physiological functions (McMahon, 1975). The second, dualistic age began with the formulations of Rene Descartes (1596-1630) who regarded mind and body as mutually exclusive entities with no interactive potential. Thus, any psychophysiological or psychosomatic event was considered to be both logically and biologically an impossibility, and mechanistic physiopathology replaced the pre-Cartesian psychosomatic approach to disease (McMahon, 1976a). Until today, this dualistic formulation has tenaciously gripped medical thought.

However, in spite of the lack of any radical and widespread change in the philosophical underpinning, the psychosomatic approach in medicine has become extremely prevalent and influential during the last few decades. For example, membership in professional societies for Psychosomatic Medicine and Psychophysiology has undergone an exponential growth (McMahon & Koppes, 1976). Also, the number of diseases placed in this category has steadily increased. Nevertheless, one notices "an increasing amount of dissatisfaction with the

Anees A. Sheikh, Department of Psychology, Marquette University, Milwaukee, WI 53233; **Phyllis Richardson,** Eastside Community Mental Health Center, Bellevue, Washington 98005; **L. Martin Moleski,** Marin General Hospital, Greenbrae, CA 94902.

progress of psychosomatic medicine" in the recent literature (McMahon, 1976b).

This paper is meant to be a preliminary and brief attempt to bring together findings from apparently diverse areas in order to show that imagery holds a significant promise in the field of psychosomatic medicine. In the first part of the paper, a brief account of contemporary views concerning psychosomatics is presented. The topics discussed in the second section include: the prevalence of theorizing about illness in terms of imagery during the pre-Cartesian period, imagery's later ostracism from the psychological scene, and the recent robust return of images. Studies dealing with the characteristics of imagery that are particularly relevant to psychosomatic phenomena are also discussed. In the next segment an overlap between hypnosis and imagination is demonstrated, and it is argued that recent success of hypnosis in the area of psychosomatics is due mainly to the imagery evoked in the subjects by the suggestions. The last section consists of a brief discussion of one of the most significant recent attempts to tackle psychosomatic problems through imagery.

Psychosomatics: Contemporary Views

Although the term "psychosomatic" was first employed in 1818 by Heinroth, a German psychiatrist, it was not until the 20th century that the complex nature of psychosomatic medicine was approached through sophisticated methods of research (Freyhan, 1976). It is gradually being realized that persons, not cells or organs, have diseases, and that human beings do not merely consist of "self-contained organs carrying out specialized metabolic processes in isolation, uninfluenced by external events" (Weiner, 1977, p. 8). Social and psychological variables now appear to play an important role in the predisposition for, and inception and maintenance of a number of diseases (Schwab, 1978; Shontz, 1975; Weiner, 1977; Wittkower, 1977). Also, several personality factors (i.e., inability to release emotions), that characterize the psychosomatic cases, have been noted (Shontz, 1975).

Various contemporary theorists seem to agree that certain stimulus situations, overt or covert, elicit a variety of internal conditions, which if sufficiently intense and prolonged, will lead to structural or physiological alterations. Which structure will undergo alterations? Focusing on this question, Lachman (1972) has classified the theories about the development of psychosomatic pathology into the following major groups.

1. *Constitutional - Vulnerability (Weak-Link) Theories.* According to these theories, stressful stimulation damages the most vulnerable organ: "the chain breaks at the weakest link" or "the inner tube blows where the rubber is thinnest." The elements that render a particular organ more vulnerable are genetic factors, injuries, diseases, and other previous influences.

2. *Organ Response Learning Theories.* Proponents of these theories hold that due to a previous connection between emotional stimulation and a reinforced response of an organ, future stressful cues lead to the same organ response. If these stressful situations are frequent, persistent, and sufficiently intense, a malfunction of or damage to that organ may result.

3. *Stimulus Situation Theories.* According to these theories, certain specific emotional stimulus situations cause specific physiological reactions and thus lead to damage to the organ structures involved. An innate relationship between various patterns of stimulation and those of physiological reaction is often implied.

4. *Emotional Reaction Pattern Theories.* Partisans of these theories contend that malfunction or damage in certain organs results from a specific pattern of physiological reaction in emotion. This view differs from the stimulus situation theory in the following ways: "First, as far as emotional reaction pattern theories are concerned, objectively identical or very similar patterns of stimulation can produce different physiological reactions in different people, and different emotional reaction pattern theories often imply some kind of cognitive-affective factor or central component that intervenes between stimulus and response and that influences or processes the pattern reaction" (Lachman, 1972, p. 59).

5. *Personality Profile Theories.* Followers of these theories maintain that various personality structures result in differing reaction tendencies, and thus different individuals are predisposed to different kinds of psychosomatic pathologies.

6. *Symptom Symbol Theories.* These theories orginated in psychoanalytic conceptions and hold that the diseased organ or system has symbolic meaning for the patient. For example, a peptic ulcer is supposed to be a symbol of internalized aggression originally directed against the mother (Garma, 1950).

It should be noted that the proponents of almost all of the foregoing theories in recognizing the role of covert stimulation have implicitly accepted the part played by cognitive variables, such as images. However, in none of these theories the role of imagination in the disease process is explicitly proposed.

Imagination and Psychosomatic Phenomena

In the premodern, holistic era of medical thought, imagination, as a faculty of the biological soul, occupied a central position. It was regarded as a psychophysiological variable of great significance. "The soul," Aristotle claimed, "never thinks without a picture" (Yates, 1966, p. 32). He further believed that the emotional system was invariably activated by mental images. Images were also called by some "the movements of the soul." According to some Renaissance physicians, as Carole McMahon (1976a, p. 180) explains, "when imagination conceived an object which was either pleasing or repellent, spirits carried activation from brain to heart, via nerves, and initiated arousal in and around that most sensitive organ . . . . Bodily functions were disordered to an extent determined by the vividness and tenacity of the image." It was also thought possible through images to develop conscious control over the autonomic or "involuntary" functions. Furthermore, mental images were considered so potent in producing somatic changes that they were believed to "imprint characteristics on embryos *in utero.*" Charron, in 1601, stated that imagination "marks and deforms, nay, sometimes kills embryos in the womb, hastens births, or causes abortions."

In Carole McMahon's words, "the key to an understanding of pre-Cartesian theory lies in recognizing that imagery was understood to be as much a physiological reality as it is today regarded as a psychological reality. When an image became an obsession it pervaded the body, bound up the heart, clutched at the sinews and vessels, and directed the flesh according to its own inclination. Soon its essence became manifest in its victims complexion, countenance, posture and gait. Imagination had greater powers of control than sensations, and thus, anticipation of a feared event was more damaging than the event itself" (1976a, p. 181). Since pathological changes were considered to be image produced, it follows that the prevalent therapies of the day were also imagination based: if images could by some mechanism produce pathology, then they could similarly restore health.

With the spreading of Cartesian dualism, imagination quickly lost its role in the disease process. Although a few attempts were made during the 18th and 19th century to approach imagination from a psychophysiological angle, they were largely unsuccessful in changing the dualistic trend. At best, parallelism, as advocated by Hartley, found some acceptance. More than two centuries later, Watsonian behaviorism (Watson, 1913) struck a final blow to the images: they were reduced to mere ghosts of sensations with no functional significance whatever (Sheikh, 1977).

However, the last decade has witnessed a marked resurgence of interest in imagery by psychologists of varied persuasions. The importance of the use of imagery in psychotherapy is being realized clearly, and a possible supremacy of images over words is being examined. It has been discovered that "images are less likely to be filtered through the conscious critical apparatus than is linguistic expression. In most cases, words and phrases must be consciously understood before they are spoken; for in order to assume a grammatical order, they must first pass through a rational censorship. Imagery perhaps is not subject to this filtering process" (Sheikh & Panagiotou, 1975, p. 556). Images have been noted to occur spontaneously at times when the subject is no longer able to formulate his/her experience verbally (Jellinek, 1949). Free imagery, an analogue of free association has been demonstrated to be extremely effective in uncovering repressed material (Reyher, 1963). Also, imagery is considered to provide access to significant memories encoded at developmental stages when language was not yet present or predominant (Ahsen, 1968; Kepecs, 1954). Furthermore, details pertaining to affect and fantasy may be contained in the image but not be available in verbal thought (Horowitz, 1968).

Numerous clinicians are persuaded of the suitability of mental imagery for dealing with psychosomatic problems (Ahsen, 1972, 1977; Dolan & Sheikh, 1977; Leuner,.1977; Sheikh & Panagiotou, 1975). Particularly the practitioners of eidetic psychotherapy, that was originated by Akhter Ahsen, have achieved stunning successes in this area.

Besides the increasing number of clinical studies, numerous laboratory studies dealing with the potential of imagination have appeared which somewhat indirectly suggest that, perhaps, a major promise of imagery lies in the area of psychosomatic medicine.

Imagery and Perception

Several studies, including those of Perky (1910), Leuba (1940), John (1967), and Segal and Fusella (1970), propose that imagery and perception are experientially and neurophysiologically comparable processes and cannot be distinguished from each other on the basis of any intrinsic qualities of either phenomenon (Richardson, 1969). Hebb's and Pribram's views tend to support this conclusion. Penfield (1963) demonstrated that the locus of image excitation corresponded to localization of sensory functions in the brain. Consequently, it is not surprising that images have been noted to possess an amazing ability to effect extensive affective and physiological changes (Paivio, 1973; Sheikh, 1977; Sheikh & Panagiotou, 1975; Zikmund, 1972).

Imagery and Affect

Images have been observed to uncover very intense affective changes or generate emotional reaction (Goldberger, 1957; Horowitz, 1972; Jellinek, 1949; Shapiro, 1970). Reyher and Smeltzer (1968) obtained higher physiological measures of anxiety for free imagery than for verbal free association. Sheehan (1968) found evidence in the literature that intensity of affect is one of the most important variables influencing the phenomenon of imagery. Goldberger (1957) suggests that elements distorted by the image are related to areas of strong affect. Also, practitioners who extensively use induced images, notice that the image, in one way or another, is capable of being the focal point of strong affect (Ahsen, 1968; Desoille, 1965; Leuner, 1969). Furthermore, "images may have a greater capacity than the linguistic mode for the attraction and focusing of emotionally loaded associations in concentrated forms: verbal logic is linear; whereas the image is a simultaneous representation. The quality of simultaneity gives imagery greater isomorphism with the qualities of perception, and, therefore, a greater capacity for descriptive accuracy" (Sheikh & Panagiotou, 1975, p. 557). Moreover, since imagery seems to be mediated by the right hemisphere, it is hardly surprising if it expresses relationships in certain areas of experience more elegantly than words do (Ornstein, 1972; Paivio, 1971; Pines, 1974).

Imagery and Motivation

Aristotle claimed that the images serve as the sources of activation, and guide and direct behavior by representing the goal object (see McMahon, 1973, p. 465). Many contemporary psychologists also view images as being capable of representing situations or objects, and as a result, acting as motivators for future behavior (Miller, Galanter, & Pribram, 1960; Mowrer, 1977; Sarbin, 1972).

Imagery and Physiology

The power of imagery to produce physiological changes has been demonstrated in a number of studies. For example, Simpson and Paivio (1966) observed changes in pupillary size during imagery. May and Johnson (1973) noticed that an increase in heart rate was produced by arousing images. Yaremko and Butler (1975) found that imagining a tone or shock and real presentation of these stimuli produced comparable habituation. Barber, Chauncey, and Winer (1964) reported that the request to imagine that a solution of tap water was sour led to increased salivation. Increases in electromyograms have also been noted by several researchers (Craig, 1969; Jacobsen, 1929; McGuigan, 1971). Furthermore, Barber (1961, 1969) reported that images could produce blood glucose increases, inhibition of gastrointestinal activity, increases in gastric-acid secretion, blister formation, salivation, and alterations in skin temperature. Several studies of meditation, and of biofeedback, which undoubtedly often involved imagery, have reported reduction in blood pressure, decreased oxygen consumption, control of gastrointestinal activity, slowing down of the heartbeat, and increase in body temperature (Allison, 1971; Bagchi & Wenger, 1972; Lachman, 1972; Wallace, 1972). Cancer remission as a function of imaging has also been reported, but the evidence is still very equivocal (Holden, 1978).

Imagery and Psychosomatic Personality

Some recent research dealing directly with the psychosomatic personality further strengthens our conviction that imagery offers a very viable approach to psychosomatic problems. It appears that individuals suffering from these problems are often unable to fantasize or daydream and have a tendency to orient themselves toward external events rather than feelings (Nemiah, 1973; Nemiah & Sifneos, 1970; Sifneos, 1973; Singer, 1976). M'Uzan (1974) suggests that there is a fundamental psychic structure unique to the psychosomatic individual and that this "structure is characterized by a deficiency, more or less marked, of the phantasmic activities which no longer, or very imperfectly, fulfill the functions of elaboration and integration" (p. 103).

In view of the finding that psychosomatic patients are unable to fantasize freely, it is important to look more closely at persons who display difficulty in fantasizing. It is interesting to note that personality characteristics of low-imagers in a "normal" population are quite similar to the characteristics of psychosomatic patients. It seems as though low-imagers are less "inner-accepting" and more likely to remain out of touch with their inner lives than those who have no difficulty with fantasy (Schonbar, 1965).

Low-imagers are said to react to their objective environment as it presents itself and are thus influenced by the appearance of things (Schonbar, 1965). This suggests a stimulus-bound cognitive style similar to field-dependence. In contrast, persons who experience a high frequency of daydreaming are more field-independent and exhibit willingness to admit anxieties and show less evidence of the use of repression and denial (Singer & Schonbar, 1961; Schonbar, 1965).

Weiner, Singer, and Reiser (1962) found that when responding to TAT, both hypertensive and peptic-ulcer subjects dealt with the physical details of the situation represented in the cards, with little or no emotional coloring or evoked fantasy. No physiological changes were reported during storytelling; this absence further indicates a lack of involved affect. A breakdown of the peptic-ulcer group into depressed and nondepressed showed some differences. Stories containing some fantasy were noted in the nondepressed subgroup, although they were neither rich nor affectladen. Depressed peptic-ulcer patients told brief and impersonal stories.

Indications concerning the relevance of mental imagery to psychosomatic problems appear to be ample. Imagery seems to have the potential to provide whatever psychosomatic patients lack. However, the major problem arises from the fact that these patients frequently are incapable of producing sufficiently vivid images. This inability to produce adequate imagery responses continues to be a nightmare for clinicians interested in using imagery as the main tool for diagnosis and treatment. Fortunately, several possibilities are opening up. For example, it appears that even those individuals who do not have vivid imagery, with some encouragement and concentration, can visualize developmentally determined images from significant life situations in the past (Ahsen, 1977, 1978; Sheikh, 1978). These images, in turn, gradually tend to open up the general imagination and fantasy process. Hypnosis can also be successfully used as an aid to induce therapeutic images or dreams. Several other possibilities exist that should be systematically explored.

Hynosis, Imagery, and Psychosomatics

The commission appointed by the king of France to investigate Mesmer's claims concluded that his cures were primarily due to the excitement of the imagination of the patient. This view of hypnosis has recently re-emerged, and there is increasing evidence that hypnosis and imagery are closely related (Barber, 1978a). It has been noted that suggestions used in the hypnotic setting generally direct the subject to imagine various situations (Honiotes, 1977; Weitzenhoffer & Hilgard, 1962). Hypnotic responsiveness and the ability to be absorbed in activities involving imagination and fantasy have been found to be positively correlated (Barber & Glass, 1962; Hilgard, 1970; Sarbin & Lim, 1963; Sheehan, 1972). Sarbin (1976) views the responsive hypnotic subject to be similar to the child engaged in imaginative play. Furthermore, several investigators, on the basis of their research, have concluded that hypnosis essentially intensifies the subject's imaginative processes (Arnold, 1946; Barber, Spanos, & Chaves, 1974; Hilgard, 1965; Sarbin & Coe, 1972).

In the light of the foregoing evidence, it seems safe to hypothesize that the wide variety of physiological effects of hypnosis are primarily due to the imagery involved. Through hypnotic suggestion, and thus perhaps through imagery, allergic reactions have been inhibited, physiological reactions to cold stress have been minimized, labor contractions have been induced and inhibited in some women, some aspects of the narcotic withdrawal syndrome and of narcotic drug effects have been produced in postaddicts, water diuresis has been elicited in some hydrophenic females, ichthyosis has been mitigated, and wheals have been produced in patients with urticaria (see review of research by Barber, 1965). Increase in gastric acidity, metabolic rate, and heart rate, reduction of blood calcium level, and alteration in spasticity of the bowels have also been noted (Gorton, 1959). Furthermore, attempts at preventing skin reactions produced by plants such as poison ivy (Ikemi & Nakagawa, 1962), producing localized skin inflammation (Barber, 1970; Johnson & Barber, 1976), stimulating the remission of warts (Johnson & Barber, 1978), and stimulating further growth of breasts (Williams, 1974; Willard, 1977) have been successful (Barber, 1978b).

It needs to be pointed out that several of the studies cited in the preceding paragraph were not well controlled and lacked waking subjects for comparison. However, this weakness is irrelevant here, for, our main goal is to simply show that some profound physiological reactions can be produced by images of various stimulus situations. Incidently, Barber and his co-workers have now demonstrated that procedures of hypnotic induction are not necessary, but they can aid in producing acceptance of suggestions (Barber, 1978b).

Eidetic Therapy and Psychosomatic Disorders

Eidetic psychotherapy (Ahsen, 1968, 1972; Sheikh, 1978) represents a true departure from dualism in the field of medicine and is in complete agreement with Plato's view found in *Charmides,* subtitled *The Mistake of Physicians:* "And this is the reason why the cure of many diseases is unknown to the physicians of Hellas, because they are ignorant of the whole which ought to be studied also; for the part can never be well unless the whole is well. It is the greatest mistake in the treatment of diseases that there are physicians who treat the body and physicians who treat the mind, since both are inseparable" (Quoted in Freyhan, 1976, p. 381).

Ahsen (1968, 1978) cogently explains how every important event in the developmental course of the individual is triadically represented by an eidetic which consists of an image or visual pattern, a somatic pattern, and a meaning or affective signification. The life-like eidetic, also called ISM (for *i*mage, *s*omatic response, and *m*eaning) is probably the only event in the psyche which is fundamentally psychosomatic and unites mind and body in a single undifferentiated whole. Therapy is based on the elicitation and manipulation of this type of images. It must be pointed out that, in eidetic psychotherapy, no distinction is made between psychosomatic and nonpsychosomatic problems, because it is noted that both psychic and somatic components are present in all problems.

The eidetic is formed and retained because it represents a highly affective and significant event or relationship, or a recurring fantasy in the development of the individual. Although fantasy determinants may overshadow the external event in creating the eidetic, it, nevertheless is a representation of the individual's perception, bodily and feeling responses, and interpretation of these responses at a particular time (Sheikh, 1978).

It has been demonstrated that at the origin of the ISM, the visual component assumes representational precedence (Ahsen, 1977). It spearheads the experience of the total event, and, thus, becomes the psychic cue for the event in its entirety. It has been reported that through the recall of the visual component, the entire composite event can be fully recalled into awareness, and the ISM can be experienced in exactly the same way as at the time of the original perception. Actually, it may even release latent affect that may have been arrested or repressed originally (Sheikh, 1978).

Initially, the image component may be relatively vague and elude focusing. Further concentration, however, makes it more precise, vivid, detailed, and stable. The image is fixed and cannot be changed at will by the subject. Even if the patient is successful in temporarily altering an image, it will revert to its original form as soon as he/she looses control or relaxes. The image can be manipulated and altered only under concentrated attention and only according to the laws under which these images function. Furthermore, when a series of changes are made, they have a corresponding impact on the individual (Dolan & Sheikh, 1976, 1977; Sheikh, 1976, 1978).

According to Ahsen (1973, 1974), the three elements of the triad become "dessociated" but not irretrievably separated; it is merely that the connection between them becomes imperceptible, although the response patterns survive and the image is readily called to consciousness. Through the visual component the connection may be recovered and the entire experience repeated (Panagiotou & Sheikh, 1977).

It is believed that at the inception of the ISM, the elements of experience tend to fission into ego-positive and ego-negative poles. In pathological conditions there is usually an exaggerated emphasis on one pole, while the other pole has been relatively neglected. In therapy, an image representing one pole is worked against an opposite image to create a movement in the psyche in a desired direction to achieve a new and balanced visiofixation (Sheikh & Panagiotou, 1975).

It has been demonstrated by Ahsen and by others who have followed his system that the symptoms are mainly caused either by "dessociation" of the three components of the eidetic, by fixation on the negative pole, or by a repression of significant experience. Therefore, the aim of eidetic therapy is to revive the tripartite unity, to shift the ego's attention to the neglected or positive pole which leads to a more balanced and realistic appraisal of the experience, and to uncover the repressed experience through progression of eidetic imagery. Since an eidetic is considered to be the psychic equivalent of the corresponding actual event, the experience in the form of eidetics is the re-experience of one's history, which thus becomes accessible for alteration (Sheikh, 1978). Discussion of specific eidetic techniques to achieve the foregoing goals is beyond the scope of this paper. The interested readers are referred to the more detailed works (Ahsen, 1968, 1972, 1977; Sheikh, 1978).

Concluding Remarks

There appears to be ample evidence, direct and indirect, to indicate the relevance of imagination to the disease process. However, the majority of the available research does not centrally deal with the problem at hand. It is primarily correlational and fails to yield causal relationships necessary to the understanding of pathogenesis and, therefore, to the development of effective treatment procedures. It is so because we have not as yet been able to escape the clutches of Cartesian dualism (McMahon, 1976b). It seems to us that great strides would be taken in the area of psychosomatic medicine, if holism ceased to receive mere lip service and a serious attempt to develop a truly holistic scientific theory were made. Eidetic theory, we feel, is a notable attempt in this direction. The triadic unit, the eidetic, may very well become the modern substitute for the pre-Cartesian biological soul.

REFERENCES

Ahsen, A. *Basic concepts in eidetic psychotherapy.* New York: Brandon House, 1968.
Ahsen, A. *Eidetic parents test and analysis.* New York: Brandon House, 1972.
Ahsen, A. Eidetics: A visual psychology. Invited address, American Psychological Association, 81st Annual Convention, Montreal, Canada, 1973.
Ahsen, A. Anna O. — patient or therapist? An eidetic view. In V. Franks & V. Burtle (Eds.), *Women in therapy.* New York: Bruner/Mazel, 1974.

Ahsen, A. *Psycheye: Self-analytic consciousness.* New York: Brandon House, 1977.

Ahsen, A. Eidetics: Neural experiential growth potential for the treatment of accident traumas, debilitating stress conditions, and chronic emotional blocking. *Journal of Mental Imagery,* 1978, *2,* 1-22.

Allison, J. Respiratory changes during the practice of the technique of transcendental meditation. *Lancet,* April, 1970.

Arnold, M. B. On the mechanism of suggestion and hypnosis. *Journal of Abnormal and Social Psychology,* 1946, *41,* 107-128.

Bagchi, B. K., & Wenger, M. A. Electrophysiological correlates of some yogi exercises. In L. Van Bogaert & J. Radermecher (Eds.), Proceedings of the First International Congress of Neurological Sciences, Brussels, 1957.

Barber, T. X. Physiological aspects of hypnosis. *Psychological Bulletin,* 1961, *58,* 390-419.

Barber, T. X. Physiological effects of "hypnotic suggestions": A critical review of recent research. *Psychological Bulletin,* 1965, *63,* 201-222.

Barber, T. X. *Hypnosis: A scientific approach.* New York: Van Nostrand Reinhold, 1969.

Barber, T. X. Suggested ("hypnotic") behavior: The trance paradigm versus an alternative paradigm. (Medfield Foundation Report 103) Medfield, Mass.: Medfield Foundation, 1970.

Barber, T. X. Imagination and hypnosis. Paper presented at the Second American Conference on the Fantasy and Imaging Process, Chicago, November, 1978. (a)

Barber, T. X. Hypnosis, suggestions, and psychosomatic phenomena: A new look from the standpoint of recent experimental studies. *The American Journal of Clinical Hypnosis,* 1978, *21,* 13-27. (b)

Barber, T. X., Chauncey, H. M., & Winer, R. A. The effect of hypnotic and non-hypnotic suggestions on parotid gland response to gustatory stimuli. *Psychosomatic Medicine.* 1964, *26,* 374-380.

Barber, T. X. & Glass, L. B. Significant factors in hypnotic behavior. *Journal of Abnormal and Social Psychology,* 1962, *64,* 222-228.

Barber, T. X., Spanos, N. P., & Chaves, J. F. *Hypnosis, imagination, and human potentialities.* Elmsford, New York: Pergamon Press, 1974.

Charron, P. *Of wisdom, Three Books.* London: Bonwick, 1601.

Craig, K. D. Physiological arousal as a function of imagined, vicarious, and direct stress experiences. *Journal of Abnormal Psychology,* 1969, *73,* 513-520.

Desoille, R. *The directed daydream.* New York: Psychosynthesis Research Foundation, 1965.

Dolan, A. T., & Sheikh, A. A. Eidetics: A visual approach to psychotherapy. *Psychologia,* 1976, *19,* 210-219.

Dolan, A. T., & Sheikh, A. A. Short-term treatment of phobias through eidetic imagery. *American Journal of Psychotherapy,* 1977, *31,* 595-604.

Freyhan, F. A. Is psychosomatic obsolete? A psychiatric appraisal. *Comprehensive Psychiatry,* 1976, *17,* 381-386.

Garma, A. On the pathogenesis of peptic ulcer. *International Journal of Psychoanalysis, 1950, 31,* 53-72.

Goldberger, E. Simple method of producing dreamlike visual images in the waking state. *Psychosomatic Medicine,* 1957, *19,* 127-133.

Gorton, B. E. Physiological aspects of hypnosis. In J. M. Schneck (Ed.), *Hypnosis in modern medicine.* Springfield, Illinois: Charles C. Thomas, 1959.

Hilgard, E. R. *Hypnotic susceptibility.* New York: Harcourt, Brace & World, 1965.

Hilgard, J. R. *Personality and hypnosis.* Chicago: University of Chicago Press, 1970.

Holden, C. Cancer and the mind: How are they connected? *Science,* June, 1978, 1363-1369.

Honiotes, G. J. Hypnosis and breast enlargement — a pilot study. *Journal of the International Society for Professional Hypnosis*, 1977, *6*, 8-12.

Horowitz, M. J. Visual thought images in psychotherapy. *American Journal of Psychotherapy*, 1968, *22*, 55-57.

Horowitz, M. J. Image formation: Clinical observations and a cognitive model. In P. Sheehan (Ed.), *The function and nature of imagery*. New York: Academic Press, 1972.

Ikemi, Y., & Nakagawa, S. A psychosomatic study of contagious dermatitis. *Kyushu Journal of Medical Science*, 1962, *13*, 335-350.

Jacobsen, E. Electrical measurements of neuromuscular states during mental activities: 1. Imagination of movement involving skeletal muscles. *American Journal of Physiology*, 1929, *91*, 567-608.

Jellinek, A. Spontaneous imagery: A new psychotherapeutic approach. *American Journal of Psychotherapy*, 1949, *3*, 372-391.

John, E. R. *Mechanisms of memory*. New York: Academic Press, 1967.

Johnson, R. F. Q., & Barber, T. X. Hypnotic suggestions for blister formation: Subjective and physiological effects. *American Journal of Clinical Hypnosis*, 1976, *18*, 172-181.

Johnson, R. F. Q., & Barber, T. X. Hypnosis, suggestions, and warts: An experimental investigation implicating the importance of believed-in efficacy. *American Journal of Clinical Hypnosis*, 1978, *20*, 165-174.

Kepecs, J. G. Observations on screens and barriers in the mind. *Psychoanalytic Quarterly*, 1954, *23*, 62-77.

Lachman, S. J. *Psychosomatic disorders: A behavioristic interpretation*. New York: Wiley, 1972.

Leuba, C. Images as conditioned sensations. *Journal of Experimental Psychology*, 1940, *26*, 345-351.

Leuner, H. Guided affective imagery: A method of intensive psychotherapy. *American Journal of Psychotherapy*, 1969, *23*, 4-22.

Leuner, H. Guided affective imagery: An account of its development. *Journal of Mental Imagery*, 1977, *1*, 73-92.

May, J., & Johnson, H. Physiological activity to internally-elicited arousal and inhibitory thoughts. *Journal of Abnormal Psychology*. 1973, *82*, 239-245.

McGuigan, F. J. Covert linguistic behavior in deaf subjects during thinking. *Journal of Comparative and Physiological Psychology*, 1971, *75*, 417-420.

McMahon, C. E. Images as motives and motivators: A historical perspective. *American Journal of Psychology*, 1973, *86*, 465-490.

McMahon, C. E. The wind of the cannon ball: An informative anecdote from medical history. *Psychotherapy and Psychosomatics*, 1975, *26*, 125-131.

McMahon, C. E. The role of imagination in the disease process: Pre-Cartesian history. *Psychological Medicine*, 1976, *6*, 179-184. (a)

McMahon, C. E. Psychosomatic disease and the problem of causation. *Medical Hypotheses*, 1976, *2*, 112-116. (b)

McMahon, C. E., & Koppes, S. The development of psychosomatic medicine: An analysis of growth of professional societies. *Psychosomatics*, 1976, *17*, 185-187.

Miller, G. A., Galanter, E., & Pribram, K. H. *Plans and the structure of behavior*. New York: Henry Holt & Co., 1960.

Mowrer, O. H. Mental imagery: An indispensable psychological concept. *Journal of Mental Imagery*, 1977, *1*, 303-326.

M'Uzan, M. de. Psychodynamic mechanism in psychosomatic symptom formation. *Psychotherapy and Psychosomatics*, 1974, *23*, 103-110.

Nemiah, J. C. Psychology and psychosomatic illness: Reflections on theory and research methodology. *Psychotherapy and Psychosomatics*, 1973, *22*, 106-111.

Nemiah, J. C. & Sifneos, P. E. Affect and fantasy in patients with psychosomatic disorders. *Modern trends in psychosomatic medicine*. London: Butterworths, 1970.

Ornstein, R. E. *The psychology of consciousness*. San Francisco: Freeman, 1972.

Paivio, A. *Imagery and verbal processes*. New York: Holt, Rinehart & Winston, 1971.

Paivio, A. Psychophysiological correlates of imagery. In F. J. McGuigan & R. A. Schoonover (Eds.), *The psychophysiology of thinking*. New York: Academic Press, 1973.

Panagiotou, N. C., & Sheikh, A. A. The image and the unconscious. *International Journal of Social Psychiatry*, 1977, 23, 169-186.

Penfield, W. The brains record of auditory and visual experience — a final summary. *Brain*, 1963, *86*, 595-696.

Perky, C. W. An experimental study of imagination. *American Journal of Psychology*, 1910, *21*, 422-452.

Pines, M. *The brain changers: Scientists and new mind control*. Bergenfield: New American Library, 1974.

Reyher, J. Free imagery, an uncovering procedure. *Journal of Clinical Psychology*, 1963, *19*, 454-459.

Reyher, J., & Smeltzer, W. Uncovering properties of visual imagery and verbal associations: A comparative study. *Journal of Abnormal Psychology*, 1968, *73*, 218-222.

Richardson, A. *Mental imagery*, New York: Springer, 1969.

Sarbin, T. R. Imaging as muted role-taking: A historical-linguistic analysis. In P. Sheehan (Ed.), *The function and nature of imagery*. New York: Academic Press, 1972.

Sarbin, T. R. The quixotic principle: Believed-in imaginings. Santa Cruz, California: Department of Psychology, University of California, 1976.

Sarbin, T. R., & Coe, W. C. *Hypnosis: A social psychological analysis of influence communication*. New York: Holt, Rinehard & Winston, 1972.

Sarbin, T. R., & Lim, D. T. Some evidence in support of the role-taking hypothesis in hypnosis. *International Journal of Clinical and Experimental Hypnosis*, 1963, *11*, 98-103.

Schonbar, R. A. Psychosomatics. *Journal of Consulting Psychology*, 1965, *29*, 468.

Schwab, J. J. *Sociocultural roots of mental illness*. New York: Plenum, 1978.

Segal, S. J., & Fusella, V. Influence of imaged pictures and sounds on detection of visual and auditory signals. *Journal of Experimental Psychology*, 1970, *83*, 458-464.

Shapiro, D. L. The significance of visual imagery of psychotherapy. *Psychotherapy: Theory, Research, and Practice*, 1970, *7*, 209-212.

Sheehan, P. W. Some comments on the nature of visual imagery: The problem of affect. Paper presented at the meeting of the International Society for Mental Imagery Techniques, Geneva, Switzerland, 1968.

Sheehan, P. W. Hypnosis and the manifestations of "imagination." In E. Fromm & R. E. Shor (Eds.), Hypnosis: *Research developments and perspectives*. Chicago: Aldine-Atherton, 1972.

Sheikh, A. A. Treatment of insomnia through eidetic imagery: A new technique. *Perceptual and Motor Skills*, 1976, *43*, 994.

Sheikh, A. A. Mental images: Ghosts of sensations? *Journal of Mental Imagery*, 1977, *1*, 1-4.

Sheikh, A. A. Eidetic psychotherapy. In J. L. Singer & K. S. Pope (Eds.), *The power of human imagination*. New York: Plenum, 1978.

Sheikh, A. A., & Panagiotou, N. C. Use of mental imagery in psychotherapy: A critical review. *Perceptual and Motor Skills*, 1975, *41*, 555-585.

Shontz, F. C. *The psychological aspects of illness and disability*. New York: McMillan, 1975.

Sifneos, P. E. The prevalence of "alexithymic" characteristics in psychosomatic patients. *Psychotherapy and Psychosomatics*, 1973, *22*, 258.

Simpson, H. M., & Paivio, A. Changes in pupil size during an imagery task without motor involvement. *Psychonomic Science*, 1966, *5*, 405-406.

Singer, J. L. Fantasy: The foundation of serenity. *Psychology Today*, July 1976, 32-37.

Singer, J. L., & Schonbar, R. A. Correlates of daydreaming: A dimension of self-awareness. *Journal of Consulting Psychology*, 1961, *25*, 1-6.

Wallace, R. K. The physiology of meditation. *Scientific American*, 1972, 64-92.

Watson, J. B. Psychology as the behaviorist views it. *Psychological Review*, 1913, *20*, 158-177.

Weiner, H. *Psychobiology and human disease*. New York: Elsevier, 1977.

Weiner, H., Singer, M., & Reiser, M. Cardiovascular responses and their psychological correlates: A study in healthy young adults and patients with peptic ulcer and hypertension. *Psychosomatic Medicine*, 1962, *24*, 477-498.

Weitzenhoffer, A. M., & Hilgard, E. R. *Stanford hypnotic susceptibility scale, Form C*. Palo Alto, California: Consulting Psychologist Press, 1962.

Willard, R. D. Breast enlargement through visual imagery and hypnosis. *American Journal of Clinical Hypnosis*, 1977, *19*, 195-200.

Williams, J. E. Stimulation of breast growth by hypnosis. *Journal of Sex Research*, 1974, *10*, 316-326.

Wittkower, E. D. (Ed.) *Psychosomatic medicine: Its clinical applications*. Hagerstown, Maryland: Harper and Row, 1977.

Yaremko, R. M., & Butler, M. C. Imaginal experience and attenuation of the galvanic skin response to shock. *Bulletin of the Psychonomic Society*, 1975, *5*, 317-318.

Yates, F. A. *The art of memory*. London: Routledge and Kegan Paul, 1966.

Zikmund, V. Physiological correlates of visual imagery. In P. Sheehan (Ed.), *The function and nature of imagery*. New York: Academic Press, 1972.

8

Mental Imagery and Psychotherapy: European Approaches

CHARLES S. JORDAN

The resurgence of interest in imagery in Europe and America in the 60's and 70's appears to be leading to the closing of the gap between the scientific and clinical interests in the role of imagery as a central integrative process in perception. Many are coming to appreciate the role of imagery in adults, as well as children, as a highly synthetic cognitive process which integrates sensation, affect, thought, and memory processes (Ahsen, 1977; Paivio, 1973; Sheikh & Panagiotou, 1975). The recognition of two encoding systems, a verbal, sequential system and an imagery-spatial-parallel processing one, has led researchers and clinicians alike to agree on the need of both for optimum functioning (Paivio, 1971; Sheikh, 1977, 1978; Singer, 1977). The interest of the psychotherapists in imagery as an effective method of uncovering repressed material and integrating cognitive, emotional, and behavioral events is indeed close to the scientists' inquiry into the role of images in memory and perceptual processes. Our progress towards integrating clinical and experimental approaches may be based on the unavoidable observation that the scientist-practitioner and the subject-patient are all dependent on a subjective approach to an objective adjustment.

In contrast to the objectivity of American behaviorism, current European schools applying imagery in psychotherapy have remained more subjective and phenomenological in theory and practice. A brief survey will be made to trace the philosophical, scientific, and clinical roots of these European schools, as well as

Charles S. Jordan, Department of Psychiatry and Behavioral Sciences, Medical University of South Carolina, Charleston, SC 29401. The author expresses appreciation to Robert S. McCully and Patsy Hicken for their aid in the preparation of this paper.

their impact on other schools of imagery. Following the development of this historical perspective, the work of Desoille (1965), Fretigny and Virel (1968), and Leuner (1969) will be reviewed, since their approaches seem to typify current European schools of imagery applied to psychotherapy.

Early Experimental Studies of Imagery

It is interesting to note the dialectical process set in motion by the European functionalist and structuralist schools of psychology employing introspection in the investigation of the role of imagery in memory, thought, and perception. The examples are found in Fechner's "memory after images," Alfred Binet's "imageless thought," Edgar Rubin's study of "figure and ground," and Jaensch's "eidetic imagery," (see Woodworth & Sheehan, 1964). As exponents of a phenomenological approach to the study of perception, these schools provided the thesis of subjectivity in experimental psychology. J. B. Watson developed the antithesis of behaviorism in 1914 with his assertion that "it is possible to define a 'science of behavior,' and never use the terms consciousness, mental states, mind, content, will, imagery and the like" (Woodworth & Sheehan, 1964, p. 112).

This dialectical struggle between behavioral and phenomenological schools of psychology provided a historical perspective which prognosticates a synthesis between subjective and objective approaches in scientific research and clinical practice. This synthesis is most evident currently in America among researchers and clinicians interested in mental imagery, whose approaches may be called cognitive (Beck, 1970), cognitive-affective (Ahsen, 1977; Singer, 1974), and cognitive-behavioral (Meichenbaum, 1977).

However, as noted above, current European exponents of the use of imagery in psychotherapy appear to have been slower to adopt operationalism and systematic investigation of imagery procedures, with only a few exceptions. Antecedents influencing this more subjective European approach to imagery in psychotherapy are many. First of all, many of the experimentalists and leading clinicians fled Europe during World War I and World War II. Secondly, the phenomenology of German and French origin permeated the philosophical roots of European clinical and scientific systems. Thirdly, Jung's subjective approaches to the understanding of symbols in fantasies, dreams, and myths had a most profound effect on many European practitioners. Finally, Europe had been subtly seeded by a rich legacy of subjective Eastern psychology which obviously directly influenced the theory and practices of Jung and Assagioli.

The Contributions of Jung, Assagioli, Freud, and Schultz in Developing Imagery Methods

Though not often noted by historians of psychology, the practical Tantric psychology of Patanjali's Yoga Sutra (1949), written the second century B.C. in India, describes the nature and function of the conscious, subconscious, and unconscious layers or Kosas of the mind. It is also interesting to note that the Hindu religious philosophy contains the ancient concept of the "collective consciousness" or "collective mind" which descriptively bears great similarity to Jung's concept of the "collective unconscious." Consciousness in Hindu and Tantric psychology includes the unconscious mind that links the individual with all creation. In fact, Jung repeats this idea when he considers the relationship between macrocosm and microcosm: "The microcosm which contains the images of all creation would be the collective unconscious"(Jung, 1952/1960, p. 494).

Miguei Serrano's (1973) interviews in 1959, with the then 84-year-old Jung, give a fascinating personal account of how Jung's rational Western intellect struggled with the paradoxical Tantric approaches to transcending the ego with the very tool of the ego, the observing conscious mind. Jung apparently consciously or unconsciously integrated many Eastern concepts into his description of universal symbols and images, archtypes, and the collective unconscious (Jung, 1927/1960). However, he regarded much of Indian philosophy and psychology as excessively irrational; and he warned westerners interested in practicing yoga that these methods were best suited for the archetypal ground of Indians.

It is important to examine Jung's contributions as a bridge between Eastern and Western psychologies. His efforts represent an intrapsychic and intercultural synthesis of the objective and subjective realities of individual and collective consciousness.

Jung gave imagery *the* central role in the dynamics of the psyche. He states, "The psyche consists essentially of images. It is a series of images in the truest sense, not an accidental juxtaposition or sequence, but a structure that is throughout full of meaning and purpose; it is a 'picturing' of vital activities. And just as the material of the body that is ready for life has a need of the psyche in order to be capable of life, so the psyche presupposes the living body in order that its' images may live" (Jung, 1926/1960, pp. 325-326). Through this recognition of the reciprocity of psyche and body, he expresses the belief in mind-body unity as a life process and suggests that the power of imagery is a means of perceiving and experiencing this life process. Jung (1926/1960) concludes that from a psychological standpoint, the validity of psychic realities which involve the immediate world of images cannot be subjected either to epistemological criticism or to scientific verification.

Jung's application of imagery in therapy is best represented by his method of active imagination that could grow out of a dream, hypnagogic image, or fantasy. However, Jung is careful to discriminate between imagination and fantasy. He states, "A fantasy is more or less your own invention, and remains on the surface of personal things and conscious expectations. But active imagination, as the term denotes, means that the images have a life of their own and that the symbolic events develop according to their own logic — that is, of course, if your conscious reason does not interfere" (Jung, 1935/1976, p. 171). He also remarks, "When you concentrate on a mental picture, it begins to stir, the image becomes enriched by details. It moves and develops . . . and so when we concentrate on an inner picture and when we are careful not to interrupt the natural flow of events, our unconscious will produce a series of images which makes a complete story" (Jung, 1935/1976, p. 172). Jung comments further that this active-imagination process is superior to dreams in "deflating" the unconscious and quickening maturation in analysis. He cautions, however, that many people are not ready for this direct confrontation with their natural flow of images until later in analysis.

Thus, Jung fostered much interest in the role of imagery in psychotherapy and his ideas served as an intellectual bridge between Eastern and Western approaches to psychology and psychotherapy. A more direct integration of Eastern and Western views of imagery in psychotherapy was undertaken by an Italian psychiatrist, Roberto Assagioli, a contemporary of Jung and Freud.

Assagioli's therapeutic system of "psychosynthesis" differed from the analytical methods of Jung and Freud in being more holistic and eclectic. Psychosynthesis includes approaches to develop man's personal and spiritual capacities by using the analytical, behavioral, and humanistic methods of the West, as well as meditative techniques from the East (Assagioli, 1965).

Assagioli proposed that there were seven dimensions of human personality. The *lower unconscious* contains bodily functions, drives, emotions, primitive dreams, and imagination. The *middle unconscious* is similar to waking consciousness. The *higher unconscious* or *superconscious* includes higher intuitions and inspirations of an artistic, scientific, or humanitarian nature. The next dimension is called the *field of consciousness* of which we are directly aware, that is, sensations, images, thoughts, and feelings. The sixth level is the *higher self* which is above and unaffected by the flow of mental life and can be attained through the use of depth approaches such as meditation. The final level is the *collective unconscious* corresponding to Jung's concept that included primitive structures or archetypes, as well as higher forward-directed activities of a superconscious nature.

Many of the imagery procedures based on the "ideal model" in psychosynthesis were oriented towards the goal of achieving increased awareness of the first three levels of the unconscious, in order to solve personal problems (Assagioli, 1965). The ideal model involved spontaneous creative imagery directed by the unconscious, just as Jung (1935, 1976) had described in the active imagination process. However, Assagioli took a step farther than Jung had dared to take: he employed yogic methods of meditation and a number of other ego-transcendant imagery techniques involving symbols to attain the spiritual goal of realization of the higher self. In the transcendence imagery exercise called the "Temple of Silence"

(Assagioli, 1965), "the subject is asked to imagine himself slowly climbing a mountain, on top of which is a temple of silence and in which he allows all the cells in his body, his heart, and his mind to be filled with silence which he then brings down from the mountain with him and radiates to the world around" (Crampton, 1969, p. 149).

Assagioli's influence upon the imagery schools of Europe has appeared to be less than his impact in the United States and Canada. His acceptance in America may be due to the current humanistic movement which embraces holistic and spiritual approaches.

In contrast to Jung and Assagioli, Freud de-emphasized the use of imagery in psychotherapy. However, it is interesting to note that Freud's use of imagery association in psychotherapy was extensive prior to 1900 (Singer, 1974). He was at first influenced by Breuer's use of the abreaction of early memories with hypnosis but soon dropped the use of hypnosis in favor of an imagery method that was more under the patient's conscious control. Freud began using a technique in which he pressed on the patient's head and instructed him/her to observe the images that appeared as he relaxed the pressure. Freud reported that, with this approach, the patient began seeing, in rapid succession, different scenes related to the central conflict. These scenes emerged spontaneously in chronological order. During the use of this imagery approach, Freud discovered and described the nature of resistance for the first time (Singer, 1974).

Freud appears to have dropped his approaches that involved touching the patient and the use of imagery associations around 1900. Thereafter he moved towards free association and dream interpretation. Freud came to regard imagery as a form of resistance to free association, which was defending the patient against unacceptable impulses containing elements of transference. Thus his influence, particularly among analysts, led to emphasis upon the secondary process or verbal content of the patient's productions. Imagery was labeled a more primitive, primary-process function associated with regressive features in the patient. This definition of imagery stood in stark contrast to that proposed by the Jungian and numerous other European schools of psychotherapy that regarded imagery as a creative process of the psyche to be used for achieving greater individual, interpersonal, and spiritual integration.

The autogenic training method of the German psychiatrist and neurologist, J. H. Schultz, is another important imagery-related therapy developed around the turn of the century. He, like Freud, was initially interested in the physiological basis of disorders, but his autogenic training method bears more resemblance to Assagioli's holistic approach in that meditative exercises are integrated into the advanced stages of treatment.

In a review article, Luthe (1963) states that the roots of autogenic training lie in research on sleep and hypnosis carried out in the Berlin Institute by brain physiologist Oskar Vogt, during the years 1890 to 1900. Vogt observed that intelligent patients who had undergone a series of hypnotic sessions were able to put themselves into a state which appeared to be similar to a hypnotic state. His patients reported that these "autohypnotic" experiences had a remarkable recuperative effect (Schultz & Luthe, 1959) which enhanced their overall efficiency.

Stimulated by Vogt's work, Schultz began to explore approaches to autosuggestions which would eliminate the unfavorable elements of contemporary hypnosis such as patient's passivity and dependence on the therapist. In this work, Schultz found that most of his hypnotized subjects reported sensation experiences of two types. One was a feeling of heaviness in the extremities and often in the whole body, and the second was a feeling of agreeable warmth. Schultz then posed the question of whether a person could induce a psychophysiologic state similar to a hypnotic state by merely thinking of heaviness and warmth in the limbs. The systematic approach to this question was the beginning of autogenic training. Through methods of passive concentration on verbal formulas implying heaviness and warmth in the extremities, Schultz's subjects were able to induce a state resembling hypnosis. Due to this self-directed method, dependence on the hypnotist was eliminated.

Luthe states (1963) that the key therapeutic factor of autogenic training lies in "a self-induced (autogenic) modification of cortical-diencephalic interrelations, which enable natural forces to regain their otherwise restricted capacity for self-regulatory normalization. The hypothesis implies that the function of the entire neurohumoral axis (cortex, thalamus, reticular system, hypothalamus, hypophysis, adrenals) is directly involved and that the therapeutic mechanism is not unilaterally restricted to either bodily or mental functions" (p. 193).

Schultz developed a number of useful verbal formulas with either a more bodily (standard exercises) or mental orientation (meditative exercises). The six standard exercises are physiologically oriented: they are focused on the neuromuscular system (heaviness) and the vasomotor system (warmth). The meditative exercises are composed of a series of seven exercises which focus primarily on certain mental functions including imagery and are reserved for trainees who master the standard exercises.

Initial training involves the achievement of muscle relaxation, slowing of autonomic and respiratory activity, and warming of the solar plexus and cooling of the forehead. To achieve these results, verbal formulas of "warming" and "heaviness" and also "passive" concentration are emphasized. Passive concentration implies a casual nongoal-oriented attitude towards the psychophysiologic effects of a given formula. Effectiveness of passive concentration on a given formula depends on two factors: a) the mental contact with the part of the body indicated by the formula, and b) the maintenance of a steady flow of a filmlike (verbal, acoustic, or visual) representation of the autogenic formula in one's mind (Luthe, 1963). These autogenic procedures have been widely applied to treating the whole range of functional and organic disorders, such as bronchial asthma, writer's cramp, hemorrhoids, brain injuries, esophagospasm, and puritus.

Imagery plays a vital role in the passive concentration procedure. However, Luthe and Schultz (1969) comment, "In order to avoid clinically undesirable possibilities of mobilization of disturbing visual discharges from overloaded brain areas, it is recommended that caution be exercised, and not to suggest the use of associated images unless the patient's history and his actual psychodynamic constellation is without potent pathodynamic elements" (p. 137).

However, extensive use of imagery is used in the treatment of psychoneurotic and psychosomatic patients by Luthe. He outlines in detail (Luthe, 1970) the stages and the levels of structual and dynamic differentiation of visual phenomena during what he calls the seven stages of visual elaboration in the process of "autogenic abreaction." These stages of brain-directed visual elaborations range from vague, cloudlike, monochromatic forms to highly realistic and differentiated filmlike productions. The movement towards an increase in the reality of features is viewed as therapeutic progress. It is assumed that the brain-directed processes of autogenic neutralization, while aiming at self-normalization, are guided by a participating "reality mechanism."

Imagery, which includes visualization of colors, concrete objects, abstract objects, selected feeling states, other persons, and "answers" from the unconscious, is central in the meditative exercises. These meditative exercises have been applied to severe medical and psychosomatic cases such as advanced cancer, ulcerative colitis, and anorexia nervosa. Routinely, the meditative exercises are used in "depth-dimensional" psychotherapy after 10 to 12 months of practice with the standard exercises mentioned above.

Schultz's autogenic training generated in the early 1900's and elaborated today by Luthe represents a significant milestone in the history of the therapeutic use of imagery. Schultz's methods may be seen as the forerunner of Jacobson's method of deep muscle relaxation therapy and the many uses of imagery in behavior modification. The autogenic method can also be seen as a self-generated and self-regulated biofeedback approach and may have inspired our more technological approach to biofeedback. Autogenic training has influenced many European and American imagery-oriented psychotherapies, and it has become a standard therapy in various fields of medicine in recent years.

The meditative approach used in autogenic training also has a strong tie with the Psychophysiologic Therapy which includes meditative exercises, of Indian physician Vahia and his associates (1973). They have applied the ancient concepts of Patanjali to the treatment of neurotic and psychosomatic disorders. An impressive and well-controlled outcome study over a 9-year period shows that this therapy produced improvement in 70% of patients in the four diagnostic categories of anxiety state, depression, hysteria, and bronchial asthma. It is noteworthy that this approach achieved significantly better results than antianxiety drugs, as measured by the Taylor Anxiety Rating Scale.

The methods of Vahia and his colleagues included the following:

1) *Asana.* Practice of certain selected postures for relaxation

2) *Pranayama.* Breathing practices for voluntary control of inspiration, expiration, and retention of breath

3) *Pratyahara.* Restraint of,the senses by voluntary withdrawal from the external environment

4) *Dharana.* Selection of an object for concentration and development of increased concentration on that object and decreased preoccupation with external stimuli

5) *Dhyana.* Development of integration with the selected object to the complete exclusion of all other thought processes and later, identification of that object with the integrating mechanism present within all of us, leading to unison with it

Patanjali's techniques outlined above begin with control over the voluntary musculature, subsequently over the autonomic nervous system, and later over the thought processes. The sequence and manner very much resemble those used in passive concentration in Schultz's autogenic training. Schultz's and Vahia's methods are further alike in their focus on the process of self-generated change, whereby extreme dependence and transference relationships with the therapist are avoided.

The goals of Vahia's psychophysiologic therapy are to minimize the preoccupation with feedback from environmental gratifications and frustrations, to increase self-awareness and thereby produce better integration of the personality, and thus to achieve actualization of one's creative potentialities.

Schultz's meditative exercises and the application of Patanjali's light limbed Ashtanga Yoga by Vahia in India and Swami Rama (1976) at the Himalayan Institute in Chicago represent systematic steps towards a workable synthesis of Eastern and Western approaches to psychotherapy.

From the above, it is not difficult to appreciate the important historical role of European imagery approaches in the synthesis of Eastern and Western views of therapy and personal growth.

Current European Applications of Imagery to Psychotherapy

Robert Desoille's Guided-Daydream Method

Ironically, among contemporary European schools, the most influential imagery-oriented therapist appears to be a French engineer by the name of Desoille. His methods, developed between 1938 and 1966, were initially influenced by Caslant, a layman who attempted to generate psychic experiences (Singer, 1974). Caslant was exploring the use of directed imagery in scenes of climbing a mountain or descending into the earth, in order to produce creative imagery not reliant on memories and possessing the potential to induce extrasensory experiences. From this technique Desoille (1965) developed the "waking dream" technique as a psychotherapeutic procedure, although he had no training in psychology.

Desoille (1965) describes his directed daydream as follows: "The basic procedure of this experiment is quite simple: it consists of having the subject engage in a daydream while he is stretched out on a couch as comfortably as possible. We give the patient a starting image, for example a sword, or possibly, a seashore where the water is very deep. We have him describe this image as thoroughly as possible and ask him questions so as to evoke details, if necessary. During the course of the first session, it may be necessary at times to remind the subject that in a dream anything is possible" (p.1).

Desoille encourages his patients during the directed daydream to let the images occur spontaneously in the absence of a conscious critical attitude. This spontaneous creative imagery, Desoille proposes, as many others have also done (Ahsen, 1968; Horowitz, 1972; Jung, 1935/1976; Leuner, 1969), is effective in circumventing resistances. The projective nature of Desoille's image themes further assists the individual in bypassing ego control in dealing with unconscious conflicts.

In the first phase of treatment, Desoille introduces, as projective stimuli, a sequence of six image themes which he feels were questions put to the unconscious. The individual's responses are regarded as diagnostic of the patient's habitual patterns in dealing with the major problems of human experience. These six themes used as starting images include: (1) the sword or vessel representing masculine and feminine identity respectively, (2) descent into the depth of the ocean in order to confront unconscious conflicts, (3) descent into a cave where a witch or magician, representing the opposite-sex parent, is encountered, (4) descent into a cave where the same-sex parent is encountered as a witch-sorceress or wizard-magician, (5) descent into a cave of a dragon which represents social prohibition, and (6) the image of the castle of Sleeping Beauty located deep in the forest, where both sexes focus on the Oedipal conflict.

The second phase of treatment involves making the patient aware of underdeveloped capacities and promoting new habits at an imagery level. While the patient has more freedom at this point to let the imagery unfold at his/her own rate and choice of direction, the emphasis remains on movement of either ascending or descending nature. Ascending images are associated with the positive affect of joy or achievement, while descending images are more likely to evoke fear. One example of this work involves a patient who meets a monster in an underwater grotto. The "guide" or therapist encourages the patient to ask the monster to give him a tour of the grotto and then to bring the monster back onto the beach with him. At this point the patient is encouraged to tap the monster with a magic wand, which has been provided — this turns the monster into an octopus. Desoille (Singer, 1974) indicates that following the appearance of the octopus, the image of the actual person in the patient's life, whom the monster represents, often emerges. In the final stage of the daydream, the patient ascends the mountain overlooking the sea, in the company of the person that the octopus represented. The patient is prepared before the descent image that he may encounter frightening images and encouraged to show a certain amount of bravery. If the patient reaches an impasse, the guide assists by suggesting different implements or techniques that the patient may use to continue his journey.

In the third and final phase of therapy, the patient is encouraged to move from imagined responses to making realistic responses in the environment. This transfer of training is augmented to some extent by having the patient write out full accounts of his/her experience and discuss them in detail with the therapist. Thus, we can see in Desoille's work, elements similar to those occurring in current behavioral methods of desensitization, cognitive restructuring, and education in developing new response patterns. Desoille's three phases of treatment closely resemble those of Meichenbaum's (1977) stress-inoculation training, which consists of educational, imagery-rehearsal, and application phases.

It might be argued that some of Desoille's imagery symbols are not universally applicable and his methods may encourage too many wish-fulfilling fantasies that the patient cannot transfer to the environment. However, with corrective factors for individual and cultural differences, his methods seem applicable to a wide variety of problems.

Hanscarl Leuner's Guided Affective Imagery

Leuner's (1969) method of guided affective imagery, while closely related to the approach of Desoille, incorporates Freudian and Jungian psychoanalysis. Leuner was trained as a psychoanalyst and traces his method to Freud's original use of imagery. However, he claims that his method requires considerably less time to be effective than traditional psychoanalysis (Singer, 1974). He reports that the average therapeutic program lasts only 40 hours, and the upper limit is 160 hours. He notes that he has achieved limited results with psychotic patients and addicts.

The method of treatment is descriptively close to Desoille but more systematized. The patient reclines on a couch and is encouraged to relax using Schultz's (Schultz & Luthe, 1959) autogenic training involving a fixed image. External stimulation is reduced in a quiet and dimly lit room. There is a series of five techniques for evoking fantasy material and interpreting it; it consists of the training method, the diagnostic method, the method of associated imagery, the symbolic dramatic method, and the psychoanalytic method.

Leuner then employs a sequence of 10 standard imaginary situations in the same style as Desoille. The drama always begins with a meadow representing a new beginning, the Garden of Eden, or the mother-child relationship. Next, the image of ascending a mountain and describing the view, is projected in order to tap the patient's feelings concerning mastery-of-life situations. Thirdly, the patient is encouraged to follow a brook upstream to its source or down to the ocean. To Leuner the brook represents the "flow of psychic energy" and the capacity for emotional development. In the course of manipulation of these first three images, the patient receives the basic training in guided affective imagery; he/she is then ready to explore the seven other areas. The patient is asked to visualize a house, a close relative, a lion confronting its enemies, a person representing the ego ideal, a situation arousing sexual feelings, a swamp in the corner of a meadow, and a dark forest or cave.

During the diagnostic phase, these images may be reviewed rapidly, but later the images are reviewed in "micro-diagnosis" for enhancing observation of emotions associated with the image and proceeding into psychoanalytic methods.

Leuner's psychoanalytic work contrasts sharply with classical psychoanalysis. Leuner feels that the patient's involvement in his/her own imagery becomes so potent that the complexity of the transference neurosis and the need to analyze it is avoided. Further, Leuner points out that confrontation with real people in the patient's life rather than fantasies about the therapist dominates the symbolic drama. Ahsen's (1972) eidetic imagery approach also maximizes the utilization of the naturally occurring parental images, thereby avoiding transference and promoting creative emanations of solutions to real-life situations. This circumvention of excessive transference made possible by the more internal and direct analysis through imagery may, in part, account for the fact that briefer periods of therapy are required.

An important feature of Leuner's approach is his systematic definition of concepts and procedures which lend themselves well to formal research. Kornadt found significant positive correlations between projective measures of striving and the height of mountains in the mountain-climbing scene, among 30 adult subjects (Sheikh & Panagiotou, 1975). In an application of guided affective imagery to psychotherapy groups, Plaum found significant improvements from pretest to posttest measures in rigidity, extraversion, neuroticism, and anxiety (Singer, 1974).

Fretigny and Virel's Onirotherapy

Roger Fretigny and Andre Virel (1968) are a psychiatrist and a psychologist who display experimental, theoretical, and clinical interests. They make ample use of Desoille's techniques, but they have generated a much more systematic experimental method in the context of a general psychotherapeutic approach.

Virel's interest and research in psychophysiology led the team to define onirotherapy as an approach dealing with "oniric" or quasi-dreamlike images as opposed to the specific guided daydreams of Desoille.

Fretigny and Virel begin treatment with a rather complete case history of the family background, psychosocial factors, physiological status, and psychological development. They then encourage the patient to relax deeply and start with imagery in the fashion of Desoille. However, they use a much more general psychotherapeutic approach to investigating daydreams, requiring the patient to prepare detailed accounts of imagery produced during the previous session. The central process in onirodrama is the vivid and dramatic confrontation through imagery of the critical problems of the patient.

This team resembles neo-Freudian psychoanalysts in their treatment of resistance and transference. These analytical approaches are integrated with procedures which tend to allow the imagery to unfold more freely than is the case in Desoille's or Leuner's procedures. Desoille refers to the therapist as "guide"; they use the term "operator," which suggests that he is someone who starts and monitors the process without very much directing of each step.

Fretigny and Virel's research efforts (1968) to validate some of their psychophysiological hypotheses regarding onirotherapy have revealed that during imagery sessions there is ample evidence of alpha rhythm and minimal orienting response to external noises other than the therapist's voice. No evidence of sleep rhythms was found while the patient's vigilance remained stable in conjunction with the production of alpha. These results led to the conclusion that while the electrophysiological characteristics of imagery resemble those of hypnosis, the close rapport with the psychotherapist during imagery sessions is of a more active nature than observed in hypnosis.

Overview and Conclusions

It appears that the European schools of imagery have been largely responsible for keeping the use of mental imagery in psychotherapy alive and well in the wake of behaviorism in the early 1900's. While these schools have contributed relatively little to the systematic investigation of imagery processes, they have provided a rich heritage in establishing therapeutic procedures that are now used in dynamic and behavioral approaches in America.

Philosophically, these European schools have kept us in touch with the unavoidable phenomenological nature of perception. The depth approaches of Jung, Assagioli, and the current work of Ahsen (1968, 1977) in this country serve as bridges between Eastern and Western approaches to understanding the nature of man's consciousness.

This brief historical account of European schools of imagery further attests to the fact that many therapists have independently discovered the power of imagery processes in promoting psychotherapeutic change. Continuing progress in the utilization of imagery in psychotherapy and understanding the role of imagery in perception will be fostered significantly by greater interdependence between clinicians and researchers.

REFERENCES

Ahsen, A. *Basic concepts in eidetic psychotherapy.* New York: Brandon House, 1968.

Ahsen, A. *Eidetic parents test and analysis.* New York: Brandon House, 1972.

Ahsen, A. *Psycheye: Self-analytic consciousness.* New York: Brandon House, 1977.

Assagioli, R. *Psychosynthesis: A collection of basic writings.* New York: Viking, 1965.

Beck, A. Cognitive therapy: Nature and relation to behavior therapy. *Behavior Therapy,* 1970, *1,* 184-200.

Crampton, M. The use of mental imagery in psychosynthesis. *Journal of Humanistic Psychology,* 1969, *9,* 139-153.

Desoille, R. *The directed daydream.* New York: Psychosynthesis Research Foundation, 1965.

Fretigny, R. & Virel, A. *L'imagerie mentale.* Geneva: Mont-Blanc, 1968.

Horowitz, M. J. Image formation: Clinical observations and a cognitive model. In P. Sheehan (Ed.), *The function and nature of imagery.* New York: Academic Press, Pp. 281-309, 1972.

Jung, C. G. *The symbolic life.* (Tr. by R. F. C. Hull) Collected works, Vol. *18,* Princeton: Princeton Press, 1976.

Jung, C. G. *The structure and dynamics of the psyche* (Tr. by R. F. C. Hull) Collected works, Vol. *8,* Princeton: Princeton Press, 1960.

Leuner, H. Guided affective imagery: A method of intensive psychotherapy. *American Journal of Psychotherapy,* 1969, *23,* 4-22.

Luthe, W. Autogenic training: Method, research, and application in medicine. *American Journal of Psychotherapy,* 17, 174-195, 1963.

Luthe, W. *Autogenic therapy, volume V: Dynamics of autogenic neutralization.* New York: Grune & Stratton, 1970.

Luthe, W. & Schultz, J. H. *Autogenic therapy, volume III: Applications in psychotherapy.* New York: Grune & Stratton, 1969.

Meichenbaum, D. *Cognitive-behavior modification.* New York: Plenum Press, 1977.

Paivio, A. *Imagery and verbal processes.* New York: Holt, Rinehart & Winston, 1971.

Paivio, A. Psychophysiological correlates of imagery. In F. J. McGuigan & R. A. Schoonover (Eds.), *The psychophysiology of thinking.* New York: Academic Press, 1973, Pp. 263-295.

Patanjali, *Yoga-Sutra* (Tr. from Sanskrit by Bengali Baba), Poona, 1949.

Rama, S., Ballentine, R., & Ajaya, S. *Yoga and psychotherapy.* Glenview, Illinois: Himalayan Institute, 1976.

Schultz, J. H. & Luthe, W. *Autogenic training: A physiological approach in psychotherapy.* New York: Grune & Stratton, 1959.

Serrano, Miguel, *C. G. Jung, & Hermann Hesse: A record of two friendships.* New York: Schocken Books, 1973.

Sheikh, A. A. Eidetic psychotherapy. In J. L. Singer & K. S. Pope (Eds.), *The power of human imagination.* New York: Plenum, 1978.

Sheikh, A. A. Mental images: Ghosts of sensations? *Journal of Mental Imagery,* 1977, *1,* 1-4.

Sheikh, A. A. & Panagiotou, N. C. Use of mental imagery in psychotherapy: A critical review. *Perceptual and Motor Skills,* 1975, *41,* 555-585.

Singer, J. L. *Imagery and daydream methods in psychotherapy and behavior modification.* New York: Academic Press, 1974.

Singer, J. L. Imagination and make-believe play in early childhood: Some educational implications. *Journal of Mental Imagery,* 1977, *1,* 127-144.

Vahia, N. S., Doongaji, D. R., Jeste, D. V., Ravindranath, S., Kapoor, S. N., Ardhapurkar, I. Psychophysiologic therapy based on the concepts of Patanjali: A new approach to the treatment of neurotic and psychosomatic disorders. *American Journal of Psychotherapy,* 27, 557-565, 1973.

Woodworth, R. S. & Sheehan, M. R. *Contemporary Schools of Psychology.* New York: The Ronald Press Company, 1964.

9

Emotive-Reconstructive Psychotherapy: Changing Constructs by Means of Mental Imagery

JAMES K. MORRISON

In the course of this paper, I would like to briefly outline two major aspects of emotive-reconstructive therapy or ERT (Morrison & Cometa, 1977): (1) the basic *theoretical approach* or the assumptions on which ERT is based, (2) the *operational approach* or the combination of clinical techniques used in ERT. In order to further the understanding of both the theory and the techniques, I will present some research findings and discuss some brief case illustrations.

Theoretical Approach of ERT

ERT is based on a cognitive model of personality (Bannister & Fransella, 1971; Kelly, 1955; Piaget, 1972; Sarbin, Taft, & Bailey, 1960) and incorporates the notion of intrapersonal variations in the level of Reticular Activating System (RAS) arousal (Dember, 1965; Fiske & Maddi, 1961; Hebb, 1955; Malmo, 1959; Schachter & Singer, 1962). The individual is thus viewed as an active organism constantly engaged in the process of monitoring and interpreting experiences so as to maintain an orderly view of the world and, concomitantly, an "optimal level of arousal" (Fiske & Maddi, 1961).

James K. Morrison, 678 Troy-Schenectady Road, Latham, NY 12110.

Within the context of ERT, clients are viewed as individuals "victimized" by their apparent inability to construe themselves and others in a congruent, personally satisfying manner. In other words, their predictions about self and others are frequently invalidated by life's experiences. I regard the behavior of clients to reflect, to some extent, the adoption of certain roles as a means of coping with stress. Finally, I assume that these inadequate self-constructs and often dysfunctional roles have their source in early childhood experiences (Morrison, 1977) which are poorly encoded in a person's memory system, and thus are retrievable only with difficulty. In order to briefly explicate ERT, it will be necessary to explore the key concepts of stress, memory, and early childhood experiences.

Stress

Following Kelly's (1955) formulation, "stress" and/or "anxiety" are treated as referents for instances wherein an individual becomes aware of an inability to integrate an event into his/her present "cognitive system." "Cognitive system" refers in general to the dimensions or criteria which individuals employ in making sense of events. Within the context of this paper, this term and equivalent notions such as categories, constructs, schemata, and frames of reference are used interchangeably. An individual may cope with discrepant events by screening out data which do not conform to existent beliefs, or may reinterpret certain portions of his/her cognitive system in the direction of achieving greater consonance with incoming feedback. Likewise, information-processing theories (Neisser, 1967) suggest that incongruent data disrupt ongoing conceptual nervous system activity levels and place an organism into a state of hyperarousal. Given that organisms seek to maintain an optimal level of arousal, one free of too much novelty or boredom, (Fiske & Maddi, 1961) and that present cognitive strategies are suspended under conditions of hyperarousal (Mancuso, 1970), ERT serves to reduce stress by encouraging the client to adopt different conceptualizations of events, and it accomplishes this process by assisting the client in re-experiencing the psychological and physiological components of arousal. Such a recreation of high-arousal states is facilitated primarily by extensive use of mental imagery, combined with other ancillary techniques, such as selective deep-breathing exercises and role playing.

For example, as children, clients may not have been able to deal with the high degree of stressful arousal induced by the perception of their parents as "nonloving." In order to cope with the physiological and psychological stress engendered by this perception, children sometimes resolve this incongruency by construing their parents as "loving," and themselves as "bad" persons, who, if only they could become "good," would be loved by their parents. Such children then undertake the role of "bad child" and, thus, camouflage ongoing family interactions. Essentially, locked into the role of "bad child" as a means of reducing the stress and confusion of paradoxical family communication, individuals' subsequent life experiences are but replays of early roles. Thus, such persons continue to construe themselves as "bad" and unworthy of anyone's love or concern and to act out the same non-productive roles.

Memory

Many approaches to psychotherapy tend to rely, albeit tacitly, upon rather static, reproductive models of memory (i.e., models wherein memory is viewed as the storage of "whole events" such that instances are either recalled intact, distorted from "pure form," or entirely "blotted out"). In ERT, however, memory is treated from within a cognitive paradigm in which "recall and problem-solving are constructive acts, based on information remaining from earlier acts. That information, in turn, is organized according to the structure of earlier acts" (Neisser, 1967, p. 292). I feel that this is a key point. Since memory is a selective, fragmented process of synthesizing events, in ERT the focus is upon the manner in which a client constructs memories (i.e., the structure of memory), rather than upon the eliciting of accurate, correct recall (Bartlett, 1932). In brief, I believe that "repression" reflects the client's use of inappropriate search strategies and/or a deliberate effort to avoid hyperarousal through the inadequate construction and encoding of stressful, incongruent events. ERT provides and encourages the use of effective search strategies so that the client can gain access to improperly construed and encoded data. Then, by understanding why certain constructs and roles were used in the past, the client can more adequately understand present experiences.

Borrowing from Jerome Singer (1974), perhaps we can bring some clarity to the manner in which ERT enables a client to recall and reconstruct early experiences:

The storage system of the brain operates through discontinuities in that many significant aspects of early childhood are stored reasonably intact, but in a "location" for which the "name" has been partially forgotten or is being systematically avoided. The ability to call forth the specific pattern of behavior that was stored at a period of childhood requires the establishment of a complex series of external circumstances that revive many of the stimuli also part of this stored schema .... Many experiences learned in childhood and much of the thinking of childhood is less organized and complex than that of the adult. Early memories are "forgotten" not so much because they are actively repressed, but rather because two different memory systems or two different systems of locating the memory are in operation .... Many of these behaviors remain encapsulated, emerging occasionally in adult life only when the adult is put into a situation that dramatically revives the early childhood experience (pp. 45-46).

In short, in ERT, I try to help the client retrieve sensorial information, especially visual, which is not used by most people in attempting to resolve their problems.

Early Childhood Experiences

At the outset, I would like to note that in ERT, it is not assumed that all stress is a function of events stemming from early childhood. Rather, I submit that early childhood experiences are *often* the *key* source of a person's inadequate construction of self and others. A brief consideration of the child as "information processor" serves to illustrate this point. As Piagetian (Piaget, 1970a, 1970b, 1972) theory clearly notes, until the ages of 7 or 8, the child is largely incapable of employing complex, adultlike cognitive operations. In a period characterized by egocentrism and an inability to consider alternative interpretations of events, a child tends to integrate experiences in a global, holistic fashion. Being unable to deal with situational factors (Morrison, 1973), a young child's interpretation of parental anger, for example, might be: "I am bad," whereas an older child is more likely to interpret the same event in a qualified, flexible manner: e.g., "Mommy said I was bad, but she was angry when she said it!" Simply stated, a child lacks the wide range of constructs necessary to deal with many of the stresses of childhood.

The chances of early childhood events having a great impact upon the individual are further heightened when one considers the limited number of roles and restricted feedback for role performance, which the child is apt to encounter. The child, cast into and maintained in the role of "dependent, weak child" by the family, continues to perform this role since the role serves the purpose of controlling arousal. As an adult, the same individual continues to construe self, and control arousal, via maintaining a dependent role in interpersonal relations. By encouraging the individual to re-experience early events under conditions of hyperarousal, ERT enables him/her to reassess these events which, as a child, were assimilated in a global, simplistic manner. The goal of such reconstruction is to liberate the client from long-held roles and self-conceptualizations.

In summary, keeping in mind the key concepts of stress, memory, and early childhood experience, I feel that it is reasonable to view the current functioning of many persons in terms of their conceptions of self and others. Further, I believe that early childhood experiences often serve a key function in the formulation and maintenance of adult conceptions. Since early childhood stress experiences are more likely to have been interpreted in a global manner, the overall impact of early events tends to persist as a vague, yet pervasive, memory which resists attempts at integration into present construct systems. Through use of imagery and other ancillary techniques, ERT enables a client to recall and reinterpret key early experiences which had been poorly encoded in the memory system.

Before offering a case illustration, I would like to mention the childhood experience, inadequately construed, which I believe to be most anxiety arousing. I consistently find in my therapy sessions that once a client has successfully dealt with feelings such as anger, fear, and sadness, he/she can then penetrate to the basic core feeling of *aloneness*. This feeling, often described as cold, empty, vague, scary, and the most anxiety arousing of all, is really impossible for a child to understand with his inadequate constructs. It is so stress inducing that many children can escape from it only through dysfunctional constructs and roles; and when these children become adults, unless they can, through therapy, immerse themselves in this core feeling of aloneness, and understand it, and walk away from it, they will continue to attempt to escape, albeit unsuccessfully, this feeling now through alcohol, drugs, work, and other means. Aloneness, once experienced and clearly understood within the context of childhood, is what I find to be the step which most consistently brings about the most radical shift of a client's constructs and subsequently a positive change in that client's behavior.

A case illustration may help to delineate the key concepts of ERT. A 27-year-old executive, who viewed himself as bisexual due to experiencing homosexual fantasies, had improperly construed his response (extreme anxiety) to a homosexual advance made to him during adolescence. To the therapist the client's hyperarousal on this occasion did not seem to reflect a homosexual orientation but rather threatening feelings of aloneness felt since childhood, and now again when he was fearful of losing a friend by failing to respond. In recreating the event via ERT, the client discovered how alone and unloved he had always felt, even in his early years. Subsequent to reconstruing himself and his parents in terms of newly retrieved data, the client embarked on a successful course of therapy which aided him in changing his life. Having synthesized a new perspective of events, the client was able to accept the fact that his parents did not love him — they appeared to have had too many problems themselves to do that — without viewing himself as unlovable. The client took ownership of his wide range of feelings for himself and others and learned to accept all of these feelings. The personality and behavior changes ensuing from therapy were quite marked and pervasive. Homosexual fantasies ceased, and the client became dramatically more self-confident, relaxed, and socially competent. A whole host of annoying *symptoms* (e.g., migraine headaches, suicidal ideation, severe sleep disturbance, stomach problems, excessive use of alcohol, timidity with women, fear of public speaking, etc.) disappeared. Long-range follow-up (after 2 years) confirmed the stability of these therapeutic changes.

Operational Approach

Most clients come for ERT once a week for the traditional 50-minute hour. In the *emotive* and first phase of therapy, the emotive-reconstructive therapist attempts to recreate the physiological and psychological stress events of early childhood through facilitating imagery, and, at times, by asking the client to hyperventilate or to engage in deep, regular breathing for short periods of time. For example, the client is asked to sensorially immerse himself/herself in past events by focusing on the contexual surround (colors, odors, noises, texture) of early experiences, and then to provide the therapist with a minimal verbal description of the same. To bring about hyperventilation, the client is requested to breathe deeply and rapidly for 20- to 30-second time periods; this is done when the therapist judges that hyperarousal would enhance the vividness of the imagery and/or facilitate the expression of a particular feeling. Many times, deep regular breathing is substituted for hyperventilation, especially where hyperventilation might be contraindicated for reasons of health. Often neither type of breathing exercise is needed because the imagery alone is vivid enough to induce strong feelings.

Thus, primarily through vivid mental imagery, the client is aided in re-experiencing the type of hyperarousal encountered in childhood. During the recreation of early stress, the client can now be aided by the therapist in applying adequate constructs in order to reduce stress. While actually feeling the stress, a client can learn effective strategies of coping with it.

It is important to note that in ERT, the client is assisted in recalling certain sensorial, especially visual, information which is not often considered in traditional verbal therapy, as Singer (1974) points out. With *eyes closed* and with a focus on the contextual surround of an event, the client begins to recall more and more detail about early experiences. Soon the client starts to experience some strong feelings about these early events and the persons connected with them. This whole process is made possible, I would contend, because in ERT the focus is on sensorial information or imagery early in the session. This information is easier to retrieve than are the early, poorly coded constructs of parents and other significant persons. But the recall of imagery facilitates the recall of never-dealt-with feelings. Once an understanding of early experiences takes place, the client can more adequately label feelings which he/she was not able to define and label in youth.

A further word is in order about the major techniques used in ERT, the mental imagery techniques. There are three basic imagery techniques.

(1) *Sensorial recreation of a perceived event.* Through imagery, the client is helped to more fully recall partially remembered, *anxiety-arousing events.* For example, through this technique one client remembered a horribly traumatic day when she was 6 or 7. At first, she remembered only awakening her father from a nap; then she recalled that her father was so angry at being awakened that he lifted her onto an electric saw and cut her severely on both hips. Until that session, the client had not known why she had such huge scars on her hips. Unfortunately, that was not the end of that horrible day. Later that day she happened to see her mother miscarry in the bathroom. Finally, because of her despair at being hated by her father, she attempted to kill hrself. It was not until that session that the client began to understand her adult pattern of suicide attempts, after being victimized by the anger of a father-figure, her husband.

Sensorial recreation of perceived events can also be used to assist the client in recalling *pleasurable* events of childhood. At times, such recreations are helpful to prevent the client from falling into the trap of construing his/her parents in completely negative terms, or of blaming parents for all problems. Taking responsibility for one's past, however minimal due to a child's inadequate coping strategies, is important in ERT. Accepting major responsibility for one's present experiences is essential.

(2) *Sensorial fantasizing of symbolic events.* Again, these exercises can deal with either anxiety-arousing or pleasurable events. A few examples will clarify how anxiety-arousing imagery can often be used in symbolic ways. One client was asked to imagine himself standing in the middle between his parents, looking back and forth between them, and being forced to go in one direction or the other. This fantasy was highly anxiety arousing and helped the client to remember the terrible feeling of being caught in the middle between two parents, each of whom was constantly trying to use him against the other.

Other clients have been asked to imagine inanimate objects (e.g., a doll) expressing feelings for them when they are unable to do so themselves in certain therapy sessions. At times, after expressing feelings, some clients are asked to imagine the reaction of parents. Lastly, still other clients seem to gain a great deal of insight by imaging a dominant mother or father shrinking in size, while they grow in size so that they can feel powerful enough to express the anger they feel toward their parents.

(3) *Some recreation of a perceived event combined with a fantasizing of a symbolic event.* For example, after a client remembers an experience where a parent had induced rage in him/her, and after he/she has expressed that rage, the client is asked to imagine a parent's reaction. Such imagined reactions often lead to new discoveries about how a client construes parents.

At the beginning of therapy, I ask the client to list as many early and emotionally upsetting experiences as he/she can remember. After going through a standard sequence (see Morrison, 1977) of scenes common to most children (e.g., upsetting scenes at school, with mother, with father, etc.), I eventually try to recreate some of the experiences which the client had listed. I do not believe that with most clients there is any one key scene or event which must be discovered and re-experienced. I usually find a whole host of scenes which carry with them the type of content and affect which enables a client to figure out the basic dysfunctional patterns of his/her life.

At times during the emotive phase of therapy, in addition to the above techniques, I will also use Gestaltlike techniques (e.g., pounding on a chair to facilitate release of verbal anger), verbal confrontation (e.g., "You're lying to your father!"), directed role playing (e.g., "Tell your mother how you feel."), and other ancillary techniques. Such techniques, although not apparently as essential to therapy as focus on imagery, nevertheless are helpful in inducing the client to express intense and complex feelings which are difficult to define until they are expressed. Along with the feeling of release which often follows the expression of heretofore anxiety-arousing feelings, the client often perceives that he/she has discovered new self-conceptualizations. These new self-constructs, along with the subsequent adoption of appropriate roles, enable the client to effectively cope with stress.

It is actually during the *reconstructive* or second phase of an ERT session that a client focuses on the reconstruction or reconceptualization of his/her life. After a client's recall and expression of feelings, he/she is asked to open his/her eyes. Then the therapist's primary task is to facilitate the integration of the new data. With assistance, the client is usually able to bring a more complex system of constructs to bear in interpreting events which were previously of a global, vague, and hyperarousing nature. In so doing, the client is able to suspend those dysfunctional constructs which were previously employed in futile attempts to resolve problems. In my opinion, in order to successfully avoid repetitions of dysfunctional behavior patterns, one must retrace and then understand basic life patterns. If those basic patterns are understood, the rest of the client's life offers opportunities for him/her to continually clarify those patterns through frequent insights or subtle modifications of the therapy-induced reconstructions.

Before a therapy session concludes, the therapist provides support to the client by means of self-disclosure and reassurance. Such therapeutic interventions are aimed at comforting the client after a moment of often dramatic and painful discovery. No one who has done this therapy has any doubt that the client's feelings of pain and distress are clear and genuine. Nor is there any difficulty for the therapist in empathizing with such a client.

Before turning to a few more case illustrations, let me clearly state that, in my opinion, emotional catharsis without construct change, and construct change not resulting from an exploration of intense feelings, are both of little value in ERT. The sessions which produce both deep feelings as well as *profound* insight are the sessions which seem to really make a difference.

Brief Case Illustrations

In separate therapy with a young married couple, a poet and a musician on the verge of divorce, I attempted to introduce both clients gradually to what I assumed was the core feeling underlying their neurotic depression. Once the clients experienced and then understood the intense emotional pain of childhood aloneness, they experienced dramatic construct change of self, parents, and each other on almost all dimensions of a 30-item Semantic Differential. These construct changes coincided with almost total symptom reduction, as evidenced by change on a symptom checklist (Morrison & Cometa, in press). The musician reported that due to therapy he no longer experienced what I had suspected to be a number of psychogenic disorders (migraine headaches, lower-back pain, frequent sore throats, asthma, acne, hay fever, and grinding of teeth). None of these conditions reappeared between discharge from therapy and a follow-up 15 months after discharge. Both clients also experienced a number of personally satisfying changes in artistic expression which fly in the face of the myth that good art can be produced only by the "suffering artist."

Another case illustration may further clarify the construct changes which can result from ERT. A middle-aged married couple, seriously considering divorce, requested individual therapy to deal with their personal problems. In the course of ERT, both discovered that they had originally been attracted to one another because the wife needed a weak, passive husband on which to work out her conflicts with her weak passive father, and the husband needed a cold, rejecting woman like his mother in his futile attempts to escape from the aloneness of being rejected by his cold mother. After this discovery, which followed upon intense feelings of aloneness as their childhood — largely forgotten — was reconstructed, both clients' constructs of parents, each other, and themselves changed radically and their large number of pretherapy symptoms (13 for the wife, 16 for the husband) were in both cases reduced to zero. Again, follow-up indicated no symptom relapse.

Finally, one young client, describing himself as a homosexual even though he had never engaged in overt homosexual behavior, reported dramatic personality and symptom changes after discovering in one session his intense, but long repressed, longing to identify with his father. This longing, constantly negatively reinforced by his mother, was discovered when the client suddenly remembered watching his father eating, at work, a butter sandwich made by the client's mother. That visual imagery awakened in the client his long-repressed anger toward his mother, a woman who could not take a few minutes more to make a decent sandwich for his father. Along with the anger came the feelings of wanting to be like his father instead of his mother. Following this session, the client experienced a positive change in his relationship with his father and an emergence, for the first time, of heterosexual feelings.

ERT: A Consumer-Oriented Approach

ERT is based upon the assumption that the client's perspective on his/her problems is of utmost importance to the therapeutic process; and unless the psychotherapist learns to understand the client's cognitive processes, the probability of therapeutic success is greatly minimized.

In ERT, the therapist who is in touch with his/her own mental imagery, is able to understand the client's imagery and lead him/her to a therapeutic resolution of problems by means of that imagery. Thus, through the use of mental imagery, an ERT therapist learns to place emphasis and value on the client's cognitive experience and by so doing can reinforce client autonomy and independence from the therapist. In ERT, the client, with the guidance of the therapist, learns to resolve problems. ERT is not a treatment wherein the therapist "cures" the patient. Rather, it is an educational experience wherein the client learns to understand himelf/herself and to resolve his/her own problems. The client is able to do so after the therapist has taught him/her to effectively use mental imagery to tap new resources of information about the self and significant others.

Also, in ERT the right of the client to evaluate the effectiveness of therapy is emphasized (Morrison, 1978a; 1979; in press). One way of systematically achieving maximum client involvement in such evaluation is through client advisory boards (Morrison, 1976) which can oversee the delivery of therapeutic services and have the potential for radically changing those services. Further emphasis within ERT on a consumer-oriented approach leads to client involvement in contracting (e.g., confidentiality contracting, problem definition, problem resolution planning) and the follow-up research.

Succinctly, in ERT the therapist emphasizes the dignity and autonomy of the client, and strives to avoid using any procedures which would minimize the ability of the client to resolve as many of his/her own problems as is possible. To make a client dependent on a therapist through the "purchase of friendship" (Schofield, 1964) would be considered a sign of the failure of the ERT process.

Research Evidence of ERT Effectiveness

Statistical Data

Before presenting some empirical evidence of ERT effectiveness, I will present some statistical data which will illuminate certain aspects of ERT.

1. 41% of those clients who begin ERT complete at least 15 sessions.[1] Because of this relatively high completion percentage and the high average number (nine) of ERT sessions completed — the national average is seven (see Sacuzzo, 1977) — one can conclude that the *dropout rate* for ERT is *not excessively high* despite the intensity of this experience.
2. Only 23% of those who complete therapy need to have more than 15 sessions. Thus, ERT appears to be a *short-term therapy.*
3. The success rate (determined by some positive change on regularly administered self-report symptom checklists and measures of construct change) for those clients who complete at least *15 sessions* is 96%. Most clients finish therapy after only 15 sessions.
4. The success rate (determined by the same evaluative measures) for those clients who complete at least five *sessions* is 91%.
5. Among those clients who complete at least 15 sessions, 73% report a symptom reduction of at least 50%.

---

[1] It was arbitrarily decided that if ERT were to be truly a promising therapeutic modality, it should be able to produce a significant reduction in client complaints within a course of 15 sessions.

Since most reports of psychotherapy indicate that about 60-80% of clients who undergo various forms of psychotherapy experience some therapeutic change, the success rates just mentioned, all based on empirical, systematic data, suggest that ERT may be a promising new mode of psychotherapy. I should mention that when I begin developing ERT 7 years ago, I made the decision that unless ERT were effective with at least 80% of my clients and unless it produced a minimum of 50% symptom reduction for clients as a whole, I would discontinue ERT. Since my recent data indicate that ERT produces a 69% overall symptom reduction rate and appears to reduce at least some symptoms for 96% of those who complete at least 15 sessions (91% for those who complete five sessions), I feel that ERT is worth considering further. A collection of such statistics, limited as it is by comparison with empirical data (which I will discuss later), can at least reinforce my enthusiasm for ERT.

Empirical Data

Although ERT may sound like an interesting form of psychotherapy, a most important question must be raised. Is it effective in inducing substantial therapeutic change? A series of studies on ERT clients can provide some tentative answers.

In most of my studies on the effect of ERT on client problem resolution, I administered the *Psychotherapy Problem Checklist* (Morrison & Teta, 1978) to a group of clients before therapy and after every five sessions up to and including each client's last session, which in most cases was the 15th. This checklist consists of 21 items or symptoms which are highly indicative of excessive anxiety (e.g., frequent headaches, sleep problems, nail biting, etc.) and/or depression. It is very reliable (r=.81) and a client's scores on the PPC are highly and significantly correlated with scores on Spielberger's scale of anxiety.

This checklist was devised in such a way that the wording of the questions and the simplified response format discourage responses indicating anything but major symptom reduction. Thus, self-help groups tend to change in a positive direction on a number of self-report measures but *not* on the PPC (Morrison & Becker, 1978b).

In one study (Morrison & Cometa, 1979), analysis of the PPC responses of clients undergoing ERT indicated that this type of imagery therapy appeared to not only significantly[2] reduce symptoms of anxiety and depression from before to after therapy, but also after only five sessions.

In another study (Morrison & Teta, 1978), analysis of the data supplied by client responses on the PPC as well as the Semantic Differential revealed that a symptom reduction on the PPC was significantly correlated (-.84, p<.01) with a positive

---

[2] When the word "significantly" is used in this presentation, it means a probability level of less than .05.

change of self-constructs. The clients involved in the study had reported a significant reduction of symptoms and an increase of positive self-constructs after 15 sessions of therapy. There was also suggestive evidence, that as clients report reduced symptoms, presumably as a result of an increase of positive self-constructs, they also tend to report a change (sometimes positive, sometimes negative) in constructs of their parents.

In a recent unpublished study of the effectiveness of ERT, data analysis indicated that the symptom and construct changes induced after short-term imagery therapy were stable, as suggested by clients' responses on a three-month follow-up (Morrison & Becker, 1978a).

Further research on ERT is currently in progress; these studies include utilization of control groups, long-term follow-up, and different measures of therapeutic change. Although the research on ERT is still in its early stages, the evidence to date suggests that this type of imagery therapy is indeed one with proven effectiveness.

In closing, let me clarify that the clients studied in research were not specially selected. I do not turn away clients, and I offer all clients ERT. The average age of clients is 33 (range of 21 to 61). The clients include an equal number of males and females, and they have an average of 14 years of formal education (range of 8 to 21 years). The vast majority of clients tends to be of the lower and middle class, and their diagnoses range from psychoses to neuroses to character disorders.

Clients Most Suitable for ERT

After close inspection of empirical data, I have tentatively concluded that the most successful ERT client tends to be young rather than old, relatively well educated (at least some education beyond the high-school level), never hospitalized for psychiatric reasons, and to have the ability to form vivid images of past experiences. Although I have used ERT with clients who might be described as psychotic, I cannot claim that I am much more successful with them than are therapists who use other types of psychotherapy.

Advantages of an ERT Approach

Some of the advantages of using an ERT approach are the following:

1. It is a short-term psychotherapy and, therefore, costs the client less time and money.

2. Because it is often capable of producing rapid results, even in the first few sessions, it provides immediate hope to those clients who are seriously considering suicide.

3. Client dependency on the therapist is rare. Focus on a client's parents[3] seems to make relatively unnecessary the transference process so common in many therapies. Clients almost never call me in crises; it has been 5 years since I received an evening or weekend call from a client in crisis.

4. ERT is an interesting process, since no sesssion is like any other. Thus, an ERT therapist is seldom bored and seems to avoid the burned-out syndrome which many therapists experience.

In spite of such advantages, I would discourage therapists from doing this form of therapy until they have confidently sorted out their own imagery and dysfunctional life patterns. Otherwise, there would be dangers for both clients and therapists. To play around with these techniques without self-analysis and some training may increase in both therapist and client, at least in some circumstances, the risk of a psychotic episode.

Special Uses of ERT

In the past 7 years I have found some specialized uses of ERT. These mini-techniques can be used by therapists of different disciplines with certain clients for whom other techniques have failed to produce the intended effect. For example, I have found ERT techniques to be very useful, in as few as one or two sessions, in inducing successful grieving for a loved one who has died (see Morrison, 1978b, for details). The imagery recreation of the death, wake, funeral, and burial events can clarify feelings about the deceased, feelings which can cause depression and other dysfunctional states.

A technique called "image comparison analysis" can be helpful when a therapist is trying to understand a client's problematic relationship with a spouse or significant other. As described elsewhere[4], often "repressed" feelings about a parent of the opposite sex can interfere with feelings about a spouse until image comparison analysis reveals the similarity on key traits between the two persons. ERT can also help illuminate the reasons behind certain artistic styles and homosexual fantasies.

Conclusions

In summary, I believe there is evidence that ERT may for some therapists and some clients be a promising therapeutic modality. Although I feel that in many ways I have just begun to clarify the assumptions I tentatively maintain, and to im-

---

[3] Notice the similarity here between ERT and Eidetic Psychotherapy (Ahsen, 1968, 1972).

[4] Write to the author for copies of the various as yet unpublished studies of ERT.

prove the techniques I use, I know that the comments of other therapists and the feedback I receive from clients will help me to continually modify, and hopefully improve, those assumptions and techniques. I would like to end by clearly stating that, despite my enthusiasm for my work, I do *not* believe that ERT is a therapeutic panacea, and my limited experience in training others to do ERT, as promising as it seems, does not yet allow me to know with any certainty that ERT is not inextricably wound up with my own personality and needs. All I can say is that I have finally found the type of therapy which is exciting and reasonably effective for *me*. It is marvelous to have found, after all my searching, the type of therapy which has consistently over the years made almost every session with a client on intriguing and fascinating learning experience.

REFERENCES

Ahsen, A. *Basic concepts in eidetic psychotherapy.* New York: Brandon House, 1968.

Ahsen, A. *Eidetic parents test and analysis.* New York: Brandon House, 1972.

Bannister, D. & Fransella, F. *Inquiring man: The theory of personal constructs.* Baltimore: Penguin Books, 1971.

Bartlett, F. C. *Remembering.* Cambridge, England: Cambridge University Press, 1932.

Dember, W. N. The new look in motivation. *American Scientist,* 1965, *53,* 409-427.

Fiske, D. & Maddi, S. *Functions of varied experience.* Homewood, Illinois: Dorsey Press, 1961.

Hebb, D. O. Drives and the C.N.S. *Psychological Review,* 1955, *62,* 243-254.

Kelly, G. *The psychology of personal constructs* (2 vols.). New York: Norton Co., 1955.

Malmo, R. B. Activation: A neuropsychological dimension. *Psychological Review,* 1959, *66,* 367-368.

Mancuso, J. (Ed.) *Readings for a cognitive theory of personality.* New York: Holt, Rinehart & Winston, 1970.

Morrison, J. K. Developmental study of person perception of young children. *Proceedings, 81st Annual Convention, American Psychological Association,* 1973.

Morrison, J. K. An argument for mental patient advisory boards. *Professional Psychology,* 1976, *7,* 127-131.

Morrison, J. K. The family heritage: Dysfunctional constructs and roles. *International Journal of Family Counseling,* 1977, *5,* 54-58.

Morrison, J. K. The client as consumer and evaluator of community mental health services. *American Journal of Community Psychology,* 1978, *6,* 147-155. (a)

Morrison, J. K. Successful grieving: Changing personal constructs through mental imagery. *Journal of Mental Imagery,* 1978, *2,* 63-68. (b)

Morrison, J. K. (Ed.) *A consumer approach to community psychology.* Chicago: Nelson-Hall, 1979.

Morrison, J. K. A consumer oriented approach to psychotherapy. *Psychotherapy: Theory, Research and Practice,* in press.

Morrison, J. K., & Becker, R. E. *Psychotherapeutic effectiveness of imagery in changing personal constructs: A follow-up study.* Manuscript in preparation, 1978. (a)

Morrison, J. K., & Becker, R. E. *A comparison of the effectiveness of imagery psychotherapy vs. self-help instruction.* Manuscript in preparation, 1978. (b)

Morrison, J. K. & Cometa, M. S. Emotive-reconstructive psychotherapy: A short-term cognitive approach. *American Journal of Psychotherapy,* 1977, *31,* 294-301.

Morrison, J. K. & Cometa, M. S. Emotive-reconstructive therapy and client problem resolution: Periodic accountability to the consumer. In J. K. Morrison (Ed.), *A consumer approach to community psychology.* Chicago: Nelson-Hall, 1979.

Morrison, J. K. & Teta, D. C. Simplified use of the Semantic Differential to measure psychotherapy outcome. *Journal of Clinical Psychology,* 1978, *34,* 751-753.

Neisser, U. *Cognitive psychology.* New York: Appleton-Century, 1967.

Piaget, J. *Genetic epistemology.* New York: Norton, 1970. (a)

Piaget, J. *Structuralism.* New York: Harper, 1970. (b)

Piaget, J. *Judgment and reasoning in the child.* Totowa, N.J.: Littlefield, Adams & Co., 1972.

Sacuzzo, D. P. The practice of psychotherapy in America: Issues and trends. *Professional Psychology,* 1977, *8,* 297-306.

Sarbin, T. R., Taft, R. & Bailey, D. E. *Clinical inference and cognitive theory.* New York: Holt, Rinehart & Winston, 1960.

Schachter, S. & Singer, J. E. Cognitive, social and psychological determinants of emotional state. *Psychological Review,* 1962, *69,* 379-399.

Schofield, W. *Psychotherapy: The purchase of friendship.* Englewood Cliffs, N.J.: Prentice-Hall, 1964.

Singer, J. E. *Imagery and daydream methods in psychotherapy and behavior.* New York: Academic Press, 1974.

10

Death Imagery: Therapeutic Uses

ANEES A. SHEIKH
GEORGE E. TWENTE
DWIGHT TURNER

Currently, a significant change in orientation is taking place in the domain of psychotherapy. Whereas the pioneers of the field sought answers in the dynamics of abnormal functioning, the recent trend is to move into the deeper realms of consciousness and strive for a clear understanding of the ultimate human potential for growth and for the achievement of a unified personality (Ahsen, 1968, 1977; Assagioli, 1973; Ichazo, 1972; Perls, 1973; Sheikh & Panagiotou, 1975; Watts, 1968, 1972).

The death imagery process, we feel, is a natural outgrowth of this new approach to human fulfillment. Our clinical work in this area has revealed it to be a dramatic way of awakening to the natural flow of life. One may say that the death imagery work, in a way, is both old and new. It is old in the sense that numerous Hindu, Buddhist, Christian, and Muslim mystics have been practicing it, in various ways, for centuries. It is new in the sense that it achieves desired results in a fashion that is inherently nonmystical. Essentially, all a person has to do is to relax, confront his/her death, let go to the natural flow, and be willing to accept responsibility for whatever arises. Ahsen (1979) in his epic poem, *Manhunt in the Desert*, memorably describes the significance of this experience:

Anees A. Sheikh, Department of Psychology, Marquette University, Milwaukee, WI 53233; **George E. Twente** and **Dwight Turner,** The Retreat Hospital, 2205 Beltline Road, S.W., Decatur, Alabama 35603. The authors express sincere appreciation to Pattie Frazier for her assistance in their work.

And then you were
To see the pitch black of true Nothingness.
When you truly died,
You saw this black,
Where all hopes are hidden,
Where all things are fortified.

Fear not this black place,
There is strength and uprightness here.
You are getting into the roots of things,
But the roots are really not
The unknown or nothingness;
It is your own Nature.
You truly are here
In this unblemished dark color.
Here things lost are recovered,
And they are revealed again.

● ● ●

The long night of rest
Is lit by brilliant stars of guidance.
As you lie restful
You are aware of these stars
Which surround you.
These are the stars of your destiny;
These stars watch over your dust.
The light of these stars
Reaches through disintegration and annihilation,
And touches your body,
Which is in deep sleep.
Your future is taught to you
During your sleep,
By these lights of Nothingness.

When you have rested
You wake up to your day,
And carry the light of these stars,
Like a fluttering flag,
To the battlefield of the day;
And war at midday
In the heat of the sun (pp. 110-111).

Confronting Death

Since ancient times, death has been the "truly inspiring genius" of philosophy, literature, art, and music. Socrates, Plato, Montaigne, Schopenhauer, and many others considered philosophy in several ways analogous to the study of the problem of death. Thomas Mann remarked, "Without death there would scarcely have been poets on earth." "No thought exists in me which death has not carved with his chisel," said Michelangelo. The earliest songs were funeral dirges; and death is the leading motif of the inspiring music of Bach, Gluck, Mozart, Beethoven, Schubert, Liszt, Verdi, Mahler, Moussorgsky, and many modern composers (Kübler-Ross, 1975).

However, the subject of death is evaded by the youth-worshipping American and European societies. Western culture has attempted to cope with death by pretending that it is not a basic condition of life, by regarding it as just another disease to be mastered, or by simply disguising it (Aguilar & Wood, 1976; Braga & Braga, 1975). When a patient dies in a hospital, the body is hurriedly whisked away; an unbelievable disappearing act does away with the evidence before it has a chance to upset anyone. The problem of death generally reaches the core of one's being only when one is forced to face one's own imminent death or the imminent death of a loved one. It is only then that one really feels the pangs of life-hunger (Kübler-Ross, 1975).

People in several other cultures, on the other hand, handle the fear and uncertainty of death quite differently. Paz (1961, p. 52) points out that the Mexican, for instance, does not attempt to forget that death awaits:

For the resident of New York, Paris or London, death is a word that is never spoken because it burns the lips. In contrast, the Mexican frequents death, makes fun of it, caresses it, sleeps with it, fetes it; it is one of his favorite games and his deepest love . . . . Our songs, verses, fiestas and popular sayings demonstrate unequivocally that death does not frighten us because "life has cured us of fears."

There is generally agreement among Hinduism, Buddhism, Christianity, Islam, and perhaps several other religions that a meaningful and purposeful life is possible only through an unflinching acceptance of death as an integral part of life. Only if one confronts death steadfastly — seeking neither to escape it nor meet it prematurely — will one learn to recognize that it is not the enemy but a constant companion and even a friend. The ultimate goal is not only to accept death as the final act in life, but also to welcome it as a persistent ingredient in the entire process of life. With the attainment of this goal, one begins to transcend both life and death and enters into unity with the Changeless Absolute (Long, 1975).

Confronting death brings one to the threshold of life. By recognizing the finiteness of one's existence, one is able to muster the strength to cast off those extrinsic roles and to devote every day to growing as fully as possible. On the other hand, the denial of death must be held at least partially responsible for the empty lives: when one lives as if one's life is everlasting, it becomes too easy to postpone the important things. One lives in anticipation of tomorrow or in reminiscence of yesterday, and meanwhile each day is lost (Kübler-Ross, 1975; Meyer, 1975).

Alan Watts pointed out that the ones who are incessantly searching for health, fulfillment, and beauty, fail to realize that they already exist on a fascinating globe floating ceaselessly in the heavens. Confronting the inevitability of death can lead to the discovery that the meaning of life is close at hand. It can make one realize the value of time and lead to a genuine appreciation for the beauty and sanctity of life (Butler, 1963; Cumming & Henry, 1961; Koestenbanm, 1976). Dostoevski writes in *The Idiot:*

This man had once been led out with the others to scaffold and a sentence of death was read over him . . . . Twenty minutes later a reprieve was read to them, and they were condemned to another punishment instead. Yet the interval between those two sentences, twenty minutes or at least a quarter of an hour, he passed in the fullest conviction that he would die in a few minutes . . . . The priest went to each in turn with a cross. He had only five minutes more to live. He told me that those five minutes seemed to him an infinite time, a vast wealth . . "What if I were not to die? What if I could go back to life - what eternity! And it would all be mine! I would turn every minute into an age; I would lose nothing, I would count every minute as it passed, I would not waste one!" (Quoted in Barrett, 1962, p. 140).

Numerous philosophers, psychologists, and literary figures have maintained that facing death gives meaning, substance, and worth to life; it opens one up to the experience of pleasure, joy, and intimacy; it opens one's eyes to the personal, aesthetic, and eternal dimensions of life. Even Albert Camus, who was convinced of the absurdity of life, considered the inevitability of death as one of the most impressive features of existence. Max Frisch, in his diary-novel *Homo Faber* (1957), makes the same significant point. The protagonist, Faber, an engineer, has tried to rid his life of everything that cannot be expressed in mathematical terms and to adhere to the principle, "No mysticism; mathematics is enough." Although he is plagued by uncertainty concerning the validity of his outlook, he stubbornly tries to cling to his fiction. His former fiancée, Hanna, counters his view with her experience of life. She feels that as a pure scientist, one who admits no approach other than that of science and mathematics, he has tried to ignore the opposition within the world, and he has made the fundamental error of attempting to live without thinking of death. She says to Faber, "You treat life not as a form, but as simple addition; it has no relation to time because it has no relation to death." Hanna's formula for life is "Life is form in time." She measures life by her suffering and by its distance from death. She knows too that aging means that each moment is irretrievable and thus valuable. Initially, Faber fails to grasp Hanna's view. He regards each year of his life merely as the sum of units of time that can be measured mechanically. He does not acknowledge his error until he is seriously ill and face to face with death. At this point, he becomes aware of the beauty of the world and begins to value life. He admits that he is not enough for himself, and eagerly opens himself up to another person. He casts off his pride and the belief that only what is measurable and mathematically expressible is valid. He yearns to be eternal (Bloching, 1974).

Death Imagery

Numerous writers agree that to be able to really *live* meaningfully, we must first learn to *die*. The final chance to grow comes at death's doorstep; however, there is no need to wait until then. After comprehending the growth-producing properties of dying, one can call upon their beneficial effect at any stage (Greinacher & Müller, 1974; Koestenbaum, 1976; Kübler-Ross, 1975). The experience of dying in imagination has turned out to be a highly therapeutic avenue in our clinical work. This is not surprising, since experience in imagery is probably the best substitute for experience or perception of an actual situation (Perky, 1910; Segal, 1971; Sheikh, 1977; Sheikh & Panagiotou, 1975).

Death imagery not only provides an opportunity for the necessary confrontation with death, but it leads to numerous other salutary effects as well. For example, it has been noted that through the use of death imagery, a person is brought into direct contact with his/her interior process in a profoundly experiential manner. Inner conflicts are effectively summoned and resolved, disowned parts are reintegrated, and thus an experience of increased self-awareness and personal unity is fostered. A more detailed account of the beneficial effects of death imagery will be presented in a later section of this paper.

It should be noted that the death imagery technique was originated by the first two authors independently; neither had any knowledge of the other's work. They accidently met and were amazed to notice the similarities in their approaches. The only common denominator that they had was their background in eidetic psychotherapy (Ahsen, 1972, 1974, 1977; Sheikh, 1976, 1978a; Twente, Turner, & Haney, 1978). One may say that the death imagery approach is a natural outgrowth of eidetic therapy (Dolan & Sheikh, 1977). The technique evolved spontaneously in the clinical setting (Sheikh, Twente, Turner, & Frazier, 1978).

In one case, an individual going through a crisis in life and feeling "so tense and miserable that he felt like dying" was encouraged to imagine, while lying in bed, that he was dead. After a brief period of increased anxiety brought on by the thought of dying, he spontaneously experienced an extreme pull of gravity, slower rate of breathing, loosening of muscles all over the body, a sensation that he was shedding off his body, and consequently a deep feeling of relaxation. Concomitant with this relaxed state, several cognitive-affective changes occurred that clarified a number of issues.

In the other case, the technique emerged while working with a 30-year-old female who had a simple mastectomy, followed by an abortion 3 months later. She experienced periods of profound grief and was subsequently involved in intensive eidetic psychotherapy. The therapist, with an intensive background in grief work, suggested that she visualize each person to whom she had a strong attachment and to take leave of them, as if she had only a few moments to live. After bidding farewell to all, she spontaneously saw her death and funeral, and experienced, in a sense, entrance into a "heavenlike world" and meeting Christ. Her fears of a breakdown of emotional dependencies were resolved spontaneously, and she felt a deep sense of peace and self-understanding.

We have been using death imagery in two major ways: as a relaxation technique and as a technique for short- or long-term psychotherapy. Some form of "spiritual" awakening is involved in both cases. A discussion of these two procedures follows. The tremendous potential of death imagery for diagnosis, self-analysis, and group therapy is also being noted and will be discussed in detail elsewhere (Twente, Sheikh, & Turner, 1979).

Relaxation through Death Imagery

In hypnosis, the subject is generally asked to experience *heaviness* and *limpness* of the body and to *let go.* Judged by these criteria, death must be the ultimate in relaxation. We have discovered that dying, in imagination at least, often turns out to be a deeply relaxing experience. Reportedly, primitive men often faked death while faced with the danger of being killed by wild animals (Musel, 1975). It seems probable that they used this technique of faking death not only to deceive the animals and thus survive, but also as an effective way of handling fear and anxiety.

In our technique, the subject is asked to lie down and is given the following instructions:

"Imagine that you are dead. You have lost all your ability to counter the force of gravity and are completely immobilized and inactive. All your muscles, even all your body cells are pulled down by gravity. You no longer have to struggle, be tense, and spend energy to stay alive. You no longer have to direct your thinking or censor your thoughts. The thoughts come and go as they like. As your 'dead' body is pulled more and more by the force of gravity, you have a feeling that you are shedding off your body. Your thoughts scatter and all the verbal chatter and commotion vanishes into thin air. As you shed your body, you become a weightless, bodiless, pure consciousness. There is stillness and quiet and a benign indifference of nature."

Initially, the subject experiences an increased amount of anxiety, especially if he/she is among those who find even the mention of death threatening. Generally, however, the initial arousal of anxiety is a temporary stage and gives way to a feeling of deep relaxation and a unique sense of being at peace with the universe. At times, the relaxed state produced by death imagery verges on the religious. A few of the subjects had an experience that could best be described in Koestenbaum's words:

I felt suddenly and inexplicably that the burden and weight of living had been lifted. I felt supported. The burden of living was no longer mine alone . . . I sensed a current stronger than me and one in which I *participated,* a current within me of which I am only a part and which supports me as the sea supports a ship . . . . At that brief moment it became intuitively clear to me that the religious position that there is a God, that I can participate in His life, and that I am not really different from God but a part of Him, made sense. I felt that as my body was supported by nature, so my individual awareness was supported by a cosmic consciousness . . . . Did I at that moment lose my freedom? No, but I did lose the sense that I was a capillary cut off from the universal bloodstream. I had a sense of continuity with all of Being, rather than the sense of separateness and alienation (1976, pp. 117-118).

A subject who is familiar with death work, often spontaneously enters the realm of "void." It is a direct experience of the ground of being. The last vestiges of all thought forms are effaced. All dichotomies pass away into nothingness. All that remains is tranquil clarity. Perhaps the old Zen song portrays the state most clearly:

> Old Pang requires nothing in the world;
> All is empty with him, even a seat he has not,
> For absolute Emptiness reigns in his household;
> How empty indeed it is with no treasures!
> When the sun is risen, he walks through Emptiness,
> When the sun sets, he sleeps in Emptiness;
> Sitting in Emptiness he sings his empty songs
> And his empty words reverberate through Emptiness.

The story of a 34-year-old man is particularly significant, because he related an actual experience with death at age 14, during a drowning incident:

After I had struggled as much as possible to stay alive, I felt a certain peace come over me. There was no longer a need to struggle. The entire scope of my awareness turned red, followed by a flowing series of visual images depicting my life experience to that point. Next, there was a point of awareness or feeling of 'I am' in an infinite void. Nothing existed — time or space had no meaning. There were no forms, no colors. My experience was that of extreme bliss and peace. After an undetermined time, I was revived by means of artificial respiration. Since that time, my life has taken on a new direction, a sense of increased spiritual awareness. In the course of my death work, I would immediately merge into that void state. I was completely at peace with no pressure to be anything or do anything . . . . My total awareness became an infinite brilliance and I felt a serene oneness with the Universe.

Psychotherapy through Death Imagery

One can use the foregoing procedure to attain mere relaxation and the accompanying unity experience. Or, relaxation may be considered as only the first step in therapy. During this state, forgotten thoughts and images, particularly of unresolved issues pertaining to parents, often emerge spontaneously. They provide valuable material for meaningfull psychotherapy, especially eidetic therapy.

We have developed certain death imagery methods specifically for continuing therapy. The procedure for the first session is relatively standard. After reclining, the clients are led through an ordinary brief relaxation exercise accompanied by deep breathing. Next, they are asked to visualize, one at a time, all those individuals, alive or dead, with whom they have or had a deep positive or negative emotional relationship. The clients are asked to visualize each person, to concentrate on the person's total body, and to look deep into his/her eyes. They are directed to let go to whatever feelings arise and abreact any unresolved emotional content. The clients are then encouraged to silently take their leave of all the individuals one by one. They are expected to keep the psychotherapist posted about their progress. Subsequently, the clients are instructed to visualize themselves as infants, as children, as adolescents, and as they are now. They are asked to say goodbye to all these aspects of their development and are encouraged to complete any unfinished tasks that arise in the content of associated memories.

After the farewell process has been completed, the clients are directed to experience their death and a departure from their body. They are requested to follow the flow of their experience, paying attention to their emotional and somatic responses as well as to visual details. During the first session, the clients are asked merely to be aware of their experience, and the fantasy process proceeds uninterruptedly. At the conclusion of the first session, the clients are instructed to write up their death experience, including details of imagery, somatic, and emotive responses. We have observed that the time spent thinking and writing about the death experience often accelerates progress through the initial stages.

Beginning with the second session, the clients' attention is directed to the processing of each significant image independently. They are provided with the following basic guidelines:

(1) Become anything in the image that seems separated. Pay attention to the somatic and emotional responses and be aware of any resistance to letting go to your natural process.
(2) While playing the part of each image, note of what the experience reminds you. Report any associated memories that emerge.
(3) Relate the empathy experience in the image to your own life. If resistance appears, notice any accompanying tension or feelings.

The therapist must remember that he/she is only a guide or a facilitator who helps the clients in the process of self-awareness, without interfering with the natural flow of their experience. The experience must proceed at its own pace. Ultimately, the clients must see themselves as the agents of change.

Illustrative Cases

Instead of wandering too far into the realm of theory and didactics, let us turn directly to the practical uses of the death imagery process in the clarification of consciousness. Numerous clients have successfully undergone death imagery work. Two representative cases follow.

The Case of Christina

Christina had undergone an abortion about 4 days before she saw the therapist and was experiencing much more difficulty in adjusting to the moral issues than she had anticipated. Considering the seriousness of the issue, she thought the decision had been made too hastily. But she had been 12 weeks pregnant, and there had been no time to lose. She mentioned that the case in favor of the abortion was quite weighty: she was single, twice divorced, and while she loved the father of the baby very much, their relationship was at a low point, and they were not ready to marry. Even though she was basically opposed to abortion, practicality outweighed her moral judgment.

Christina reported that she could deal with the experience on a rational level fairly well, but suddenly, the night before she saw the therapist, she found herself somewhat hysterical, full of anger and rage. She felt that the world was exploding around her. She realized that she had not been dealing with death as well as she had thought and decided to seek help. She describes her experience with death imagery thus:

"When asked if I wanted to experience dying, I was at first taken aback. I was tense and on the verge of tears and exhausted from lack of sleep. At that point I couldn't imagine anything that I wanted to do less. Only my trust (in the therapist) made me willing to try. He told me briefly that he wanted me to relax by deep breathing; then I was to say goodbye to those who mattered to me and to begin to die. I took off my shoes, stretched out on the couch, and skeptically began.

"Relaxation did not come easily. After many breaths and muscle twitches, I began to ease out of my tension. I then began the second part of the exercise. I had anticipated having a difficult time saying goodbye to the people that I love, but I found instead that it was surprisingly painless. Visualizing the whole person, I looked straight into their eyes, told them that I loved them, that I had to die now. Only with my daughter, my parents, and my brother did I have much trouble, and that was because I wanted them to know how much they had meant to me. When the goodbyes were complete, I was ready to go on.

"The therapist instructed me to now experience my death. A surge of initial fear was dispelled by a deep breath, and I began to let go. My first sensation was an intense uterine cramp which moved downward to my legs, then dispersed and diminished. Coldness chilled my feet and began moving upward. At the middle of my body, this feeling began to become increasingly warmer, and when it reached my head, it became a ball of fire. My body became lighter and lighter, until I began to float up and away from my body. Suddenly with one deep breath, I was adrift in a quiet world of blue-white light. At first, my body would tug at me and try to bring me back, but I was not willing to come. I knew intuitively that there was a separate peace out of the boundaries that my body tightly guarded.

"As I floated, I first had the shape of a ball, warm and alive. But as I soared through the windless space, I began to expand creating new shapes, existing in new space. Suddenly I separated into a billion particles, mixing with the light and energy, and experienced an exhilaration at being able to do so.

"I crossed vast expanses of space, infused with a feeling of being part of the light. Time became meaningless . . . I moved farther and farther away from earthly existence. The sound of the world around me — the slamming of doors, footsteps, the sound of a voice — all became muted and distant. Peace and serenity flooded my being.

"Soon physical reality tugged me back. My contact lenses, well moistened all day with tears, had suddenly become dry, and I needed to blink. Reluctantly, I opened my eyes.

"When the therapist said smilingly, 'Now what was your problem?' I had no answer. The mounting tension had dissipated, and I no longer felt troubled. I had a few questions about death, and the death of the baby I had carried, but the answer was the same. Death is just another door through which we pass on our journey through eternity, and, while our waking rationality rails against it, our souls accept it."

Christina described the aftereffects of the experience in the following words:

"All senses became acute. The lovely spring breeze caressed me gently. Colors were bright and clear. Sounds blended into each other. The only other time I have experienced this kind of high was once on a mountaintop in Switzerland, on a beautiful June day. Inside I was renewed, freshly arrived into the world and totally at peace, not only with the decision I had made but with my life in general. Each person I met seemed special.

"I spent the evening with my daughter, touching and sharing. When I went to bed, I slept easily and peacefully and awakened to a beautiful spring morning outside and inside myself."

The Case of Allen

Allen, a 20-year-old, attractive, bright, and outgoing young man was first seen as an outpatient. His main complaint centered around a conflict over his sexual identity. He feared that he might be a homosexual. His parents were divorced while he was still a small child, and he was left in the care of his mother. The mother, herself in emotional distress, was unable to relate well to Allen. She married, several years later, a man who, though thoughtfully attentive and a good provider, was unable, in Allen's eyes, to take the place of his father. Shortly after graduating from high school, Allen left home to attend college. He was forced to drop out of college due to increasing inner conflict and unexplainable physical symptoms. Soon after his return from college, he moved out of the house to live with the maternal grandfather who was in need of some assistance in his daily activities. Allen took a part-time job in a fast-food outlet and hoped to return to school "as soon as he got his head together."

During the first therapeutic session as an outpatient, Allen was given the abbreviated Eidetics Parents Test (Ahsen, 1972). His responses were lengthy and at times bordered on the bizarre. In the second session, while processing the primary response to the first item (Parents in House), Allen became irrational, violent, and openly hostile. The imagery responses were clearly indicative of homosexual rage, which culminated in the complete, ritualistic mutilation of the stepfather. Beneath Allen's veneer of sanity, there appeared to be evidence of frank psychosis. Allen was advised of the possible severity of his condition, educated in the symptomatology of oncoming psychotic break, and placed on a regime of mega vitamins in an attempt to avert an acute breakdown.

Three days later, Allen was admitted to the hospital, after increased anxiety, marked auditory hallucinations, and an overt suicidal gesture. Because the therapist was forced to be out of town for several weeks, Allen was discharged 4 days later on a low dose of Navane and scheduled for follow-up therapy with the covering physician. Allen's condition, though it had stabilized somewhat during his brief hospitalization, rapidly degenerated after his discharge. He was readmitted to the hospital, where he received individual counseling, group psychotherapy, relaxation therapy, and a continuation of the eidetic analysis work. Upon discharge, Allen was functioning well on a low maintenance dose of Navane and agreed to continued work in outpatient psychotherapy.

Two weeks after discharge, Allen continued his outpatient work with his original therapist. His condition was stable, and he was easily able to process the content of his imagery work. He talked frequently during these sessions about his conflict in regard to religious matters. He spoke of a lack of continuity in his thoughts and actions on this topic and expressed a feeling of inner despair: "I sometimes feel its OK to drink a beer or two, or sleep with a woman. But then I feel I'll die in hell if I carry through with these thoughts." His imagery too reflected a pattern of inner conflict, self-judgment, and debasement. This pattern was accompanied by a rejection of any thoughts, feelings, or impulses that were not "biblically correct." Based on our past experience with similar types of conflict, we felt that intervention with death imagery was indicated.

The day of his initial death imagery session, Allen was calm and alert. The therapist talked casually with him for a few minutes, answering any general questions concerning the approach to be used. Then Allen was asked to lie down and led through deep breathing and relaxation exercises. After a sufficient degree of relaxation had been established, he was asked to spend a few minutes imagining that he was faced with death, to incorporate into his being the fact that he was going to die and that he had no control over this reality.

Next, Allen was asked to think of all the people with whom he had an emotional bond, either positive or negative. He was encouraged to interact with the persons to finish up any unresolved feelings or situations from the past, to make his peace with them, and to take leave of them. He was instructed to visualize them one at a time and concentrate on them for a moment, paying attention to his emotional and somatic response. He was to look at the person's feet, then very slowly direct his gaze upward until he reached the person's face, where he was to look deeply into his/her eyes. He was directed to concentrate on the eyes, allowing his feelings to intensify.

Allen spent approximately 20 minutes saying goodbye. In general, he experienced only minor difficulty, but he did become overtly apprehensive when dealing with his mother. He related that he was feeling some ambivalence toward her and, at this point, felt guilty about still being angry with her. He revealed that he was unsure of their present relationship and cited several incidents of conflict that had occurred during the past few weeks. Allen made several attempts to say goodbye to his mother but was unsuccessful. His anger and frustration increased, and he finally asked the therapist for assistance in making peace with her. The following dialogue ensued:

T — See your mother in front of you.

A — Yes.

T — Can you see her now? What is she doing?

A — She is standing there and crying a lot. She won't look at me directly. She stands at my side.

T — How do you feel when you see this?

A — I am upset by it, but I am not sure what is happening to me.

T — Just keep looking at her, concentrate on her in the picture. Just let whatever happens inside, happen. Let go to it.
(Long Silence)

A — I feel some tension in my throat and jaws. I am beginning to get a headache.

T — Just let go to it. Let these physical responses build up. Just be open, see what comes to you.

A — God, my head hurts.

T — Let go to it. Follow it. See what happens next.

A — (Tearfully) I feel guilty. She always makes me feel guilty.
(Pause)

T — What's happening now? Are you still experiencing the guilt feelings?

A — Yes, they are getting worse now.

T — Can you elaborate?

A — My mother has had emotional problems as long as I can remember. She usually cries a lot, when she has these fits. And let me tell you, her fits are awful. She screams and cries; I just freak out when she does that.

T — Look at your mother in the image. What is she doing now?

A — She is having one of these fits.

T — How do you feel as you see this?

A — I think I am angry, but I feel confused.

T — Get into it. Experience the confusion. See what it means to you.

.,   (Pause)

A — It's guilt. I feel guilty, and I pity her.

T — Can you talk about that?

A — Yes, I hate to see her experience so much mental pain. She has been through so much.

T — Look at your mother in the picture. Watch what she is doing.

A — I want to tell her, I understand. She needs to know I am sorry.

T — Go ahead.

A — (To mother) Mom, I am sorry if I have caused you all this turmoil and difficulty. You know I have been upset myself.

T — What happens inside when you do that? Do you get relief?

A — No, my throat and jaws are beginning to hurt.

T — Let go to the feeling; let it get so bad you can hardly bear it. Try something else. Experiment with her a little. See what works for you.

A — Damn! You know, she always blames me for these fits. She always has. Hell, it's not my fault. I get tired of it, you know?

T — Can you tell her that?

At this point Allen abreacted pent-up frustration and resentment toward his mother. Subsequently, he felt a sense of deep relaxation and peace with her. In his image, she turned to face him, and though still sobbing, they embraced.

T — How does that feel now?

A — It feels wonderful. We used to do this when I was young.

T — Stay with it; enjoy it until you are completely satisfied.

Allen remained with the image of his mother for about 5 minutes; then he said that he was ready to tell her goodbye. Shortly thereafter, however, feelings of conflict began to re-emerge.

A — You know what just occured to me? It was not my mother who put that guilt trip on me. I laid it on myself.

T — You sure did. How does that awareness strike you?

A — I have mixed feelings. I am pleased to know that I have found the source of the guilt. That part feels really good. But I don't know why I need to feel guilty. Why would I need to do that to myself?

T — You tell me.

A — I really don't know, maybe because of my pattern of judging myself. I am comfortable with that for now, can we go on?

T — Sure, let's go on.

Then Allen was directed to relax by performing several minutes of deep breathing. He was asked to visualize himself as an infant, a young boy, an adolescent, and as the young man he was now. He was encouraged to concentrate on each image and be aware of whatever feelings arose. He was then directed to say goodbye to each of these stages of his development and to bring to completion any unresolved feelings and associated memories. He chose to do this silently. He experienced no difficulty in making peace with his past.

Death Imagery

During the ensuing phase, Allen was asked to relax and let go to his own natural feelings and experience his death. He was reminded to remain aware of his feelings, thoughts, body responses, and visual details and to relate his experience verbally. The therapist assured Allen that he would be present during the experience but would remain in the background for the most part unless intense confusion, blocking, or resistance occurred.

Allen lay quietly for 5 to 6 minutes. During this time, the therapist observed marked tension on the forehead and some involuntary shaking in the lower right leg. Allen described his death experience in these words:

"After completely letting go, my first image consisted of me soaring above a city. Simultaneously, I was aware of the actions of everybody to whom I said goodbye. During this period, I felt free and considerably powerful.

"Next my self - not my physical body - was rushing through a tunnel of unfocused vision. I could see no end and only enjoyed feelings arising from this image - feelings of power again, physical elation because of the fast pace of the surroundings.

"Suddenly the self was merely floating against an intense blue background; a mountain appeared underneath the self. Now my feelings were ones of curiosity and helplessness.

"Thunder and lightning began slashing about the self, and the mountain split down the middle. The storm became more turbulent as an eye appeared where the mountain split. The self hovered, then gently floated towards the eye, which now was radiate. The self stopped directly in front of the eye, and the power of the eye absorbed all of my self. I felt very helpless and awed by the eye.

"Next, I appeared as a white dove - I felt pure and free. A tree grew out of the top of the mountain - it was brilliant white. I, in the form of the dove, started flying upward; the tree followed in growth. I exploded - my fragments penetrated everything. I was everywhere.

"The ensuing feelings are remotely describable. I could feel the gravitational pull on earth, moon, sun, stars, etc. It seemed, my heartbeat regulated the seasons; in short, I was time, or, rather, I did not fear time anymore because all stemmed from me."

Allen emerged from his death experience with a feeling of inner calm and a sense of unity with others. The therapist and Allen then briefly discussed the essentials of the death experience and also the path of future death work.

During the next two sessions, the goal was to bring the death imagery into clear focus in order to personalize or "reown" it. Allen was directed to repeat the farewell scenes of the initial session. He was again asked to relax, let go, and experience his death. As the imagery began to appear, Allen was asked to study each image individually. He was told to concentrate on the image, to be aware of his emotional and somatic responses, and then to "become" the image itself. An exerpt from the conversation follows:

A — The dove has appeared first.

T — Look at the bird. Can you describe it?

A — Yes. It's a white dove. It is floating and soaring against a pale sky.

T — Concentrate on the dove. How do you feel?

A — I feel good - as if I am weightless.

T — Now I want you to play that part. Can you become the dove?

A — I am the dove. I am weightless and agile. I feel free and alive.

T — Just spend a few minutes experiencing yourself as the dove. Note your experience as the dove - your existence as the dove.
(Pause)

T — How does your experience as the dove remind you of yourself? Are there any patterns in your life that are similar to your experience as the dove?

A — As the dove, I am myself as a free spirit. I feel this way when I am creative, when I am painting or involved with music.

T — How do you feel as you say this?

A — It feels good now. I am peaceful and full of energy.

T — Let that feeling be with you for awhile. Stay with it. Let it grow and follow it wherever it takes you.
(Pause)

A — Things are dark now. I am in the tunnel. Things are moving too fast. I am mildly frustrated by this. I can't make out the images and colors as they pass by.

T — Focus on the tunnel and your movement. Stay with your feelings and let them intensify.

A — I am getting more upset now. I need to slow things down.

T — Can you become the tunnel?

A — I am the tunnel. But my experience is confused.

T — Experience this part of yourself. See what it's like.

A — I have the tendency to let things get out of focus sometimes.

T — How do you feel now?

A — I am not sure of anything. I doubt myself and get down on myself. I think it all goes back to my concept of time; I am confused about time.

T — How do you feel as you say this?

A — It's interesting: I am not too bothered by it. Its easier to see it now for some reason.

T — Stay with the feeling. Just follow it.
(Pause)

A — I see the mountain now. It has a giant purple peak.

T — Concentrate on the mountain. How do you feel?

A — Nothing really. But I seem to be drawn toward it.

T — Let go to it. See what happens.

A — I am the mountain now. I know myself and my limits. I feel solid, stable. I know all the answers of life lie within me. I feel a kinship with everyone.

T — Let that feeling build up. Go with it, and let it take you wherever it wants to take you.

A — The mountain is splitting now. I am splitting into two parts. One part seems free and the other part in bondage. I lose confidence in myself. I am losing my stability.

T — Are you like that at times?

A — Yes.

T — Do you feel that way now?

A — I feel as if there are two selves in me. Yes, I feel that way.

T — Just let go to the feeling. See what happens next.

A — A big luminous eye comes out of the mountain. It radiates warmth and color. I am floating toward the eye.

T — Concentrate on the eye as that happens. Let go to it.

A — I feel drawn into the eye. I am the dove now. I feel better.

T — Can you become the eye?

A — I am the eye. I have just absorbed the dove. My feelings resemble those God must have. But it is not all pleasant. I feel like I am holding court.

T — How are you like that?

A — I overjudge myself a lot. When I do that, I am not spontaneous; I am more calculating and deliberate.

T — What does all this mean to you?

A — I am not sure.

T — Just be quiet awhile and see what comes to you.
(Long silence)

A — Well, when I was the dove, I had my freedom. But when I went into the eye, I lost my freedom. When I overjudge myself, I lose my freedom. And I do that all the time.

T — How do you feel now?

A — Sort of empty. I feel a sense of real loss.

T — Let it intensify. Follow it. See what comes next.
(Pause)

A — I feel tension in my head. I am getting a slight headache.

T — Let go to it. Let it get worse. Just follow it.
(Pause)

A — The dove is breaking free now. I'll be the dove again. It's like a liberation.

T — Stay with it. Let go to those good feelings.

A — I explode. I am a part of everything and time does not exist. I feel no conflict. I am everything and everything is me.

T — Just stay with that as long as you like.

The case of Allen illustrates several significant facets of the death imagery process. The farewell scenes gave Allen an opportunity to abreact longstanding resentment and achieve a degree of peace with his mother. Also, we witness the beneficial character of the personalization of the reowning process. By playing the parts of the individual images, Allen was able to gain a deep awareness of his own dynamics. Through this experience he was able to accept his creative potential and his feelings of unity. He reowned those parts of himself the rejection which kept him out of focus and prevented the sense of unity from being a more frequent reality in his daily life. As a result, he began to see that he was responsible for his state and that if he let go to his potential, he would grow in the experience of unity. In short, he achieved a wholeness of personality that he formally did not have.

Some Benefits of Death Imagery Work

Numerous clients have undergone the death imagery work: the aim of some has been merely to achieve relaxation or the experience of an altered state of consciousness; the goal of others has been to resolve a number of different problems. We have noticed a wide variety of beneficial effects. Currently, we are planning controlled investigations to systematically study the various outcomes of the application of this technique. The following brief account, however, is based primarily on our informal observations and the subjective reports of our clients.

During relaxation through death imagery, the clients generally experience a fully conscious, creative, dreamlike state which is profoundly soothing at both the physical and mental level. Our preliminary laboratory work indicates a slowing down of the heartbeat and a flattening of the galvanic skin response. Also, we have often noticed that in this condition, some trapped air escapes the body, producing a tension-releasing effect. Spontaneous remission of some minor psychosomatic symptoms has also been noted (Sheikh, 1978b).

The feeling of relaxation, especially among experienced subjects, often blossoms into a metaphysical awakening, a blissful experience of pure consciousness that has integrative aftereffects in the subjects' lives. These experiences open the clients to natural change resulting in deeper awareness and a surge of freedom. Also, these experiences assist the clients in seeing that they still possess a center of unity in their personality.

The work with death imagery indicates that personal integration is dependent on willingness to let go, take a chance, and accept whatever emerges. Unfortunately, this open, nonjudgmental, and accepting attitude is not common. In learning to cope with the world and its demands, one learns to disown parts of oneself. One projects these unacceptable parts onto others, institutions, fate, or the gods. As a result of this tendency, one cannot experience the totality of one's being. In the course of working with death imagery, one often becomes aware of this selective rejection and begins the process of reintegration.

We have observed that death imagery is especially useful in helping the normal grief process to proceed. Persons with unresolved grief reactions usually meet the deceased in their images, and these encounters frequently result in a spontaneous resolution of the conflicts. Furthermore, several people with significant death fears have achieved greater confidence and less obsession with death and have realized the importance of intimacy in their lives. It should also be noted that several clients had imagery experiences that were in many ways very similar to the experiences described by Moody in his book, *Life after Life* (1975).

Spontaneous images that emerge during death work often lead to instantaneous insight into blocked areas and also bring to the surface various unfinished emotional life situations. Further imagery work can help bring about catharsis of affect and closure to the situations. We have also been encouraged by our very preliminary work with schizophrenics, which will be discussed in a later paper.

Above all, however, death imagery provides the individual with an excellent opportunity to confront death, accept it, and come into contact with his/her deepest human feelings. For, death "explains what it means to be human (searching for meaning, immortality, freedom, love, and individuality) far better than the psychological principles of sex and aggression, the biological instincts of survival and procreation, the utilitarian theories of happiness and approbation, or the religious ukase of God's will" (Koestenbaum, 1976, p. 7).

Other Related Approaches

Since the development of our death imagery procedures, we have perused the literature for any approaches that fall within the same general category, and we found several. The following account, however, is by no means intended to be a comprehensive review of the litterature.

Meditation on Death. This is one of the most commonly used forms of meditation among Buddhist monks. The monk seats himself in the graveyard or the crematorium and contemplates the corpses and the ashes of the bodies. This meditation is believed to make him profoundly aware of the brevity and uncertainty of life and the inevitability of death. He frequently imagines his own body to be among the corpses. Through these exercises, he achieves the realization that human beings and their objects of pleasure are not enduring entities. This insight leads him to abandon the ambition to shape the world in accordance with his own will. "And, with the passing of this habit of living a life of willfulness (and its offspring, anxiety and fear) will come automatically a peace of mind and tranquility which will abide unaltered in all conditions of life and all states of mind" (Long, 1975, p. 69).

The Tibetan Book of the Dead. This book presents, in a highly imaginative manner, the various Buddhist teachings pertaining to death. It describes the most effective method of "living toward death", and it teaches the readers, especially those who are approaching death, "how to die well" (Evans-Wentz, 1960).

The clients are asked to remain calm and alert in the face of death and to avoid distraction and confusion. They are instructed to realize that their life-forces are about to disengage from their bodies and that they should focus their consciousness upon the event of their passing. They are further prepared for the meeting with death by its description: death is "the brilliant light of Ultimate Reality" or "the luminous splendor of the colorless light of Emptiness." They must drown themselves in that supernatural brilliance, shedding all belief in an individual self and realizing that "boundless light of this true Reality" is their own true self (Evans-Wentz, 1960; Long, 1975; Rahula, 1959; Robinson, 1970).

Sufi Contemplation upon Death. The Sufis have emphasized the importance of the contemplation on death. Taking to heart the Prophet Mohammad's advice, "Die before you are dead," they contemplate the inevitable future decay and disintegration of all living beings. They remind themselves that soon their own bodies too will be nothing but rotten flesh and dry bones on which worms will feed. This meditation leads them to the clear awareness of the impermanence of temporal life. For the Sufis, the contemplation upon death is an essential step towards beatitude — the ultimate goal of all spiritual striving. Death symbolizes the dismemberment of the present unwholesome state, which in turn renders possible the rebirth of a personality with spiritually healthy and stable characteristics (Ajmal, 1979).

Practicing Death. Plato, in the *Republic,* argues that there are four stages of cognitive development: (1) in the first stage the individual has a perception of only shadows and other superficial or insubstantial things; (2) the second stage is characterized by the perception of reality of physical objects; (3) the third stage involves abstract mathematics and deductive reasoning; (4) the fourth stage deals with the experience of the Forms, the eternal archetypes or potentials that structure all our thinking and perceiving. Plato claims that these Forms are properly known only by the experience of the highest level of reality, after one's physical and mental activity stops. In his dialogues, such as *Phaedo, Meno, Theaetetus,* and

Phaedrus, he equates "true knowledge, knowledge of the Forms, with knowledge of the world experiencable 'after death' " (Shear, 1978). In the *Phaedo,* he clearly states that the philosopher's true method and occupation, the method of gaining knowledge of the Forms, resides in practicing death, that is in accustoming the soul "to withdraw from all contact with the body and concentrate itself by itself . . . alone by itself" (see *Collected Dialogues of Plato,* edited by Hamilton & Cairns, 1973).

It should be noted that the above description of "practising death" closely resembles the process of achieving "samadhi" through Patanjali's *sutras* (1949).

Death and Immortality Exercises. Koestenbaum (1976) mentions a number of death and immortality exercises which he feels to be very effective. Some he has originated and others he has borrowed from Herman Feifel and Robert Kastenbaum. Koestenbaum (1976) feels that the composition of one's own obituary is very effective; for it amounts to writing out the meaning that one's life has had. It may answer the most sensitive question - the question of what it means to be a human being, of how to live well - and the deepest question of all - what it means to be *you.* Other exercises consist of (1) imagining that one is attending one's own funeral and hearing a friend talking honestly about the significance of one's life, (2) going through a rebirth fantasy, (3) writing a script for one's own death including *how, when,* and *where* the death would occur, (4) reading a moving and vivid account of the death of a 6-year-old abandoned boy and, subsequently, completing seven incomplete sentences. Koestenbaum claims that, through these exercises, it is possible to courageously face the reality of one's own death and thus to make powerful discoveries.

Koestenbaum also describes in detail an immortality exercise in the form of a guided daydream or fantasy. In the first part of that fantasy, he encourages the subject to picture himself/herself as a dying patient in a hospital. Then he describes to the subject the thoughts he/she will have immediately before death. During this stage, the subject is told, all the worldly objects, events, and values recede into a meaningless distance, and he/she now feels more "like a god in outer space observing life than a human being participating in the affairs of the world." Suggestions of this type are followed by suggested images in which the individual is reconciled with death, feels at peace, experiences himself/herself as universal, and has "a sense of eternity of pure consciousness." Through this exercise, Koestenbaum claims, one can have a premonition of the experience of immortality. "The key dynamism bringing about this realization is relinquishing the sense of being an individual" (p. 189).

Successful Grieving. Generally, our society protects the bereaved from facing the reality of death by taking over for them and inviting them to be mere observers. This practice makes it increasingly difficult for the grief stricken to come to grips with the death of their loved one (Nichols & Nichols, 1975). Aguilar and Wood

(1976), Ahsen (1968), and Morrison (1978) suggest imagery techniques that, in combination with other therapeutic interventions, reconstruct death-related events and, thus, facilitate the grieving process. Although these techniques do not deal directly with the client's own death, they are bound to bring the client to confront his/her own inevitable end.

Concluding Remarks

The death imagery procedure is still in its early stages. Only a limited number of therapists have employed it, and no controlled studies of outcome have yet been completed. However, the initial indications are highly promising. We feel that we have only begun to see the enormous potential of this dynamic technique for the clarification of human consciousness and for tapping the innate capacities of the mind.

Of course, we have had clients who, because of an intense anxiety about death, refused at the very outset to participate in death imagery work. But, out of a wide variety of individuals who went through this process, a significant majority emerged "healthier" and favorably impressed by this simple yet profound technique. We must point that, while dying in imagination has been a blissful experience for a number of subjects, it should not be construed as a revelation of what lies after death. We, by no means, intend to present it as a "temptation from the ever after" (Kastenbaum, 1977a).

The question has often been asked, "Can one actually die while experiencing death in imagination?" This question takes on further significance when one considers the literature on "psychic deaths," that suggests that the timing of death may at times be influenced by psychic factors such as an attitude of calm acceptance (Garrity, 1974). However it seems to us that it might be more reasonable to attribute these instances of "psychic deaths" to "giving up" and resignation to ill fate, rather than to acceptance of death as a fact of life (Engel, 1971). In our work, death imagery has been nothing but a life-giving experience. Nevertheless, considering the seriousness of the issue, a note of caution is probably in order. Until much more is known about the procedure, clinicians should perhaps be reluctant to employ it with extremely suggestible, superstitious, and overly death-anxious clients. Since death imagery seems to considerably lower the activity level of the body, its use in conjunction with a sedative should also be avoided.

We have noticed significant individual differences in response to death imagery. A host of variables that seem relevant include: age, sex, religious beliefs, style of ego defense, ethnic background, nature of interpersonal relationships, and life style (Chiapetta, Floyd, & McSeveney, 1976; Kahoe & Dunn, 1975; Kastenbaum, 1977b). The effect of these factors is among the issues which we wish to examine in our future clinical and laboratory work.

REFERENCES

Aguilar, I., & Wood, V. N. Therapy through death ritual. *Social Work,* January, 1976, 49-54.

Ahsen, A. *Basic concepts in eidetic psychotherapy.* New York: Brandon House, 1968.

Ahsen, A. *Eidetic parents test and analysis.* New York: Brandon House, 1972.

Ahsen, A. Anna O. - patient or therapist? An eidetic view, in V. Franks and V. Burtle (Eds.), *Women in therapy.* New York: Bruner/Mazel, 1974, pp. 263-283.

Ahsen, A. *Psycheye: Self-analytic consciousness.* New York: Brandon House, 1977.

Ahsen, A. *Manhunt in the desert.* New York: Brandon House, 1979.

Ajmal, M. Sufi contemplation upon death. Unpublished paper. National Institute of Psychology, Islamabad, Pakistan, 1979.

Assagioli, R. *Psychosynthesis: A collection of basic writings.* New York: Viking, 1965.

Barrett, W. *Irrational man.* New York: Anchor Books, 1962.

Bloching, K. The reflection of death in contemporary literature. In N. Greinacher and A. Müller (Eds.), *The experience of dying.* New York: Herder and Herder, 1974.

Braga, J. L., & Braga, L. D. Foreword. In E. Kübler-Ross (Ed.), *Death: The final stage of growth.* New Jersey: Prentice-Hall, 1975.

Butler, R. N. The life review: An interpretation of reminiscence in the aged. *Psychiatry,* 1963, *119,* 721-728.

Chiappetta, W., Floyd, H. H., & McSeveney, R. Sex differences in coping with death anxiety. *Psychological Reports,* 1976, *39,* 945-946.

Cumming, E., & Henry, W. E. *Growing old.* Illinois: The Free Press, 1961.

Dolan, A. T., & Sheikh, A. A. Short-term treatment of phobias through eidetic imagery. *American Journal of Psychotherapy,* 1977, *31,* 595-604.

Engel, G. Sudden and rapid death during psychological stress. *Annals of Internal Medicine,* 1971, *74,* 771-782.

Evans-Wentz, W. Y. *The Tibetan book of the dead.* New York: Oxford Universities Press, 1960.

Frisch, V. M. *Homo Faber.* Frankfurt: Suhrkamp Verlag, 1957.

Garrity, T. F. Psychic death: Behavioral types and physiological parallels. *Omega,* 1974, *5,* 207-215.

Greinacher, N., & Müller, A. (Eds.) *The experience of dying.* New York: Herder and Herder, 1974.

Hamilton, E., & Cairns, H. (Eds.). *Collected dialogues of Plato.* New Jersey: Princeton University Press, 1973.

Ichazo, O. *The human process of enlightenment and freedom.* New York: Arica Institute, 1972.

Kahoe, R. D., & Dunn, R. F. The fear of death and religious attitudes and behavior. *Journal for the Scientific Study of Religion.* 1975, *14,* 379-382.

Kastenbaum, R. J. Temptations from the ever after. *Human Behavior,* September, 1977, 28-33. (a)

Kastenbaum, R. J. *Death, society, and human experience.* St. Louis: C. V. Mosby Co., 1977. (b)

Koestenbaum, P. *Is there an answer to death?* New Jersey: Prentice-Hall, 1976.

Kübler-Ross, E. (Ed.). *Death: The final stage of growth.* New Jersey: Prentice-Hall, 1975.

Long, J. B. The death that ends death in Hinduism and Buddhism. In E. Kübler-Ross (Ed.). *Death: The final stage of growth.* New Jersey: Prentice-Hall, 1975.

Meyer, J. E. *Death and neurosis.* New York: International Universitis Press, 1975.

Moody, R. A. *Life after life.* New York: Bantam Books, 1975.

Morrison, J. K. Successful grieving: Changing personal constructs through mental imagery. *Journal of Mental Imagery,* 1978, *2,* 63-68.

Musel, R. Primitive man played dead to live, theory suggests. *Milwaukee Journal,* August 5, 1975.

Nichols, R., & Nichols, J. Funerals: A time for grief and growth. In E. Kübler-Ross (Ed.), *Death: The final stage of growth.* New Jersey: Prentice-Hall, 1975.

Patanjali, *Yoga sutra* (Translated from Sanskrit by Begali Baba) Poona, 1949.

Paz, O. *The labyrinth of solitude.* New York: Grove Press, 1961.

Perky, C. W. An experimental study of imagination. *American Journal of Psychology,* 1910, *21,* 422-452.

Perls, F. *The gestalt approach.* Palo Alto, California: Science and Behavior Books, 1973.

Rahula, W. *What the Buddha taught.* New York: Grove Press, 1959.

Robinson, R. H. *The Buddhist religion: A historical introduction.* Belmont, California: Dickenson Publishing Co., 1970.

Segal, S. J. (Ed.) *Imagery: Current cognitive approaches.* New York: Academic Press, 1971.

Shear, J. Plato, Piaget, and Maharishi on cognitive development. Paper presented at the American Psychological Association Convention, Toronto, September, 1978.

Sheikh, A. A. Treatment of insomnia through eidetic imagery: A new technique. *Perceptual and Motor Skills,* 1976, *43,* 994.

Sheikh, A. A. Mental images: Ghosts of sensations? *Journal of Mental Imagery,* 1977, *1,* 1-4.

Sheikh, A. A. Eidetic Psychotherapy. In J. L. Singer and K. S. Pope (Eds.), *The power of human imagination.* New York: Plenum, 1978. (a)

Sheikh, A. A. Mental Imagery and psychosomatic illness. Paper presented at the American Psychological Association Convention, Toronto, August, 1978. (b)

Sheikh, A.A., & Panagiotou, N. C. Use of mental imagery in psychotherapy: A critical review. *Perceptual and Motor Skills,* 1975, 41, 555-585.

Sheikh, A. A., Twente, G. E., Turner, D., & Frazier, P. B. Death Imagery: Clinical use for personal growth and awareness. Paper presented at the Second American Conference on the Fantasy and Imaging Process, Chicago, November, 1978.

Twente, G. E., Turner, D., & Haney, J. Eidetic in the hospital setting and private practice: A report on eidetic therapy procedures employed with 69 patients. *Journal of Mental Imagery,* 1978, *2,* 275-290.

Twente, G. E., Sheikh, A. A., & Turner, D. Therapy through death imagery. Manuscript in preparation, 1979.

Watts, A. *The meaning of happiness.* New York: Harper and Row, 1968.

Watts, A. *The book on the taboo against knowing who you are.* New York: New York: Random House, 1972.

11

The Experience of the Holistic Mind

JOHN T. SHAFFER

"I've got to get my head together" may mean far more than many people realize. The popular expression reflects in metaphoric terms a consciousness of what brain researchers have known for more than 100 years: both the left and right hemispheres take on different and complementary functions. When and how and why this specialization happens is not known; that it takes place is well documented (Ahsen, 1977a, 1977b, Bogen, 1969; Gazzaniga, 1967, 1970; Sperry, 1961; Zangwill, 1964).

Authorities, such as Ornstein (1973) and Samples (1976), believe that the left hemisphere is the center of practical, linear, problem-solving activities. It is relatively finite, enclosed, and, generally speaking, in our culture the more developed hemisphere. By contrast, the right hemisphere is intuitive, creative, philosophical, free, and relatively infinite. According to the investigators, these descriptions of the two hemispheres hold true for most people. However, the characteristics are usually reversed in the left-handed person. Among my clients under guided fantasy, there is a minority who claims to be right-handed or left-handed and yet reports reversed functions of the two hemispheres. Although the clients do not always give the traditional left hemisphere-right hemisphere descriptions, they always report a clear distinction between hemispheric functioning.

My purpose here is not to discuss the validity of localizing specific brain functioning. I am interested in sharing the self-description of many clients in guided fantasy. The starting image used was a "visit" to the left and right hemispheres of the brain. It not only is a viable and effective tool for therapy but also provides in personal terms, a rich variety of descriptions of how the left hemisphere-right

John T. Shaffer, The Well-Being Center, Inc., 349 West Morgan, Jacksonville, Illinois 62650.

hemisphere function as a team. Whether the descriptions are an accurate picture of brain functioning or a symbolic representation of total body-mind functioning, I do not know. However, when clients visit the two hemispheres, *they* have no difficulty believing in the assessment they themselves make of their experiences. Even the incredulous soon come to hold that their experiences reflect directly physiological and psychological functioning.

A Particular Use of Guided Fantasy

By my focus on the "visit" to the left and right hemispheres, I do not mean to suggest that I employ it exclusively or that is the only starting image to produce good results. I have long used a variety of such images, but my present preference is for starting images which are personal images of body, mind, and spirit. I believe these images bring me and my clients into more direct contact with mental processes including the transpersonal. For me, the image of left hemisphere-right hemisphere and the accompanying personal images from within are the most powerful; they seem to embrace ontological as well as metaphysical concerns.

Also, I prefer to use the same starting image over and over again in a continued-story form. Rarely can the experience of the holistic mind occur in a single trial and then only with persons trained in guided fantasy. When the "visit" is the starting basic model, other stages or starting images are added; for example, "the hallway of the mind," where rooms represent any personal problems; "central control," where all mind-body functions are coordinated; "the inner chapel," where transpersonal experiences begin; a visit to any place in the body or brain; age regressions to bring the past into live focus and free the person from the grip of the past. I call this process the continuing, multiple-stage fantasy[1]. I find it to be far more creative and therapeutic than either the single episode or the one-stage continuing model (Shaffer, 1972, 1978).

A Model for the Exploration of the Left and Right Hemispheres

The structured model which I have developed to explore left hemisphere-right hemisphere functioning has nine parts, which I frequently present in the following sequence in both group and individual sessions:

1. A visit to the left hemisphere
2. A visit to the right hemisphere

---

[1] Progoff (1963) was the source of inspiration for the development of this model. For an overview of the fantasy - imaging process in psychotherapy see Singer (1974), Sheikh (1978), and Sheikh and Panagiotou (1975).

3. Finding and going through the corpus callosum from the right hemisphere to the left hemisphere

4. A return visit from the left hemisphere to the right via the corpus callosum

5. Asking for a gift from the right hemisphere and taking it, if possible, to the left hemisphere

6. Asking for a gift from the left hemisphere and taking it, if possible, to the right hemisphere

7. Being in the center of the corpus callosum and experiencing the left and right hemispheres

8. Looking down through the body to say "hello" to any organ or function; then looking for trouble spots

9. The integration or synthesis of left and right hemispheres to achieve the holistic mind; for some, the experience of transcendence

Some of my experienced clients are able to make the entire nine-step journey in one session. More frequently, clients can take only one or two steps at a session, especially in group therapy. A few find they are incapable of visiting more than one hemisphere, or they meet such great resistance that they require many sessions to get through to the other hemisphere.

The process may be illustrated through a transcript of a single session. In this, one of my clients went through seven of the *nine steps* and achieved an experience of the holistic mind. He previously had had a massive heart attack and a subsequent long, slow healing process. His medical doctor had worked out an exercise program which resulted in his ability to run five miles a day with no apparent problems with his heart. But he did develop trouble with his left knee, then his left heel. He could not imagine why they were paining him, nor did he believe that he should stop his exercise program. He remarked: "I have said many times, 'I've got to run this morning. My body is screaming for attention.' My body lets me know when I do not run my regular schedule. My body feels slimy and needs to be cleaned out. But the pain in my knee and heel really bothers me."

Step I.
Guide: Be in your left hemisphere and get the feel of it.
Client: Surrealistic, spacious, stark, surrealistic figures. Sharp focus and detail.
Guide: How do you feel there?
Client: Not uncomfortable, but a little uneasy. It's difficult to get into a relaxed mood. (Pause)

Step II.
Guide: That's a good beginning for the left hemisphere. Now, be in the right.
Client: It's totally different. Tropical, lush, sunny, soothing, sensuous. Reminds me of Jamaica, totally relaxing. I feel totally at ease.
Guide: What do you feel like doing?
Client: I thought I felt like painting, but I don't want to do that. I just want to explore the beauties of all this. I just want to enjoy it. (Pause)

Step III.
Guide: The corpus callosum is the opening between the two. See if you can find it and go from one side to the other.
Client: I see it's there. It's dark, cool, dark, and damp. It's not difficult to go through. Just enough room for me to walk through comfortably.

Step IV.
(For some reason, I did not ask him to exchange gifts. Instead, I asked him to walk back and forth through the corpus callosum.)

Step VII.
Client: I can see both sides from the middle. They're both getting brighter now. They understand they each have a function to serve. A strange thing happened right now: while I'm standing off looking at both brains in my mind's eye, I'm squinting on my right side because of the sharp light. They both are light now, but the contrast is greater — significantly lighter on the right side.

Step VIII.
Guide: Let's try an experiment. Look down from that perspective in the center, to your heart.
Client: O.K. I can see it but both the right brain and left brain are having difficulty. They can't look at the heart directly. They have to run away. They feel a little guilty.
Guide: In what way?
Client: For not being in harmony with it, for one thing.
Guide: How do they look back on the catastrophe that happened?
Client: They feel guilty about moving on without full authority, for not being in consort, for not consulting the rest of the organs. The heart is smiling. (Laughs) Telling me, "It's O.K., guys, now that we're all together." The heart appears to be very happy, very, very content, very strong. As a matter of fact, I can see the scar, and it's not really that bad. It's healed. It's kind of a tough bruise. It says it wasn't concerned about itself; it was concerned about the other parts.
Guide: Can you see all the other parts from the center of the corpus callosum?
Client: The other parts seem to be blurred out, because they seem to be without problems. Except, I'm looking down the left side of the body, some throbbing in the left knee.
Guide: There's something that really isn't functioning well. You're running with pain.
Client: There's throbbing. It's a little red, a little swollen.
Guide: Are you looking at it from the brain, or are you down there now?
Client: No, I'm looking at it from the top. The heel looks like it has a sharp stone inverted in it. The left brain says the heel cannot support the extra weight I've gained, and the knee's been trying to tell me that for a long time. It is unable to absorb the pain. Now, they're giving me a sharper response to get my attention.
Guide: If one signal doesn't work, the other will.
Client: Yeah, they're saying that there's not an Ace bandage big enough to get rid of it, so I might as well work on the problem.
Guide: So, symptomatically speaking, there's no use doing a thing with your knee or your heel. They're calling attention to the weight problem, and that's the threat to the well-being of the body. They're going to keep "yakking" until you do something about your weight.
Client: Right! (Pause) I'm still at the top. The body is somewhat transparent. I really don't see any other areas that are glaring out.
Guide: O.K., maybe you could go down and talk with your knee a bit.
Client: I'm there. It's showing me the soreness. It's nothing serious, but it can develop into

more. I'm telling it, it can relax now because I'm going to do something about the weight problem. We're not that far gone.

Guide: You might thank it for being such a loyal servant.

Client: I've done that and the redness is gone. The stone in the heel is dissolving. (He puts his left heel on his right and presses hard against it.) The funny thing is, I haven't gained that much weight. The throbbing is gone. The inverted stone is gone. They said everything would be all right. I can put pressure on my heel without pain.

Step IX.

Guide: Let's go back up to your head and have a little celebration. Mind and body working together is beautiful.

Client: I'm up there and the heart seems to be the life of the party —big and beautiful.

This session represents the "classic" movement from left hemisphere to right hemisphere toward integration. It is important to keep in mind that such progress in one session is the exception. More typically, clients experience a variety of difficulties as they try to move from one step to another. Indeed, even the first two steps can be a problem. Although clients invariably can fantasize the existence of the two hemispheres, many experience difficulty in visiting both. All clients, however, are able to visit at least one.

Difficulty in Visiting Both Hemispheres: Blocking

Although clients generally have no problems using this starting image, almost everyone has some difficulty somewhere along the way. For a few, it begins with the experience of not being able to be in the brain but only on the outside looking in. However, without being there, they "know" what it is like. Later, when they are able to enter, their "sensing" proves to be correct. For some, it is the left hemisphere, they cannot enter; for others, it is the right. Nevertheless, all clients are able to be in one hemisphere or the other on the first visit. However, the ability to be in either or both hemispheres is no guarantee that a person can go from one to the other by way of the corpus callosum. Even though they have been in both hemispheres and have explored them, many clients cannot pass out of a hemisphere into the corpus callosum, or they can go one way through the corpus callosum but not back the other way. A few examples will illustrate the problem.

Lynn could not enter into his left hemisphere. However, his right hemisphere was comfortable, spacious and peaceful. After exploring it for awhile, he saw that there was a window overlooking the left side. He could see various machines working fast and furiously. A great throbbing sound came through the wall and the window. "Everything is too fast," he said, "much too fast." No matter how or what he tried, he could not enter the left hemisphere to visit. He very much wanted to slow it down, but he found himself unable to do so. When he could not make any progress in the second session, I introduced the "house fantasy." Consequently, he was able to overcome these difficulties. During the third session and the second "house fantasy, an interesting development occurred: he was on an elevator in a castle (his house) going up — where he did not know. For some reason, he opened a trap door in the top of the elevator, and there he was in his left hemisphere. It was dark, however, and there was nothing he could see or do.

Angie found that she could easily enter her left hemisphere. It was light, roomy, and comfortable. There was a little man with a feather duster keeping the place orderly and clean, but she could not visit the other hemisphere. She remarked, "I somehow know it's dark, and fat, and crowded. It feels very uncomfortable over there. There's a keeper there, but he's sound asleep. Somehow, I woke him up, but he says, he's too tired and is back asleep again." In the second session, she tried to pass through the door which she first visited, without success. Later in the fantasy, she found the door open, but there was another door in the middle of the corpus callosum, and beyond that still another door. After passing through the middle door, she came to another door — the entrance to the right hemisphere. "I'm not going to be able to go in that door, it's a foot thick. The door won't do anything. It won't talk to me, it won't listen, it won't open." However, in the third session, after working through two other fantasy models or starting images, she said, "I just walked through the door this time."

Ann had had serious attacks of depression. She had been unable to function normally for many years. When in the middle of a long depression, she could minimally care for herself, let alone anyone else. On her first visit, she said, "There's no way to get into the right brain. There's a passageway from the left brain into the hall, but there's no way to get into the right brain. I couldn't possibly get in there."

There are many others who cannot enter one or the other hemisphere in the initial two sessions. What does this mean? In the first place, I believe the blocking is a signal from the psyche that something is seriously wrong with the total organism — mind, body, spirit. Something is amiss with the free functioning of the being, if not with the mind itself. The "plot" to catch the person's attention is being staged in the brain.

One can also regard blocking of any kind, but especially in the left and right hemispheres, as a situation which provides the client with a good workshop. Blocking presents a challenge to the person to explore and understand. Blockage is a danger signal; it is also an opportunity to try, even to experience failure. I like to call these blocks "learning dilemmas." They give excellent practice in overcoming problems. Moreover, there is a double benefit: not only do clients gain confidence in their own initiative and strength, but the overcoming of a block helps them feel good. Often it results in healing, as we will see later.

Experiencing Differences between the Hemispheres

Characteristic of the process of the fantasy "visit" to the left and right hemispheres is that all clients experienced sharp differences in sensing or seeing the two hemispheres. One client visualized the left hemisphere as a room with a big computer on the left wall. The wall in front of him was glass through which he could see "out over the universe." In the corner of the glass, he could see the curve of the earth. He described his right hemisphere also as a room with a computer, but this room was "teeny tiny." The computer operator was squeezed so tightly against the machine, that he could not read anything that came out of it.

Another client described her left hemisphere as a place that looked bloody, with blue and dark red lines (arteries and veins) running through it. Her right hemisphere she reported to be more comfortable, a place with a warm quilt, feather mattress, rocking chair, and something that resembled an old steamer trunk.

Again another client said of his left hemisphere, "I found it kind of a rubbery substance — a cross-sectional view with the outside hard and the inside a gray-to-white color. It's a control center. I definitely know that. It's a clearing house, a message center. The right brain seems to be darker; it has an air of mysticism, like a waiting room of a hospital. You know something important is going on, but all you do is wait and wonder. I experience this as an uncharted, unexplored cave. It also seems much of it is hidden."

I have not had a client who did not experience a rather immediate sense of the difference between the two hemispheres. Some described the difference in purely emotive terms, others did so in more objective terms. They were even able to describe a hemisphere which they could not enter! Generally, the difference as they perceive it, reflects that which the experts believe to exist.

Most of my clients have a preference for one hemisphere or the other. Smitty definitely preferred her left hemisphere to her right one because it was "so clear and so far ahead" in its mode of operating. Her right hemisphere was painfully slow.

Mike favored his right hemisphere. He mentioned that "anything from the left brain was just out of place" when he tried to take a gift over to the right hemisphere. However, later in the fantasy, he reported, "Eventually I moved a small computer in there and left it for a long time. Behold! The first philosopher-computer was born! When I moved it back to the left brain, it began to preach the good of such a fusion — that is, the integration of cold, calculating technology with such transcending things as philosophy and love and emotion. It really stirred up those poor technicians. The philosopher-computer is still contaminating the left brain. Perhaps I'll have to get some new technicians — the old ones are too stuffy."

Pete had a preference for the left brain. Of it, he said, "It's functioning really nicely and smoothly. All the blood is going through it nicely. There is a little bit of static towards the bottom. My feeling is that it is really solid, and I can depend on it. You know, I really feel nice about my left side." On the other hand, the right is very different: "Darkness all over. It's kind of like a burning log in the fireplace. It's not a hot fire but smoldering, and you put this dark piece of plastic on it. It's like different shades of darkness. I feel like I have to do a lot of work. I've done a lot of work, but I've got to do more. I feel like the right brain is leaning on the left brain . . . I feel sad."

In general, I found that anyone who was blocked in visiting one or the other hemisphere preferred the hemisphere open to him/her. However, I also believe that each is saying, "This is the situation in which I find myself. This is the way things are." Then they go on to try to gain entrance and resolve problems.

Generally, it is true that each person liked the side that was more interesting, peaceful, calm, light, open, pleasant, colorful, large, etc. The preference for the left hemisphere or the right one was perhaps based on the individual's greater appreciation of linear versus intuitive functioning. This preference seemed to have little relation to the functions of either side. It was the *quality* of the functioning that made the difference.

It seems to me that an equal number of persons, although they sensed sharp differences in the qualities of the two hemispheres, either had no real preference or did not state one. Pete may have appreciated his left hemisphere more at first, because he knew it better, or because it was functioning very well. However, later he came to more highly esteem the functioning of the right hemisphere. Finally, as the fantasy continued through several sessions, he came to a realization of their unique functioning and then of their holistic functioning.

Pete's experience seems to be somewhat normative. At first glance, a person may simply experience the way things are. Then, as a client becomes better acquainted, he/she begins to explore more, know more, and expect more of the two hemispheres. Consequently more is achieved. When both hemispheres are functioning equally well, there is little or no preference.

Experiences in the Corpus Callosum

The ability to move into Steps III. and IV., that is, from one hemisphere to another through the corpus callosum, varies significantly from one client to another. Indeed, the nature of the passageway is strikingly different. It may be a bridge, a road, a tunnel, an elevator, stairs, a hole, a trapdoor, or a doorway with different kinds and thicknesses of doors.

Many persons have no trouble being in either hemisphere at the direction of the therapist but have difficulty going through the corpus callosum between the two hemispheres. Drea, whose immediate problem was a very sore neck, described her difficulty as follows: "It's like a split . . . in the earth, a crevice in the wall. It's connected to the bottom. I can hardly get there. Now, it's blocked. There are spaces that go from the right hemisphere to the left hemisphere but they're too small." When the therapist suggested that she try moving from the left to the right hemisphere, she said, "It's blocked, but there's a small opening from right to left. It has something to do with blood flow. Maybe it's related to the heartbeats." She discovered that the sore neck was congested and blocked the way. On her second visit, the passageway from left to right was also open but smaller than the one going in the opposite direction. Eventually, she was able to move freely between the two hemispheres.

When asked to find and go through the corpus callosum, Ward said, "I don't know; it doesn't seem possible to do. I kind of get the feeling I can reach right through and touch the matter on the right." After the therapist suggested that he go from the right to the left, he replied, "No, there's an imagined barrier. Although when I get up to look, there's nothing there." After other attempts to get through, he said, "I can walk through at least halfway. But it's tight." The therapist then instructed Ward to ask it to open up. He reported, "Yeah, it's complying easily." From that moment on, he had no difficulty.

Angie knew something about her right hemisphere even though she could not go in either by "being there" or by going through the corpus callosum. While exploring her left brain, she saw a door to the right one. She could not pass through the door into the corpus callosum the first time. While she was visiting in the hallway of her mind, the imp (a central character from her house fantasy, who had come over into the brain to help) picked the lock for her. She found the door wide open but in the center of the corpus callosum was another door surrounded by extinguished light bulbs. She and the imp corrected the lighting short and found new bulbs for the sockets. Then this door opened, but only to reveal another door at the entrance of the right brain. She described it: "I've crossed the center between the two sides, and now I'm standing in front of another door. On this one, all the light bulbs are out. I'm not going to be able to get in that door. It's a foot thick. The imp is beginning to replace all the bulbs. The door won't do anything. It won't talk to me, it won't listen, it won't open." That was all we could accomplish in the session. However, at the beginning of the third session, she said of the door which previously had been completely black, "I believe I have a little bit of white on the right side. I just walked through the door this time, so I must have done something right."

These are only a few examples of the varied experiences clients have while learning to travel between their hemispheres. Once again, it appears that the major reason for difficulty is to provide a test. It is a learning dilemma, a practical workshop for learning to take control of one's life, to develop confidence. The ability to cross over from one hemisphere to the other by way of the corpus callosum in every case resulted greater self-confidence and control. Clients reported that their brains seemed to be working better.

Exchanging Gifts between the Hemispheres

After several sessions, most clients are able to move on to Steps V. and VI.: they give and receive gifts freely in both hemispheres and also have free access both ways through the corpus callosum.

Liz took some softness from her right side and tossed it among all the boxes that crowded the right side. Immediately, the boxes became smaller, lost the sharp edges, and resembled marshmellows. Her left brain said, "Now you won't have those headaches in the back of your left side of your head!" She took some of the order from the left hemisphere to the right one. It received the order graciously and converted the swirls of color into a more orderly style. She did not understand what this action meant, but she felt good about it.

Asked to take a present from the right to the left hemisphere, Bert replied, "I've got a windmill as a present. The left hemisphere receives it with no problem and places it where the streams of wind from the right hemisphere are strongest. It changes the course of the wind." The therapist then instructed him to ask the left hemisphere for a present for the right hemisphere. He reported, "I've cut off some plants and grass and shredded them up. I've taken them over to the right hemisphere and threw them all over the place. Green shoots are growing in the former arid sand of the right hemisphere." He also mentioned that the right hemisphere was very happy about the change.

Pete took a truckload of white corpuscles from the left hemisphere over to the right hemisphere. The white corpuscles looked like those little men scrubbers in the cleanser commercial. They began to eat the black plastic off the charred area. Then they began to munch on the charred area itself. "They're trying to clean it all up. Now, the right side is thinking about what it wants to give . . . . The best present I can give my left side is a big hug."

Drea instinctively felt that the relationship between the two hemispheres was strained. "I'd like to do something about the left hemisphere. It looks terrible. The right hemisphere has a lot of color to it. It feels healthy, but the left hemisphere doesn't at all. It seems as if there's a void there, something not functioning right." The therapist recommended that she ask the right brain to share some of its health with its sister brain. But she replied, "No, it doesn't work that way! It seems almost like a different voltage. I think that's why I'm having trouble with it because it needs something different, but I don't know quite what to do." In the next session, she continued with the problem: "The right brain says it wants to push things through to the left brain, but the left brain can't receive . . . . Hm, I got a really odd picture of something like gold pouring through from the right hemisphere. I think it's good for the left brain. That's strange, the left half of my brain feels warmer. Hm, it's too heavy. It's good but it's too heavy. I think I'll put in a vacuum so there's less gravity. No, I don't think that'd work. It might collapse." The therapist suggested that she ask the left brain what it would like. She answered, "Oddly enough, to get rid of the gold. I don't know why. It looks all right." The therapist proposed that she ask the right brain to take it back. She reported, "Yeah, the right brain took it back. You know what? I think it did some good. It left behind a fine film of gold dust. The flow was what was important. Just the process of bringing it from right to left and back again to right." Later, after an involved discussion with both hemispheres, she said, "The right brain feels overtaxed. The left brain isn't too bothered. It doesn't see itself as sick. I don't think they are saying to leave things as they are. It's just that I can do something, but no sudden changes."

One general principle emerges from these varied experiences: if there is a free exchange between the two hemispheres, it generally feels good. If the exchange is faulty or lacking, the person has work to do before he/she can proceed. Another outcome of the exchange of gifts or of the inability to make the exchange is the accentuation of the difference between the two hemispheres.

Experiencing Health or Illness in the Hemisphere

Generally, clients feel that one hemisphere is either healthier or sicker than the other, depending on their general assessment of self. Often it is possible to take a gift from the healthy hemisphere to the sick one. The gift may improve the condition of the sick hemisphere. Sometimes, however, the sick hemisphere is too ill to receive it, or the gift feels too alien to be of use.

Ann never said that her left brain was sick. However, her description of it was extremely negative. "It's so cold and bleak. It chills me right down to the marrow just standing here in front of the open door. It's so very cold. Even my stomach is cold." (She shivers and holds herself.)

Richard, at one point, said, "We discover the left brain is feeling cocky and especially lively at the expense of the right, which is hurt and threatened."

Pete, who actually had had one operation for a brain tumor and had recently had a brain scan, which was indecisive, said of his right brain, "First of all, you know how a charred log looks. He's a real pal, but he's been hurt."

Drea described her feelings by saying, "I'd like to do something about the left hemisphere. It looks terrible. The right hemisphere has a lot of color to it. It feels healthy, but the left hemisphere doesn't at all. It seems as if there's a void there, something not functioning right . . . . One more interesting thing: I had meningitis when I was a child. The feeling was the same as the one that just came over me." On her next visit to the left hemisphere, she said, "It's really sore to the touch. I don't think I should touch it. It seems to bleed."

Usually, I do not take the description of a brain in a literal sense. In most cases, I believe the psyche is simply using the brain as the site of the sickness. Drea said at the conclusion of her statement about meningitis, "I got a picture of my spiritual self crying." The visit to the left and right hemispheres is an excellent model to test relative health. My tentative hypothesis is this: if the hemispheres are closed off from each other, or unacquainted with each other, or dislike each other, or will not work together, or if one is completely subservient to the other, there is a problem of some kind in body, mind, or spirit.

Serious Problems Symbolized in the Visit

Relatively healthy persons may encounter blocks and hindrances in the course of the visit, but, in general, they are able to move freely in each hemisphere and through the corpus callosum. They soon feel some empathy with each hemisphere and some relationship between them. In addition, they sooner or later experience some control of the mind processes. However, those with serious emotional or physical problems will experience one or more of the following symbols:

1. The client encounters an inability to enter either or both of the hemispheres. It is rare for a person to be long blocked from visiting both hemispheres. However, one hemisphere may be blocked for a lengthy period during therapy.

2. The client is unable to pass through the corpus callosum at all or to go through in one direction but not in the other. This block appears to be the most serious symbol of an illness.

3. Both conditions 1 and 2 exist at the same time. It is fairly common for a person to be unable to find the opening to the corpus callosum or to go through it in the direction of the closed hemisphere. Conversely, it is always easy to go through the corpus callosum to the open hemisphere.

4. The client may feel that one hemisphere extends beyond the middle of the brain. Here, the corpus callosum does not feel right, or there is no true center. This lack of a true center is very disturbing to the client.

5. The corpus callosum may appear to run up or down hill, or even both at the same time. Or, one hemisphere feels heavier than the other and thus tips the corpus callosum.

Whenever a combination of the above is present, the state of health appears to be serious. In one cancer case, most of the above conditions were present, but the worst symbol was an impregnable, black, lead plate between the hemispheres blocking off the corpus callosum. Another person with cancer reported, "When I'm in my left hemisphere, I don't even know I have cancer; when I'm in my right hemisphere, I know I have cancer, but I can't get to it to do anything about it." A client suffering from multiple sclerosis reported an impassible chasm, "dry as a desert," between the two hemispheres. Although clients sense that something is wrong when one of these symbols is present, they may be unaware of a malfunctioning of the brain or of an immediate relationship to an existing disease. Also, they often do not recognize that the symbols indicate a split between mind and body. However, I believe, not only are these true symbols of illness of body, mind, or spirit, but, even more to the point, they are symbols of the "unholistic" mind. Any of the symbols may or may not be indicative of a split between the mind and the body.

The Experience of Centering

It is not yet clear to me whether the left hemisphere or the right is dominant within the guided-fantasy experience. However, what is clear in the initial experience and what is very surprising to many is the sense that no one is in control. Whenever dominance of one hemisphere occurs, it is still up to the client to be the go-between to aid each hemisphere become acquainted with the other, to initiate cooperation between the two, and to work out the maximal and most natural process of interaction between them. Symbolically, this result is achieved within guided fantasy by establishing the center of the corpus callosum as a personal space or area. Here the client learns to be friends with both hemispheres, appreciating both equally for their specific and unique functioning. The more the client learns about each hemisphere, the more "control" he/she has over the processes. Eventually even the so-called autonomic systems respond.

Generally, the center is relatively easy to establish. The client is asked to be in the center of the corpus callosum and become acquainted with that center. Then the client can furnish the area as desired. I sometimes suggest a bed or recliner or table and chair. The experience of resting or sleeping in the center is, by and large, refreshing and recreating. In fact, I advise my clients to visualize themselves in their centers when they go to sleep at night. Subsequently, the center becomes a conference area where both hemispheres can meet. A surprising degree of objectivity can be gained from this conference. Finally, the center becomes a quiet place to meditate and to integrate experiences.

A very practical activity which takes place at the center is self-healing. From the center, most clients are able to look down through their bodies. They can see and talk with any organs, identify trouble spots, and may be able to "heal" the troubled area. This self-healing is sometimes done from the center and sometimes by an on-the-spot visit.

Toward the end of a group session, Sally looked down through her body and saw a strange sight. She could see her whole circulatory system except for her hands and feet. It ended at her wrists and ankles. She exclaimed, "No wonder I have cold hands and cold feet!" Unfortunately, there was insufficient time to work on this problem. However, she did feel that from the center, she could learn to work more closely with her body to improve the circulatory system.

Mary's left and right hemispheres used the corpus callosum as a place where they could meet freely. At the same time, they valued their individuality. This common room grew larger and larger, until it was larger than both remaining hemispheres. It became her favorite area. On one occasion, inhabitants from both sides were jitterbugging in mixed pairs. "Amazingly, I see them as bright forms now." After enjoying watching them, she called them over and talked with them about her physical problems. A professor among them was their spokesman. He explained in symbolic language the injury to her heel. Then she went down to the heel and looked at the spur from that perspective. "There are flashing red and green lights. The red flashing lights look like danger to me." She came back up to the common room and shared her experience. They told her, there was inflammation and pain, but it would not last long. The green was overcoming the red. She then asked about her weight problem. They showed her a series of images — first in slow motion and then gradually more quickly until it made an interesting design. The professor explained the event as a symbolic acceleration of her metabolism. I saw her a month later. She reported that her heel spur was all healed, a weight reduction of about thirty pounds, and a greatly increased feeling of total well-being. She considered the visit to her left and right hemispheres as the most significant influence among the various fantasies she had experienced.

Ward initiated a flow between the left and right hemispheres. A week later he reported, "The flow keeps going in both directions. Now the flow has carried me into my body, where there's a muscle spasm. The muscle is asking me to take care and be in control of more situations. The flow is advising me to take better care of myself. It warns me not to feel total rejection. That aspect has been too dominant in my life." He gained new confidence, took a long training course for a new position, and upon completion passed all the tests.

The Experience of Transcendence

Perhaps even more importantly, this merging of the two hemispheres, or this integration of brain functioning, leads to the experience of self-transcendence. Clients report "peak experiences" of various kinds. Richard, the skeptical college professor, is a case in point. Initially, he had no difficulty entering his left hemisphere but was unable to gain access to his right. After several sessions, he was able to enter the right hemisphere as well. Nevertheless, conflict persisted until the fifth session, when he was able to achieve a comfortable merging of the two hemispheres.

He discribed the merger of left and right hemispheres as the creation of a new entity; the familiar, left hemisphere with its grey, stoney exterior, now had a warm red interior. The corpus callosum had been transformed from an eight-foot bridge into a suspension bridge, larger than the Golden Gate or George Washington bridges. The entire structure was supported on one column only, and this column was the "peanut-sized," combined left-right brain. The bridge lay suspended in a pale grey sky. Eager to explore this new area, Richard went out to the end of the bridge and saw nothing but space or sky all around him. The plot development from that moment was fascinating. He began a journey that was to take him to a remote island, where he was welcomed as a godlike ruler. The natives had been awaiting him and were eager to hear his message: "Rise up. Stand on your own two feet. Look at the sky. You are your own greatest strength. You have that within you which will make you great. You have waited a long time for me, and now I have come. And you will know that the message I have to bring you is of your salvation. Rise up and meet your own destiny." The message was electrifying to the natives. They held a grand procession, elevating the king on their shoulders. The fantasy concluded with the king being given a gift of a beautiful woman, with whom he spent the night in splendid lovemaking.

After returning to the bridge, Richard reported feeling a tremendous pull, a force coming from the outer reaches of the space he had explored. He found both the left and the right hemispheres constricted and narrow, even in their merged state. More significantly, they seemed to have had no part in this experience. Richard emerged from the fantasy experience with a feeling of exhilaration, and he felt that in some special way his experience had been profound. He felt as if he had become part of a reality infinitely larger than himself.

Richard's experience is somewhat unusual in that it seemed to take place apart from or outside of both hemispheres. More often, the hemispheres are enhanced by the transcendent experience, although they seem not to directly participate in the experience. The experience of transcendence is sometimes felt to occur within one of the hemispheres. However, the focal point is the Self experiencing the transcendent quality rather than the hemisphere giving rise to a transcendent experience.

Spontaneous models like Richard's cosmic bridge bring on the experience of transcendence. However, a model or starting image can be induced, for example, in the following way: "Be in your center. Above you is a chapel, a holy place, a meditation center, a temple. Explore it as you wish." A rich variety of transpersonal experiences are felt as the individual explores freely. If, however, a person is blocked from entering this experience or encounters blocks inside the chapel, the guide simply proceeds on the basis that another learning dilemma is present. For example, a woman found her chapel completely closed to her. There were two-by-sixes across the front and back doors and across all the windows. She was saddened by this sight and sat weeping in front of the chapel. To her surprise, a warm nose nuzzled her hand; there was a fawn beside her. She was greatly comforted and set to work on the chapel. It took several sessions before she could unbar the doors and windows. Now the chapel and her fawn are a constant source of comfort and strength. Her experience is quite a contrast to Richard's; yet, both appear to be equally valid.

Additional experiences can be induced within both the spontaneous and the given starting image: "Wherever you are in your experience, you notice a beam of sunlight from above you; it forms a cone of light large enough to enclose you completely. Walk into it and feel its richness."

Generally, this image is a fruitful one, although it may not have the power of some of the purely spontaneous ones. Participants describe the ensuing experience as "comforting," "cleansing," "warming," "peaceful," "enriching," "strengthening."

The feeling of transcendence also may be initiated by the following instructions: "You feel a presence near you, or you may see a picture or a statue of an admired figure. Ask the presence to become visible, or ask the figure in the picture or the statue to come alive and talk with you."

Some talk with deceased loved ones, others to guides or religious personages. Most find the experience to be rich and meaningful. Once again, for those who are unable to enter into any of these relationships, the exercise becomes a learning experience in overcoming blocks.

The rich variety of transpersonal experiences attests to the functioning of the holistic mind. The transcendent experience is greatly enhanced when the two hemispheres are friends, when the center is well established, and when the person is able to move freely between the hemispheres. Of course, these three qualities are hallmarks of the holistic mind.

Summary

Most participants in the "visit" were surprised to find initial hindrances, blocks, and difficulties in moving freely. For some, the lack of a sound relationship between the hemispheres was unexpected. Still others were not prepared for the indifference or hostility which the hemispheres expressed for each other. However, a minority had little or no trouble in achieving some degree of holism during the first session. By and large, the excitement of all participants was related to both the resolution of the problems and the experience of various qualities of the holistic mind — openness, centeredness, integration, and transcendence.

One outcome of the "visit" is greater left hemisphere - right hemisphere integration. Many clients reported that one hemisphere seemed to function at the expense of the other. Others sensed that one hemisphere was too practical and the other provided little or no creativity. As a result, there was little real productivity. Later, when the clients reported that the two hemispheres were working together, there was a substantial improvement in functioning. Within the guided fantasy, this cooperation is often symbolized as a flow back and forth between the two hemispheres, producing a unity of functioning. This unity is one aspect of the holistic mind.

A very practical result of taking control of the mind from within or of experiencing the holistic mind, is both mental and physical healing. Such healing seems to be an automatic consequence of the increased feeling of well-being. It may be initiated by overcoming blocks within the corpus callosum, or by gaining entrance into a hemisphere which previously had been closed, or by establishing a friendship with a previously unknown or unfamiliar hemisphere, or by simply learning the individual functions of each hemisphere. The symbolism most directly related to increased mental health is seen in the experience of healing a sick hemisphere. In my opinion, emotional and mental health are related directly to the free and equal functioning of the two hemispheres. If the relationship of the two hemispheres meets the client's approval, then he/she testifies to good mental health.

The "visit" has been valuable to my clients in other ways. The starting image provides them with a workshop to improve the functioning of the brain. They experience a clarification of purpose and direction which allows them to use their brain to engage in activities previously thought too difficult or even impossible. In addition, they feel that they are taking control of their hemispheres and thus achieve a fuller utilization of the brain potential. Many clients testify that one of the most beneficial outcomes of the holistic-mind experience is in the release of hidden potential. The possibility of taking control of the brain's functioning is a major revelation for those who often feel that they are not in control of themselves. It is important to know that the brain as well as the body is one's servant and not one's master.

Finally, the experience of the holistic mind brings about a feeling of body-mind-spirit unity. But first, one must experience a direct relationship individually with these three aspects of the self. In the visit to the hemispheres, one senses the distinctive quality of each. Then, through the exercise of centering, particularly, one becomes aware of the unity of the mind. A new appreciation of the body is gained both from looking at the body and its functioning from the vantage point of the center or by a visit to any part of the body. The experience of transcendence brings a conviction of the reality of the spirit. The three experiences are unified or blended in the centering experience in the corpus callosum, and thus the person becomes aware of the oneness of body, mind, and spirit.

REFERENCES

Ahsen, A. Eidetics: An overview. *Journal of Mental Imagery,* 1977, *1*, 5-38. (a)

Ahsen, A. *Psycheye: Self-analytic consciousness.* New York: Brandon House, 1977. (b)

Bogen, J. E. The other side of the brain, II: An appositional mind. *Bulletin of the Los Angeles Neurological Society,* 1969, *34*, 135-162.

Gazzaniga, M. S. The split brain in man. *Scientific American,* August, 1967, *217*, No. 2, 24-29.

Gazzaniga, M. *The bisected brain.* New York: Appleton-Century-Crofts, 1970.

Ornstein, R. E. *The psychology of human consciousness.* San Francisco: Freeman, 1973.

Progoff, I. *The symbolic and the real.* New York: Julian Press, 1963.

Samples, B. *The metaphoric mind.* Reading, Mass.: Addison-Wesley Publishing Co., 1976.

Shaffer, J. T. *Induced guided fantasy: Therapist's kit.* Jacksonville, IL: Psychologists and Educators, Inc., 1972.

Shaffer, J. T. *Psychefeedback: The use of induced guided fantasy as a creative therapeutic process.* Unpublished manuscript, 1978.

Sheikh, A. A. Eidetic Psychotherapy. In J. L. Singer & K. Pope (Eds.), *The power of human imagination,* Plenum Publishing Corporation, New York, 1978.

Sheikh, A. A., & Panagiotou, N.C. Use of mental imagery in psychotherapy: A critical review. *Perceptual and motor skills,* 1975, *41,* 555-585.

Singer, Jerome L. *Imagery and daydream methods in psychotherapy and behavior modification.* New York: Academic Press, 1974.

Sperry, R. W. Cerebral organization and behavior. *Science,* 1961, *133,* 1749-1757.

Zangwill, O. L. The current status of cerebral dominance. *Research Publication Association Research Nervous Mental Disorders,* 1964, *42,* 103-113.

12

Between Wakefulness and Sleep: Hypnagogic Fantasy

PETER McKELLAR

I often get a bit angry with people who think psychology began with Wilhelm Wundt and Leipzig. Two and a half thousand years ago Aristotle had observations to make about the subject I will be discussing in this paper. I quote: "To some young people, even when their eyes are wide open, if it is dark, many moving images appear" (Parva Naturalia). Aristotle added, "Often they cover their heads in fear" of them. Let us zoom in and have a good look at these oddities of mental life: these eruptions of imagery into drowsy conscious before sleep. From Aristotle to Chaucer, from Spinoza to Freud, many people have found them interesting, amusing, or terrifying. Finally in 1848, Alfred Maury gave them a name: "hypnagogic imagery." They have been known under many names. Even today people with appropriate belief systems sometimes view them as "glimpses of another world," "visions from a previous incarnation," or clairvoyant "pictures of some other place." For my own part, I prefer Maury's name, "hypnagogic imagery," together with the framework of naturalistic science to these alternatives. Surrealist painters have made use of the imagery, as Max Ernst has testified (McKellar, in press). Wagner composed his Rheingold overture from auditory hypnagogic imagery. Wordsworth, Coleridge, Poe, Hoffmann, and others used them in literature. Three terrifying, imaginative novels have had partly hypnagogic origins: *Dr. Jekyll and Mr. Hyde, Frankenstein,* and *The Castle of Otranto* (McKellar, 1957, 1975). The full contribution imagery has made to visual and literary art has not yet been fully examined. And as regards science, we all know about Kekule, his dozing on the top of

Peter McKellar, Department of Psychology, University of Otago Dunedin, New Zealand.

a London bus, and the benzene ring. The startling creative originality of the imagery has impressed many. Subjects have often told me that they wished they had the talent to paint the beautiful hypnagogic landscapes and moonscapes they have visualized. Freud (1923) referred to dreams as "something alien, arising from another world, contrasting with the remaining contents of the mind." Hypnagogic imagery has this same quality, indeed more so. To use Morton Prince's (1909) analogy: "It is like putting your hand into someone else's pocket, and taking out something not your own." My own preferences lie with Morton Prince rather than with Freud. The imagery seems to erupt into consciousness from some dissociated subsystem of the personality.

Warren's *Dictionary of Psychology* defines it as "imagery of any sense modality, frequently of hallucinatory vividness, occurring in the drowsy state before deep sleep." Certainly the images may be very vivid indeed. As Aristotle observed, the visual ones are sometimes experienced open-eyed in a darkened room. Auditory hypnagogic imagery is often confused with real perception. I have many instances of would-be sleepers who have risen from bed to answer telephones, turn off television, or respond to purely hypnagogic doorbells. Yet, by contrast, hypnagogic imagery can be unobtrusive. It is going on but passes unnoticed until people are alerted to attend to it. During our first research project in the 1950s, Lorna Simpson and I obtained reports from Aberdeen University students: a majority of them, 63%, reported the imagery. We as researchers possessed a good combination of qualifications: Lorna did not have the imagery, I did. But we had not gone far into the study, before she realized she did have it also. This figure of 63% is almost certainly an underestimate. Errors of exclusion are probable. I have encountered individuals who have denied having the imagery, only to later discover that they did have it regularly, even nightly. In one smaller study, of 60 subjects with the imagery, half reported it once a month, 17 reported it once a week, and 13 declared they had it several times weekly.

From various data (e.g., Leaning, 1925; McKellar, 1957, 1968, 1977; Schacter, 1976; Sheehan, 1972), let me distinguish two kinds of visual hypnagogic imagery. Type A are hypnagogic sequences. These take the form of rapidly changing successions of familiar and unfamiliar objects, persons, or scenes; for example, a snowscape, wharf, head of bird, old Victorian building, various marine shells, a tall tree, more shells, etc. Their changes of shape and their three dimensionality led an imager to liken them to "things stuck on, or hanging from, a mobile." Words like "bizarre" and "random" accurately describe these Type A, hypnagogic sequences. I tend to think of them as a pile of lantern slides that have tumbled on the floor, been picked up and then shown in an utterly random order. The Type B images are different: they are hypnagogic episodes, scenes or mini-plays of longer duration; for example, one imager reported "a family of skulls in a car, driving along." He added, "I could see the expressions on their faces. I could tell it was a friendly family. They were all skeletons . . . no, it wasn't at all frightening. On the whole it was rather jolly." Whether they are Type A sequences or Type B episodes, hypnagogic images exhibit what one subject described as "endless variety." Landscapes are common: some subjects report they tend to occur later rather than earlier in the hypnagogic period. Disneylike cartoons often occur, taking the form of visual jokes. Imagers are often amused by them; for example, "A cartoon sabretoothed tiger tiptoes on hind legs up to some unseen victim, paws held up near face . . . suddenly a striped tiger's arm comes around from behind and covers the sabre-toothed tiger's eyes." Maury himself, like many imagers, often saw grotesque and distorted faces. His usually had bizarre hairstyles. He never saw the face of anybody he knew. My own hypnagogic faces likewise involve an internal population other than my personal friends and acquaintances. It is easy to understand how, with appropriate belief systems, such faces could be given occult interpretation. In some societies, and for some individuals, clearly they are evil spirits, demons malevolently waiting for sleep to occur, then moving in to possess the sleeper.

I have been discussing content. We have already noted some of the emotional responses to such content; for example, amusement and fear. Another emotion is anger. I am still quite cross about one of my own hypnagic images. In it I saw a group of people: as usual they were strangers. Then another stranger appeared, produced a handgun, and proceeded to shoot them down. Although the image was the product of some subsystem of my own mental life, I was very indignant. These people were doing nothing to hurt anybody: they were innocent victims of unprovoked aggression. It will be remembered that the novel *Dr. Jekyll and Mr. Hyde* was itself, in part, a product of Stevenson's own hypnagogic imaging. In my case, as a kind of Dr. Jekyll, I wished to disown the hypnagogic Mr. Hyde who had emerged from myself and done the shooting. One does feel responsible. Such concern is another of the emotional reactions reported; at times the imager on return to wakefulness feels an obligation to doze off again and put things right in some previous hypnagogic episode. Overall, like the content, the emotional reactions provoked by the imagery vary widely.

For the most part, the imager himself does not appear in the imagery. "I watched but did not participate" is a typical comment. There are exceptions. The following example is of interest in that it also involved changing into an animal. In his hypnagogic nightmare, the imager found himself a member of a group of sheep standing outside a slaughter house. He told me, "I was one of them. We moved up the gangway. I could feel what all the sheep felt." In the image, he saw the slaughterman's face and the expression on it. The image was very frightening indeed.

Let us now turn to the relationship between hypnagogic fantasy and perceptual origins of the content. Some hypnagogic imagery is of the flashback kind. Subjects report that their hypnagogic sequences include memory images of past events, often childhood events. These images are suggestive of the brain stimulation phenomena that had interested Penfield at McGill (see Ahsen, 1977; Sheikh & Panagiotou, 1975). My own subjects also report, within sequences, flashes of memories of dreams they have had in the past. Sexual imagery and sexual symbolism may likewise occur within sequences, though often in this rather casual flashback form. More generally, we can make a distinction between two main types of hypnagogic visualization. These I have labelled "perseverative" on the one hand, and "impersonal or archetypal" on the other. In the perseverative type, the perceptual origins are obvious. The imagery relates back to events of the day or at least to recent events. Many people who have done fruit picking are familiar with it. After a day of berry picking, one imager reported seeing "raspberries, endless raspberries." One regular imager, a science student, can very largely predict his perseverative imagery. On the evenings of Tuesdays, after 3-1/2 hours of laboratory work, he will see shells: "It will be a night of shells." These perseverative images will be known to many gardeners. Those who weed their gardens by species may report how that specific weed, and that one alone, will loom up as a hypnagogic perseveration. Recently I did a "mixed" weeding. The night that followed was a veritable hypnagogic botany lesson on the weeds of a New Zealand garden. There they all were: docks, dandelions, convolvulus roots, and others I could not name but with which I had been dealing sternly that afternoon. They surged up to my drowsy consciousness without any control on my part. I watched the botany lesson with interest.

In contrast to the perseverative kind, the impersonal type of imagery has an archetypal quality. It exhibits Freud's feature of "something alien;" it seems to come "from another world." Origins in previous perception are difficult, sometimes impossible to locate. They are interestingly, amusingly, or alarmingly foreign to the imager's usual mental life: they are "places I have never visited," and "people I have never met." This quality may tempt some imagers to suspect an occult or otherworldly source. It is easy to at least half believe that the images are glimpses of some other place; for example, the imager saw "a young girl, a princess, dark skinned (probably Aztec), lying on the ground, head towards me, yawning and wearing a brilliant headdress of predominantly scarlet, blue, and yellow, with a front-piece of beaten metal," with plumes. My own interest in hypnagogic imagery first arose during a series of experiments we were doing at Aberdeen with mescaline and LSD (Ardis & McKellar, 1956). As subject in one early mescaline experiment, I sought to communicate my drug-induced imagery to the experimenters. I found an analogy with hypnagogic imagery. Later I learned from the research literature that very many other researchers had similarly, and independently, noted this same resemblance. In one of the earliest reported mescaline experiments, Weir Mitchell reported that, after taking the drug, he found the visions increased when he lay down and relaxed in a darkened room and almost fell asleep

(Ardis & McKellar, 1956). From these and other data I conclude three things. First, there are strong resemblances between these types of imagery; secondly, drug and hypnagogic drowsiness may summate; thirdly, hallucinogenic substances may alert us to notice psychological processes that are already there and going on all the time. Among them I would include hypnagogic imagery.

Whether they are perseverative or impersonal and archetypal, hypnagogic visualizations exhibit a marked degree of autonomy. They erupt spontaneously. The imager, though their author, lacks control over their occurrence and content. In this they resemble typical dreams, though in the case of dreamlife there is the interesting exception of lucid dreams. In these, the sleeper knows that he is asleep, knows that he is dreaming, and may have some control over dream events. There are some exceptions to the generally autonomous character of hypnagogic imagery also. Some of my subjects reported a measure of control. One subject — he has the imagery more or less nightly — defined his control in these terms. He told me that he sees a lot of landscapes. He said, "The scene is going on of its own accord, but I can put something in." He gave an example: "I can't say, 'I'll have a square cloud,' but I can say, 'I'd like a different one, thanks.' And a different one will come. You can't specify." His gratitude and word of thanks towards his obligingly autonomous imagery system may be noted!

Somebody is bound to ask, "How do we know a person is having, or reporting, a hypnagogic image and not a dream?" A short answer is that you can sound record hypnagogic experiences at the time. I have done this often. I have yet to encounter an introspective, as opposed to merely a retrospective, tape recording of a dream. Even lucid dreamers might find this difficult. In the research literature, there is an account of one regular lucid dreamer who, in his dream, would cry out, shout, and even sing. But he never broke through to his adjacent sleeping wife, who heard nothing. As regards introspective tape recordings of hypnagogic experiences, my work recently has been heavily indebted to two subjects. They are science students at Otago University, though neither is a psychology student. I gratefully acknowledge the help of Mr. Rob Guyton and Mr. Phil Scadden, who have — as regular hypnagogic imagers — systematically studied their own images. They have been coinvestigators rather than mere subjects. They have drawn their imagery, painted it, tape-recorded it, and patiently gone over these visual and auditory records with me. I will now add some additional observations, drawn largely from their work and our interview, making use of other data as necessary.

(1) The distinction between hypnagogic (presleep) and hypnopompic (postsleep) imagery does not lie merely in the former being evening images and the latter being morning images. One can doze off in the morning and have a hypnagogic rather than hypnopompic image. My two observers find a difference in character between typical nightly and typical morning hypnagogic imagery. The sequences of images occurring at night seem to proceed to form themselves before the gaze of the would-be sleeper. In the mornings, when the imager has had a

period of sleep and his mind is less cluttered with the day's events, the images tend to appear more ready-made rather than to form themselves.

(2) My observers suggest, that, at least in their own cases, there appear to be layers and layers of the imagery. Beneath those in the foreground, are additional ones to be examined. There is the strong impression that the imagery is, in some sense, there to be noticed or overlooked.

(3) During a hypnagogic sequence of imagery, introduction of eyelid pressure may produce some additional effects. There occurs, as a result of this inadequate stimulation, an orange blob. This assumes the function of a television screen.

(4) My two observers, though they usually enjoy their imagery, report that on occasion it can still be frightening. Sometimes it is intrinsically terrifying. Sometimes, however, an aura of fear becomes attached to neutral imagery. Here I suspect the emotion is free-floating and the imagery itself more secondary. In less sophisticated adults and children, the relations to superstition, fears of psychosis, and nightmares seem obvious.

(5) The beauty of much of the imagery merits emphasis. As with mescaline imagery, the colors may be described in such terms as "strange luminosity," "liquid fire," "bathed in fiercest sunlight," or "moonlit." My subjects described their own dream imagery as inferior in color qualities to the imagery. One added that he often saw the images as though "through a gauze curtain — like a poorly adjusted television set."

(6) Polyopia may occur: multiple repetitions of some figure or object may be present; for example, one imager saw "hundreds of pink cockatoos, on an outdoor table, by a hedge talking."

(7) Micropsia may figure in the imagery; for example, an imager reported "antlike figures carrying something," and "something tiny will wriggle and turn into something: a milk bottle with tiny bubbles."

(8) Several hypnagogic synaesthesias occurred. Mr. Guyton had a series of these while dozing and listening to Ravel's "Bolero." He saw bubblelike figures that would run in slow motion in time with the music, and also a pale skeleton figure, and later a stick insect, rocking in time with the bass. Ardis and I cited some other instances of hypnagogic synaesthesias in our article comparing mescaline and hypnagogic imagery.

(9) Duration aries. We have noted the rapid sequences on the one hand and hypnagogic episodes on the other. One of my earlier subjects had an image of an alligator which he timed to last for 2-1/2 minutes, a field of wheat lasting 50 seconds, and a pencil shape which lasted 18 seconds. My two subjects reported that their images, in longer sequences, seemed to last about 10 seconds. One had evolved a method of timing from his own breathing. On his tape he reported, "I've just watched one which lasted 10 breaths."

(10) It is possible to study source material of the imagery through free association. In order to illustrate let us take a hypnagogic image of a woman feeding a black cur-

rant pie to a fish. The associations which had produced the image did these: that evening a little girl had showed the imager her new dress with a fish design on it, and the meal that night had included black currant pie. Hypnagogic juxtaposition had done the rest.

Their availability of the imagery to introspection, not mere retrospection, gives it advantages over dreams. The 10 points upon which I have commented, all arise from the possibility of such introspection, including sound recording.

Well, what is it? How do we explain it? In any case, do we need to explain it at all? It seems to me probable that such imagery reflects the pulse beat of spontaneous mental life. It is there to be noticed if we are introspectively literate, or ignored if we have not become aware of it, or are preoccupied with outward events. I suspect — along with Ian Oswald and some other researchers — that hypnagogic imaging is a universal human phenomenon. Not everybody notices it. The imagery differences which may divide a husband from a wife may, for years, also pass unnoticed. Some people's ears exhibit fixed lobes, others have free lobes. They do not cease to have these anatomical structures simply because they have not been alerted to them.

If some explanation is necessary, I think again of Galton who distinguished a "presence chamber of consciousness" and a nearby "antechamber." He discussed the processes of creative thinking in terms of these chambers in which "one portion of the mind communicates with another portion, as with another person." For my part, I am delighted that Hilgard is doing so much to bring dissociation theory back into psychology. In my own forthcoming book on *Dissociation and Multiple Personality*, I intend to give him a helping hand. As Hilgard (1977) has put it, "Daily life is full of many small dissociations, this is provided we know how to look for them." Among them are many interesting forms of autonomous mental imagery of which hypnagogic fantasy is an excellent example. In one of his tape recordings, Mr. Scadden reported of his hypnagogic imagery: "carrying over things I had been dreaming about . . . a state of oscillating between half consciousness and unconsciousness." The recording stopped at this point and sleep ensued. This reference to oscillating between the hypnagogic and sleeping state is of interest. On the one hand there is normal waking consciousness, on the other the dreaming subsystem, with a fragile hypnagogic bridge between them. Memory may, or may not, link full wakefulness with dreamlife. On waking we are often conscious of having forgotten the dream we have been experiencing. In the hypnagogic bridge between the two, we may be able to recall a little of it and resist this slipping away into total forgetfulness. It is like tuning in to one television station and thus excluding an alternative program. In the intermediate hypnagogic state we are able, sometimes, to switch back to the other station and continue the program. In Morton Prince's famous case, we encounter the introspections — not mere retrospections — of the Sally subsystem who was able to remain awake while B.1 or B.1V slept and dreamed. Sally, an acute introspectionist, was well placed to testify that much more dreaming occurred than the waking Miss Beauchamp was able to remember. That was all recorded at the start of this century. It was not until 1953 that other evidence — from Aserinsky and Kleitman — confirmed or rediscovered this important finding for imagery research. Eventually we may be able to make a distinction between those who notice, attend to, and recall their hypnagogic imagery, and those to whom it passes unnoticed and forgotten.

Psychologists like Lawrence Kubie postulate a "preconscious stream" of continuous information processing. This continues for 24 hours a day. In dreams and waking hallucinations we are aware of it, when external perception does not blot it out. There are, as C. W. Savage has said, images that "flow on by their own law." He adds, "I can terminate my visual perceptions by closing my eyes, and I can terminate visual fantasies experienced with eyes closed by opening my eyes" (Savage, 1975, p. 273). There is a great deal of what Granit has called "spontaneous activity of the sense organs" themselves, which as he says make them "one of the brain's most important energizers" (Granit, 1955). There is a great deal of "visual noise" going on, and many investigators regard entoptic activity of the visual system as contributing to hypnagogic visualizations. In imaging, as in dreaming, we are not projecting memories of past experience onto a blank sheet. We are doing something more like responding to a Rorschach ink blot. This may have something to do with the autonomy, originality, and archetypelike quality of hypnagogic fantasy. In his important early paper on these phenomena — Wundt called them "luminous dust" — G. T. Ladd (1892) wrote, "There is no shape known to me by perception or by fantasy, . . . that has not been schematically represented by the changing retinal images" (Ladd, 1892, p. 300).

This process of interpretation of the visual Rorschach takes place in a drowsy state in which higher brain activity is relaxed. Random bits of memory are there to provide a loose schema, a dim but broad rather than narrow-beamed searchlight. This aids fantasy, but, as the early studies of Silberer on autosymbolic processes showed, it does not assist precise, conceptual thought. As Silberer (1909) wrote, "The tired consciousness switches to an easier mode of mental functioning." The work of Herbert Silberer, a man of genius and great originality, is well worth additional study by those of us who are unashamedly fascinated by the beauty, creativeness, and intrinsic interest of hypnagogic fantasy.

REFERENCES

Ahsen, A. Eidetics: An overview. *Journal of Mental Imagery*, 1977, *1*, 5-38.

Ardis, J. A. & McKellar, P. Hypnagogic imagery and mescaline. *Journal of Mental Science*, 1956, *102*, 22-29.

Aserinsky, E. & Kleitman, N. Regularly occurring periods of eye motility and concomitant phenomena during sleep. *Science*, 1953, *118*, 273-274.

Freud, S. The ego and the id. (1923), in J. Strachey (Ed.), *The standard edition of the complete works of Sigmund Freud*, Vol. 19, London, Hogarth, 1955.

Granit, R. *Receptors and sensory perception,* New York: Yale University Press, 1955.

Hilgard, E. R. *Divided consciousness.* New York: Wiley, 1977.

Ladd, G. T. Contributions to the psychology of visual dreams. *Mind* (New Series), 1892, *1,* 299-304.

Leaning, F. E. An introductory study of hypnagogic phenomena. *Proceedings of the Society for Psychical Research,* 1925, *25,* 289-403.

Maury, A. *Le sommeil et les rêves,* Paris: Didier, 1861.

McKellar, P. *Imagination and thinking.* New York: Basic Books, 1957.

McKellar, P. *Experience and behaviour.* Harmondsworth: Penguin Books, 1968.

McKellar, P. Autonomy, imagery, and dissociation. *Journal of Mental Imagery,* 1977, *1,* 93-108.

McKellar, P. Twixt waking and sleeping. *Psychology Today* (U. K. Edition) 1975, *4,* 20-24.

McKellar, P. *Mindsplit: Dissociation and multiple personality.* London: J. M. Dent (in press).

McKellar, P. & Simpson, L. Between wakefulness and sleep: Hypnagogic imaging. *British Journal of Psychology,* 1954, *45,* 266-276.

Prince, M. *The dissociation of a personality.* London: Longmans, 1909.

Savage, C. In Siegel, R. K. & West, L. J. *Hallucinations: behaviour, experience, and theory,* New York: Wiley, 1975.

Schacter, D. L. The hypnagogic state: A critical review of the literature. *Psychological Bulletin,* 1976, *83,* 452-481.

Sheehan, P. W. (Ed.) *The function and nature of imagery.* New York: Academic Press, 1972.

Sheikh, A. A., & Panagiotan, N. C. Use of mental imagery in psychotherapy: A critical review. *Perceptual and Motor Skills,* 1975, *41,* 555-585.

Silberer, H. Report on a method of eliciting and observing certain symbolic hallucination phenomena (1909). In Rapaport, D. (Ed.), *Organization and pathology of thought.* New York: Columbia, 1951.

Warren, H. C. (Ed.), *Dictionary of psychology.* Boston: Houghton Mifflin Co., 1934.

13

Art, Mental Imagery, and Cognition

GISELA E. SPEIDEL
ALEXANDER L. PICKENS

The visual arts have been relegated to an insignificant role in American education. Emphasis is placed on "academic" learning — the language arts, arithmetic, and more recently science. Thus, in most elementary-school programs, art instruction is the responsibility of the classroom teacher and occurs toward the end of the school day, once or twice a week. The art projects generally revolve around seasonal holidays and are initiated by the teacher who often has prepared some of the components ahead of time for the children. Although this arrangement might not be considered ideal by most educators and parents, the priorities within the short school day seem appropriate. The children must first learn the necessary skills to cope with our technological world. In contrast to other countries and other times, aesthetic experiences and aesthetic education play only a minor part in our lives. The one arena in education where the visual arts have assumed a more significant role is in nursery school and kindergarten programs. The purpose of art instruction there has been to develop perceptual and motor skills to aid reading readiness and to develop creativity.

The present writers, however, believe that engaging in the visual arts may develop skills and cognitions that are relevant to other areas of intellectual functioning. To find support for this notion, we are conducting a long-term project exploring the effects of instruction in specific art activities on cognitive development, for instance, on creative thinking, concept development, visual-motor skills, as well as on reading and arithmetic achievement.

Gisela E. Speidel, The Kamehameha Schools, 1850 Makuakane Street, Honolulu Hawaii 96817; Alexander Pickens, University of Hawaii, Honolulu, Hawaii.

How might skills and cognitions acquired in working in a particular art medium facilitate learning in other areas? One possibility is that the skills are directly transferable and applicable to other tasks. For example, we have found that instruction in printmaking developed visual discrimination (Speidel & Tharp, 1979), a skill considered basic to reading acquisition. Another possibility is through the mediation of visual memory and imagery. More and more evidence is accumulating in the learning research literature concerning the importance of visual imagery in learning. The following paragraphs will describe briefly the findings relevant to the present discussion.

Imagery and Learning

Evidence that visual imagery and nonverbal memory are processes separate from verbal, symbolic processes is strong and comes from a variety of sources. Reaction time studies have shown that response time is faster when stimulus letters are physically identical as well as nominally equivalent — for example, AA — than when the letters are only nominally equivalent — for example, Aa — (Posner & Keele, 1967). The explanation given for this finding is· that processing the former type of stimulus pairs requires only the visual processing system, while processing the latter type of stimulus pairs requires both the visual and the verbal processing systems.

Another line of investigation is based on an interference paradigm: the rationale is that the processing of an ongoing task by the visual system interferes with the construction of a visual image of an immediately preceding stimulus. Thus, if one memory is held in visual form and another in verbal form, and the subject subsequently is given a task requiring visual processing, he/she will remember the verbal form better than the visual image. On the other hand, if he/she were given a subsequent verbal task, the reverse would be expected. Several studies based on this particular paradigm have found such modality specific interference effects, confirming that visual imagery rather than implicit verbal responses may mediate certain memories (Brooks, 1968; den Heyer & Barrett, 1971).

The evidence for long-term visual memory processes is even more powerful. The memory capacity for pictures appears to be higher than for words. This is the case for recognition (Shepard, 1967) as well as for recall (Bevan & Steger, 1971). The function of visual imagery in long-term memory is particularly evident in paired-associate learning and free recall. Paivio (1971), who has conducted a long and systematic research program on the function of visual imagery in memory, has found that rated imagery or concreteness is the single best predictor of associative learning with meaningful material (Dilley & Paivio, 1968). In other words, the more concrete or imagery eliciting a stimulus is rated, the better it is remembered. This finding is upheld even when meaningfulness or Nobles' "m" is held constant

(Paivio, 1969). Furthermore, when the stimulus is rated high in imagery, it is not only remembered better, but subjects also report using images more often as their memorial strategy (Paivio, Smythe, & Yuille, 1968).

Rohwer (1970, 1973) has systematically investigated the effectiveness of different types of mental imagery strategies on paired-associate learning. It appears that the most facilitative imagery is one in which there is an interaction between the two items (the shoe taps the chair), while the least effective one is an image that is static (the shoe and the chair). Rohwer (1970) contends that "the relevance of imagery research for education lies in the fact that such research is concerned on the one hand with properties of learning materials that facilitate acquisition, and on the other hand with the mental activities of learners that make for efficient performance." Furthermore, he maintains that children should be taught to engage in imaginal or verbal elaboration activities to increase their learning potential. Much of the earlier research on imagery processes in paired-associate learning, including Paivio's as well as Rohwer's work, is presented in a symposium, "Imagery in Children's Learning" (Reese, 1970).

Levin (1976) has expanded the research on imagery-facilitated learning and on the manner in which imagery strategies can be applied to educational situations. For instance, Levin and his associates (Lesgold, Levin, Shimron, & Guttman, 1975) have shown that children's recall of narrative-prose passages is substantially improved when pictures accompany the oral presentation. Furthermore, when upper elementary-school children are given visual-imagery instruction before reading prose passages, their comprehension scores improve (Lesgold, McCormick, & Golinkoff, 1975; Levin & Divine-Hawkins, 1974).

Independent from the above investigations, Piaget and his associates have conducted a line of study on mental imagery, particularly on its developmental characteristics (Piaget & Inhelder, 1971). On the basis of many systematic observations of children of varying ages, Piaget contends that there are two broad categories of mental images: (a) reproductive or copy images which are based on previously perceived events, including static configurations that are the result of changes in position and changes in form, and (b) anticipatory images, which envision movements, transformations, and the results of transformations.

In Piaget's theory of cognitive development, a child progresses from sensorimotor intelligence and prelogical or preoperational thought to logical or operational thought. An important milestone in the transition phase from prelogical to logical thought is the attainment of the concrete operations as reflected in the conservation tasks. The concept of conservation refers to the ability to recognize that a certain property (such as mass, quantity, volume) remains unchanged even though other properties (such as shape, spatial position, color) are transformed. For example, in one of the tasks for volume conservation, two identical glasses are filled with liquid to an equal level. After the child has agreed that the two glasses contain an equal amount of liquid, the liquid from one of the glasses is poured, before the eyes of the child, into a large flat dish. A child who conserves will state that the two differently shaped glasses still have the same amount of liquid, in spite of the fact that they now have different shapes, and appearances suggest they are unequal.

Piaget and Inhelder (1971) maintain that the reproductive images are developed early, during the preoperational years, while the anticipatory images only begin to appear during the level of concrete operations, around the age of 7 or 8. In order to determine the function that anticipatory imagery plays in the development of operational thought, Piaget and Inhelder compared children's ability to anticipate the results of a particular transformation with their ability to conserve upon seeing the transformation actually performed. On the basis of these observations, Piaget concludes that anticipatory imagery is not sufficient to give rise to operatory level of comprehension but does serve to refine the child's awareness of states which operative thought will later connect by means of reversible transformation. In other words, imagery "becomes an instrument of representation capable of serving the operations" (Piaget, 1964, p. 31) — "a symbolic tool that is complementary to that of language and, like language, promotes the progress of thought" (Inhelder, 1965, p. 18).

Levin has set out to integrate the Piagetian conceptualization of anticipatory imagery with the imagery elaboration idea in paired-association learning discussed earlier. Thus, Levin and Pressley (1978) found, just as would have been predicted from Piaget's theory, that older kindergarten children benefited more from imagery instructions on a paired-associate task than younger children; furthermore, the ability to benefit from imagery instructions was dependent upon age and age-related experiences rather than upon the effects of schooling per se. In another series of experiments, Wolff and Levin (1972) found support for Piaget's hypothesis that mental imagery, like operational thought, grows out of the early sensorimotor activity and actually represents internalized motor activity; in other words, overt motor activity provides the basis for covert imagery. Specifically, they discovered that kindergarteners who did not benefit from imagery strategy instruction on a paired-associate learning task were able to do so when allowed to generate the visual interaction externally by manipulating the stimulus materials, as well as by merely manipulating the interaction without visual input.

We have briefly summarized a number of findings which lend support to the functional existence of mental imagery as a process separate from verbal, symbolic processes. In citing this accumulating evidence, we hope to have made a case for the general importance and relevance of mental imagery to learning and education.

At the Kamehameha Early Education Program, we have launched a programmatic study to assess the effects of instruction in various visual-art media on selected cognitive skills. We are hypothesizing that it may be mental imagery that is mediating some of the learning observed in children on their performance of certain specified cognitive skills following their participation in a defined art activity.

An Exemplifying Study

The first study in this series, investigating the effects of instruction in the visual arts on selected cognitive skills in children, had shown that participation in a unit on printmaking enhanced kindergarten children's performance of two perceptual-motor skills generally considered to be part of their intellectual functioning. The present study was conducted to assess the effects of instruction in clay forming on the visual-motor development, conceptual development, and creative thinking of first graders.

Subjects. The children participating in the study were 28 first graders enrolled in a research and development school for mainly Hawaiian or part-Hawaiian children from low-income families. The children's IQ scores, as measured by the WPPSI, ranged from 89 to 127. Two groups of relatively equal intellectual distribution were constructed on the basis of the IQ scores and then assigned by means of a coin flip to treatment and nontreatment conditions. During the period that the treatment group (clay group) received intensive instruction in clay forming, the nontreatment group (nonclay group) remained with the regular classroom teacher and engaged in social studies, music, or general art projects.

Test Battery and Administration. The 28 children were pretested and posttested on the following tests: (a) Goldschmid and Bentler's Concept Assessment Kit — Conservation, (b) The Frostig Developmental Test of Visual Perception, (c) The Torrance Test of Figural Creative Thinking, and (d) The General Concept section of the Tests of Basic Experiences. Except for the Conservation Test, which was individually administered, all tests were given in small groups of 9 or 10 children.

Instruction in Clay Forming. The children in the clay group were instructed 2-1/2 hours weekly for a period of 10 weeks. Materials used during the investigation included Cone 5 stoneware clay with grog, boxwood and wire loop clay tools, and Cone 06 to 04 opaque and transparent glazes.

The concepts emphasized in instruction were pinching and joining clay material through a series of increasingly complex problems. The children were first introduced to simple pinching and pulling techniques for forming bowl shapes and animals, and then they built upon these concepts and developed increasingly complex levels of understanding. Forming clay through pinching was explored through a variety of problems, each designed to reinforce previous learning. Pots were made as symmetrical and as tall as possible; the surfaces of some pots were ornamented with decorative patterns. Individual skill developed, and many of the pieces completed during the 2nd and 3rd week of instruction were imaginative and well-crafted.

As reinforcement and refinement of the concept of pinching and pulling form from a mass of clay, the children were asked to create a face from a flattened mass. For some, it was a difficult problem; others grasped the concept easily.

When the pieces were dry, they were bisque fired to Cone 012. Following bisque firing, each child was instructed in techniques for glazing. Since it was not possible to differentiate the colors of the liquid glazes, glazed tiles were fired to provide samples of the colors being used. The pots were glazed by pouring the inside and brushing the outside surfaces. The children were instructed to keep the bottoms of their pieces free of glaze to prevent dripping on the shelves. Subsequently, the pieces were glost fired to Cone 05 and allowed to cool. Opening and drawing of the kiln provided considerable excitement.

The concept of joining parts with slip was introduced and, when this method was combined with pinching techniques, the children were able to produce more complex animal forms having longer legs and necks. Parts were added carefully using slip as a binder. A series of turtles produced from the combined techniques of pinching and slip joining illustrated the comprehension of the problem.

Hollow forms were reintroduced when an animal made from two parts became the problem. Most had slip-attached appendages, some balanced on three legs. Only one child chose to conceal the joining seam. At this point, an explanation of the expansion of heated air was given. Holes were made in the hollow forms to allow this air to escape during firing. The subsequent problem required joining two hollow forms to create a head. The proximity of Easter provoked a variety of rabbits, some with texture, all with holes for the heated air to escape. Considerable aesthetic strength was evident in many of these heads.

In an effort to identify the skills which the children had developed in using clay, a final figurative problem was assigned. Emphasis was placed on animation within the figure. The children worked independently, and from a thick coil of clay the figures began to emerge. The results of their efforts indicated an understanding of the processes which had been introduced and the attainment of skills required to transform an idea into reality.

Test Results. Accompanying the presentation of the findings will be a brief description of each test to provide information regarding the skills and behaviors required by the tasks presented. A more expanded presentation of the results and the analyses conducted on the test scores can be found elsewhere (Speidel, 1979).

According to its authors, the General Concept subtest of the Test of Basic Experiences, may be used as a gross measure of a child's knowledge and experience with various concepts. Since this test measures a very broad range of experiences, no difference was expected as a result of clay forming; the test had been selected as a control measure for any extraneous effects on the clay group, such as a halo or Hawthorne effect. It was found that both the clay group and the nonclay group increased slightly from pre- to posttest. An analysis of covariance showed no significant group differences on the posttest scores.

The Frostig Developmental Test of Visual Perception measures the development of various components of visual perception in the young child. The test consists of five subtests: (a) Eye-Motor Coordination measures fine motor coordination and requires the child to draw lines from one point to another point both with and without the help of guiding lines; (b) Figure-Ground measures the ability to separate a figure from its ground by having the child find hidden figures and outline figures that are intermeshed with other figures; (c) Form Constancy involves the recognition of circles and squares presented in a variety of sizes, shading, textures, and positions in space, as well as their discrimination from similar geometric figures; (d) Position in Space assesses the discrimination of reversals and rotations of figures; (e) finally, Spatial Relations measures the analysis of simple forms and patterns by asking the child to reproduce patterns of lines connecting series of dots.

Since the pre- and postexperimental scores were skewed, the data were analyzed by means of Mann-Whitney U tests on the change scores rather than by means of analyses of covariance. The only subtest on which the clay group performed significantly better was Form Constancy. Thus, instruction in clay processes did not facilitate figure-ground separation, discrimination of spatial position, recognition of spatial relationships, or even eye-hand motor coordination.

The Concept Assessment Kit — Conservation measures a child's ability to conserve on various Piagetian conservation tasks. Form A and Form B, which are parallel forms, measure conservation of two-dimensional space, number, mass, continuous and discontinuous quantity, and weight; Form C measures area and length conservation. The tasks are similar to the example described earlier in the brief discussion of Piaget's theory. Form A and Form C were given as pretest, Form B and Form C as posttest. The clay group increased their conservation scores by more than 5 points on the average from pretesting, while the nonclay group increased their scores only by 1/2 point. The analysis of covariance using pretest performance as covariate showed that the clay group performed significantly better on posttesting than the nonclay group. An analysis of item performance showed that the increased success of the clay group was fairly evenly distributed among the different types of conservation tasks, suggesting that instruction in clay forming had a general effect on the ability to conserve.

The Torrance Figural Tests of Creative Thinking, parallel Forms A and B, present the individual with three sets of stimuli to which he/she is to add lines to create interesting and unusual objects or pictures of which no one else will think. The three sets of stimuli are the following: (a) a free form, (b) a series of incomplete figures, and (c) a series of parallel lines (Form A) or circles (Form B). The Figural Tests yield four scores: (a) Fluency, or the number of items completed; (b) Flexibility, or the number of different conceptual categories upon which an individual has drawn in completing the stimuli; (c) Originality, or the frequency/infrequency with which a particular stimulus is made into a particular object; and (d) Elaboration, or the extent to which an individual has included details and embellishments in his basic idea.

Figural Test Form A was given as pretest and Form B as posttest. Analyses of covariance using the pretest scores as covariate showed that the clay group performed significantly better on the posttest than the nonclay group on Fluency, Flexibility, and Originality, though not on Elaboration.

Discussion

Art activities, such as clay forming, are usually included in nursery school or kindergarten programs with the purpose of developing visual-motor skills. Surprisingly, in this study with first graders, clay instruction did not appear to foster eye-hand motor coordination nor most of the other visual skills, even though there was room for improvement, particularly on the eye-motor test. Rather the effects of the clay instruction appeared on conceptual-ideational learning. Thus, the only subtest of the Frostig Test on which the clay group performed better than the nonclay group was the Figure Constancy subtest, which requires learning to discriminate the essential dimensions of a geometric figure from the irrelevant dimensions which can be changed without destroying the concept. In other words, the clay group performed better than the nonclay group on a form of geometric-figure conservation.

The effects of participation in clay forming on the development of operational thought are very encouraging. They appear not to be restricted to conservation of mass, the conservation task most closely related to the clay group's instructional experience, but appear to have generalized to the other conservation tasks.

Other attempts to teach a nonconserving child to conserve have centered mainly on rule instruction — providing the child with the rules underlying conservation — or feedback. Both approaches have led to successes as well as occasional failures in training five- to seven-year-olds. However, the generality of the learning and the depth of comprehension of the conservation rules are questionable. The training situations in these studies are highly similar to the testing situation. For instance, in Brainerd's studies (1972, 1974, & 1976) on the effects of feedback on the development of conservation, the training and testing situations are identical except that during the training trials the child is given feedback for correct and incorrect responding: "You're right. That is the correct answer," or "You're wrong. That is not the right answer." All the child needs to learn, in order to increase his/her conservation score, is to which questions the response is "yes" and to which the response is "no." For example, the child must learn to always say "yes" to questions such as "Do these (glasses) have the same amount (of liquid)?" and "no" to such questions as "Does one of these (glasses) contain more (liquid) than the other (glass)?" Also, in a study by Denny, Zeytinoglu, and Selzer (1977) comparing the effectiveness of feedback and verbal-rule instruction, highly similar training and testing stimuli were used. As "yes" was the appropriate answer to the testing as well as the training questions, all the child had to learn in order to perform appropriately was the response set "yes" and to memorize the rule verbalized by the experimenter. Such an experimental situation seems to test the child's ability to memorize a rule rather than a deeper understanding of the concepts involved in conservation problems. In other words, the success of many of these brief conservation training studies may be due to the similarity of the intervention to the testing situation — to the child's learning of specific responses to specific test situations and awareness of the demand characteristics of the experiment. Little generalization to other conservation tasks in other settings would be predicted.

In line with this criticism, Hunt (1969) does not believe that there is a sudden change in operational thought, that the child suddenly accommodates and assimilates the necessary knowledge, but rather that, as the child develops operational thought, he/she is able to conserve with greater likelihood on a greater variety of tasks, of less and less familiarity.

In light of the above discussion on the questionable external validity of many conservation training studies, the findings of the present study are particularly significant; here, the tasks and the setting in which the increase in ability to conserve was noted were completely different from the training setting.

Support for the effectiveness of clay-forming activities in developing operational thought processes comes from a cross-cultural study by Price-Williams, Gordon, and Ramirez (1969). These anthropologists found that children from pottery-making families in Mexico performed significantly better than their peers from similar SES backgrounds on tasks of conservation of mass. The potters' children also performed better on other conservation tasks, though not statistically significantly. We may therefore conclude that intensive experiences in clay forming, whether in the form of family influence or educational experience, lend themselves to the acquisition of concrete operational thought.

The assumption that forming clay would foster creativity was also supported by the present data. Characterizing creativity is complex, and there exists a diversity of definitions and measurement instruments. The Torrance Figural Test of Creative Thinking was chosen for measuring development of creativity, because it has relatively adequate reliability and validity. Furthermore, Torrance's definition and manner of measuring creativity imply that creative thinking can be fostered through educational experiences. In reviewing 142 studies which described an attempt to teach or otherwise manipulate creative thought, Torrance (1972) found many of the approaches successful in facilitating one or more of the dimensions of creative thought. In most of the studies, the Torrance Tests for measuring creativity were used.

Although the visual arts and creativity seem to be closely related, surprisingly, only a handful of studies have investigated the effectiveness of visual-art activities on the development of creativity. Frankston (1963) found that bright 11th graders who scored below the mean on creativity tests benefited from specifically designed art activities. On the other hand, with a group of eighth graders, creative visual-art experiences did not facilitate creative writing. A study more similar to the present one (Grossman, 1969) did show that a 12-week developmental art program with kindergarten children enhanced creativity, as measured by the Torrance Tests.

The results of the present study support the finding of this last study that certain forms of visual-art instruction may foster creativity in early elementary-school children. In particular, the clay group performed significantly better than the non-clay group on Fluency, Flexibility, and Originality aspects of the Torrance Figural Test of Creativity. The increase in Fluency is by itself a meaningless change, as impulsive and commonplace thinkers can produce many ideas of low quality and no originality. However, the clay group also had become more flexible in viewing and manipulating figural elements and was more original in that they produced more unusual, novel ideas. The aspect of creativity which appeared not to be affected by clay-forming activities was the ability to elaborate, to develop, or embellish a basic idea. However, as Torrance (1974) argues, if a child spends his/her energies creating many original responses from a large variety of conceptual categories, he/she will not have much time left for elaborating each individual response. This circumstance seems to be a plausible explanation for the finding that the Elaboration score was not raised in the clay group.

Let us now speculate about what may be mediating the learning observed in the clay group. We hypothesize that forming and creating with clay develops imagery processes. Molding a lump of clay into an object requires that the child draw upon his/her store of images, interrelate these images in new ways, anticipate what changes the clay must undergo in order to create a form or figure of his/her intention. These experiences and creations in turn shape new images upon which the child can later draw.

Thus, the clay-forming experiences seem to lend themselves to creating appropriate images, which foster the acquisition of concrete, operational thought. The children begin with a lump of clay and imagine what they want to make from it. With a particular image in mind, they transform their piece of clay into an object, while realizing that their creation is still the same piece of clay with which they started. Often they are dissatisfied with their creation — it does not appear to match the image they had in mind — and they pound it back again into a ball to begin anew. When new pieces of clay are attached, it is a discriminable operation, as the children must use slip to make the new addition stick to the original. Such a sequence of transformations might be expected to produce images, linked to one another, which foster an awareness in the children of reversibility, inversion, and compensation — the underlying concepts of conservation.

Similarly, in forming objects from clay, children learn that larger balls of clay allow them to make larger objects. They learn to estimate lengths, for instance, while making a four-footed animal: if the legs are of different lengths, they obtain immediate feedback as the animal then tips over. They learn about proportions of parts of their figure to one another, and to predict the amount of material needed for a part of a particular size. Initially, they may be choosing too much clay and make the arm or leg too large, but with repeated experiences, a sense of the correct amount of clay needed to make an arm of appropriate size develops. If we postulate the existence of a visual encoding process, it would seem logical that this emerging awareness is based on the acquisition of appropriate images formed from these experiences.

As mentioned earlier, Piaget argues that imagery plays an important yet secondary role in the development of operational thought. He maintains that anticipatory mental imagery supports but does not lead to operational thought. The relationship between anticipating imagery and operational thought, however, may be more complex than Piaget holds. First, in Piaget's series of experiments conducted on this topic, there were several studies in which the ability to correctly anticipate the results of a transformation actually preceded in many children their ability to conserve. Second, Piaget's assertion that the logical operations emerge quickly and simultaneously is doubtful. Hunt writes on the concept of structures d'ensemble: "They appear to emerge tentatively from coping with a given kind of problem in one situation, then again with that kind of problem in another situation, in another, and in another, and so on, then from coping with related kinds of problems in a variety of situations until the rules for the solution become generalized" (1969, p. 54). This argument is supported by the observation that nonconserving children (as defined by their performance on the traditional conservation tasks) are able to conserve when the misguiding perceptual cues are screened; for example, when the test glass into which the liquid is poured from one of the two standard glasses is screened so that the child cannot see it, nonconserving children will make conservation judgements. Miller and Heldmeyer (1975) found that under such screening conditions the children not only gave a high proportion of conservation judgements but also logical explanations. The authors argue, "If logical explanations reflect operations, then these children possessed the underlying cognitive operations normally attributed only to 'true conservers'" (p. 591). However, many children reverted to nonconservation as more of the perceptual cues usually present in the regular conservation tasks were introduced.

The Miller and Heldmeyer findings suggest that the basic rule for equality and conservation appears to be present quite early in development; yet, initially the perceptual cues of the typical conservation tasks are misleading, confusing the children and preventing them from retaining their initial conservation judgment. Therefore, we suggest the hypothesis that success on the traditional conservation tasks is dependent upon the acquisition of a stock of interconnected images formed from a variety of experiences with transformations, inversions, and reversions, and so on — images which allow the individual to discern those perceptual cues which are relevant and those cues which are irrelevant to the property or dimension in question.

We propose that not only the development of understanding the conservation rules, but also the changes noted in the clay group on the creative measures are mediated by mental imagery. Since the assumption that the availability of a wide store of vivid mental images is important for figural creativity seems so ready at hand and plausible, it is surprising that there exists so little information in the literature connecting imagery to creativity. Durio (1975) has found several writings linking imagery to creativity, but few are of an empirical nature. In line with our hypothesis of imagery as an explanatory construct, we propose that it is plausible that clay forming fosters the development of visual imagery both by creating new mental images and by making those images already in memory more available, perhaps more vivid. Creating a picture out of an incomplete or undefined figural stimulus seems to require the ability to visualize, to call forth an appropriate mental image. To find unusual and uncommon solutions to the Torrance items would thus seem to demand a large, readily available store of images.

The attempt to relate the improvement in the cognitive skills of the clay group to the development of visual imagery is highly speculative, and, due to the nature of the construct, must to some extent remain inferential. Imagery can never be directly observed. This is why imagery for so many years was not considered to be a credible area for research in psychology, why Watson (1930) argued that imagery had no functional significance, and why verbal mediation emerged as a frequently called upon explanatory construct. However, verbal mediation is similarly inferential and unobservable.

In discussing this issue of verbal and imagery processes, Paivio (1971) writes, "Both are theoretical constructs and whether or not it is useful to postulate either, or both, depends on the adequacy of the defining operations and the research procedures used to test the properties that have been theoretically attributed to them" (p. 6). He continues, "The ultimate question to be faced concerns the scientific usefulness of postulating such a process. This question can be answered only within a framework based on an empirical foundation and constructed according to a theoretical blueprint. Imagery, like all inferential concepts, can have functional significance only to the extent that it can be differentiated from other concepts theoretically, and to the extent that these distinctive theoretical properties are open to empirical test. It is essential, therefore, to compare and contrast the concept of imagery with other concepts that have distinct theoretical properties and at the same time can be distinguished operationally from imagery" (p. 7-8). Paivio, upon reviewing the functional significance of imagery and verbal processing with regard to meaning, perception, memory, learning, and language development, concludes that the phenomena in each area studied could be conceptualized and explained within the framework of a dual processing system.

As described briefly above, there exists already a fairly large nomological network of indirect evidence for the function of mental imagery. By relating the effects of clay forming to this nomological net, a variety of hypotheses and predictions emerge. Thus, one could compare the effects of two instructional procedures, one emphasizing verbal instruction and the other presumed to facilitate appropriate imagery development, on the acquisition of a particular skill. For example, conservation could be taught by means of abstract rules or by instruction in clay forming. In an even more elaborate design, one could compare the effects of the two modes of instruction on two cognitive skills: one presumed to be more dependent on visual imagery, the other more dependent on verbal processing. For example, one could compare the effects of brainstorming and the effects of clay forming on the development of verbal and figural creativity. Indirect evidence in support of a dual processing system would be provided if the verbally based instruction was found to be more effective in fostering the verbally mediated cognitive skill, and the imagery-developing instruction turned out to be more effective in fostering the imagery-mediated skill.

Summary

The findings show that working intensively with clay, molding it, shaping it, glazing it, firing it, and coming to understand its nature, develops logical thought as defined by Piaget and enhances creative thinking in a figural medium. Surprisingly, from our data it appears that this particular form of art activity — clay forming — is not conducive to the development of fine motor coordination and to the development of other perceptual skills measured except for Form Constancy. Thus, the study supports the hypothesis that instruction in certain forms of visual art not only develops task-specific skills but may also foster performance in other selected cognitive areas, so that art instruction can be an effective and important means for developing certain cognitive skills.

A brief summary was given on the relevance of visual memory and visual imagery to learning. The possibility that imagery mediated the learning observed in this study was discussed. Further research should attempt to discover which forms of visual-art instruction will foster each of the various cognitive skills. Furthermore, the hypothesis that imagery is a functional mediator for learning induced by art instruction should be tested systematically.

REFERENCES

Bevan, W., & Steger, J. A. Free recall and abstractness of stimuli. *Science*, 1971, *172*, 597-599.
Brainerd, C. J. Reinforcement and reversibility in quantity conservation acquisition. *Psychonomic Science*, 1972, *27*, 114-116.
Brainerd, C. J. Training and transfer of transitivity, conservation, and class inclusion of length. *Child Development*, 1974, *45*, 324-334.

Brainerd, C. J. Does prior knowledge of the compensation rule increase susceptibility to conservation training? *Developmental Psychology*, 1976, *12*, 1-5.

Brooks, L. R. Spatial and verbal components of the act of recall. *Canadian Journal of Psychology*, 1968, *22*, 349-368.

den Heyer, K., & Barrett, B. Selective loss of visual and verbal information in STM by means of visual and verbal interpolated tasks. *Psychonomic Science*, 1971, *25*, 100-102.

Denny, N. W., Zeytinoglu, S., & Selzer, S. C. Conservation training in four-year-old children. *Journal of Experimental Child Psychology*, 1977, *24*, 129-146.

Dilley, M. G., & Paivio, A. Pictures and words as stimulus and response items in paired-associate learning of young children. *Journal of Experimental Child Psychology*, 1968, *6*, 231-240.

Durio, H. F. Mental imagery and creativity. *Journal of Creative Behavior*, 1975, *9*, 223-244.

Even, R. L. An experimental study of the comparative effect of selected art experiences on the creative performance and attitudes of academically superior students (Doctoral dissertation, University of Minnesota, 1963). *Dissertation Abstracts*, 1964, *24*, 4470A-4471A. (University Microfilms No. 64-4062)

Frankston, L. Some explorations of the effect of creative visual art experiences upon the poetry writing quality of eighth grade students (Doctoral dissertation, Columbia University, 1963). *Dissertation Abstracts*, 1964, *24*, 2856A-2857A. (University Microfilms No. 64-1475)

Grossman, M. J. Developing aesthetic and creative visual abilities in kindergarten children through a structured developmental art program (Doctoral dissertation, University of Georgia, 1969). *Dissertation Abstracts*, 1970, *30*, 3375A. (University Microfilms No. 70-1157)

Hunt, J.M.V. The impact and limitations of the giant of developmental psychology. In D. Elkind & J. H. Flavell (Eds.), *Studies in Cognitive Psychology: Essays in Honor of Jean Piaget.* New York: Oxford University Press, 1969, pp. 3-66.

Inhelder, B. Operational thought and symbolic imagery. In P. H. Mussen (Ed.), European research in cognitive development. *Monographs of the Society for Research in Child Development*, 1965, *100*, 4-18.

Lesgold, A. M., Levin, J. R., Shimron, J., & Guttman, J. Pictures and young children's learning from oral prose. *Journal of Educational Psychology*, 1975, *67*, 636-642.

Lesgold, A. M., McCormick, C., & Golinkiff, R. M. Imagery training and children's prose learning. *Journal of Educational Psychology*, 1975, *67*, 663-667.

Levin, J. R. What have we learned about maximizing what children learn? In J. R. Levin & V. L. Allen (Eds.), *Cognitive Learning in Children: Theories and Strategies.* New York: Academic Press, 1976.

Levin, J. R., & Divine-Hawkins, P. Visual imagery as a prose-learning process. *Journal of Reading Behavior*, 1974, *6*, 23-30.

Levin, J. R., & Pressley, M. A. A test of the developmental imagery hypothesis in children's associative learning. *Journal of Educational Psychology*, 1978, *70*, 691-694.

Miller, P. H., & Heldmeyer, K. H. Perceptual information in conservation: Effects of screening. *Child Development*, 1975, *46*, 588-592.

Paivio, A. Mental imagery in associative learning and memory. *Psychological Review*, 1969, *76*, 241-263.

Paivio, A. *Imagery and verbal process.* New York: Holt, Rinehart, & Winston, 1971.

Paivio, A., Smythe, P. C., & Yuille, J. C. Imagery versus meaningfulness of nouns in paired associate learning. *Canadian Journal of Psychology*, 1968, *22*, 427-441.

Piaget, J. The development of mental imagery. In R. E. Ripple & V. N. Rockcastle (Eds.), *Piaget Rediscovered.* Ithaca, N. Y.: Cornell University School of Education, 1964.

Piaget, J., & Inhelder, B. *Mental imagery in the child.* New York: Basic Books, 1971.

Posner, M. I., & Keele, S. W. Decay of visual information from a single letter. *Science,* 1967, *158,* 137-139.

Price-Williams, D., Gordon, W., & Ramirez, M, III. Skill and conservation: A study of pottery-making children. *Developmental Psychology,* 1969, *1,* 769.

Reese, H. W. (Chairman). Imagery in children's learning: A symposium. *Psychological Bulletin,* 1970, *73,* 383-385.

Rohwer, W. D., Jr. Images and pictures in children's learning: Research results and educational implications. In H. W. Reese (Chairman), Imagery in children's learning: A symposium. *Psychological Bulletin,* 1970, *73,* 393-403.

Rohwer, W. D., Jr. Elaboration and learning in childhood and adolescence. In H. W. Reese (Ed.), *Advances in Child Development and Behavior.* New York: Academic Press, 1973.

Shepard, R. N. Recognition memory for words, sentences, and pictures. *Journal of Verbal Learning and Verbal Behavior,* 1967, *6,* 156-163.

Speidel, G. E. *The instruction in clay forming and its effects on selected cognitive skills* (Kamehameha Early Education Program Technical Report 87). Honolulu: The Kamehameha Schools, 1979.

Speidel, G. E. & Tharp, R. G. *The effectiveness of art and language instruction on the intelligence and achievement scores of disadvantaged dialect-speaking kindergarten children* (Kamehameha Early Education Program Technical Report 84). Honolulu: The Kamehameha Schools, 1979.

Torrance, E. P. Can we teach children to think creatively? *Journal of Creative Behavior,* 1972, *6,* 114-143.

Torrance, E. P. *Torrance Tests of Creative Thinking: Norms-Technical Manual.* Lexington, MA: Personnel Press/Ginn and Company, 1974.

Watson, J. B. *Behaviorism.* New York: Norton, 1930.

Wolff, P., & Levin, J. R. The role of overt activity in children's imagery production. *Child Development,* 1972, *39,* 449-465.

14

Visual Thinking in Education

RUDOLF ARNHEIM

In recent years the notion of visual thinking has made its appearance every-where. This cannot but give me some personal satisfaction (Arnheim, 1969). But it also astonishes me because according to the long tradition of Western philosophy and psychology the two concepts, perception and reasoning, do not belong under the same bedcover. One can characterize the traditional view by saying that the two concepts are believed to require each other but also to exclude each other.

Perceiving and thinking require each other. They complement each other's func-tions. The task of perception is supposed to be limited to collecting the raw materials for cognition. Once the material has been gathered, thinking enters the scene, at a higher level of the mind, and does the processing. Perception would be useless without thinking; thinking without perception would have nothing to think about.

But according to the traditional view, the two mental functions also exclude each other, since perception, supposedly, can deal only with individual instances. George Berkeley (1910) extended this belief to mental images and insisted that nobody can picture in his mind an idea, such as "man," as a generality: one can visualize only a tall or a short man, a white or a black one, but not man as such. Thinking, on the other hand, is said to handle only generalities. It cannot tolerate the presence of particular things. If, for example, I try to reason about the nature of "man," any image of a particular man would lead me astray.

This supposed incompatibility of mental functions that nevertheless cannot do without each other has disturbed philosophers throughout our history. It led to an underestimation of the senses and promoted thought to a splendid isolation that

Rudolf Arnheim, 1133 S. 7th Street, Ann Arbor, Michigan, 48103.

threatened it with sterility. In education it made for a strict distinction between the necessary and honorable study of words and numbers and the luxury of a slightly indecent concern with the senses. When nowadays the budget for the teaching of the arts is the first to be cut as soon as the school system of a city is in financial trouble, we are still heirs to the pernicious split that has hampered our educational thinking for so long.

In psychology, the mental image has returned from half a century of exile and enjoys an attention that cannot but help our efforts. But I have the impression that the best of these studies are still limited to mental imagery as a substitute for direct visual perception, that is, to experiments showing that some of the things done in direct perception are also attainable in imagery (Shepard, 1978). This is useful enough, but theoretical and experimental psychology has still much to explore about direct and indirect perception as the principal instrument of problem solving.

Developmental psychology has been much impressed by attempts to distinguish three stages through which the child's mind passes as it grows from birth to maturity. There is, in the beginning, a motor stage at which coping behavior relies on bodily action; there is, in the second place, a perceptual stage, during which the child manages his/her affairs by what he/she can see, hear, or touch; and there is the third stage, namely reasoning, which operates at the level of abstract thinking. What matters for our purpose is to what extent the three types of behavior are assumed to be mutually exclusive, and especially what happens to the behavior mode of an earlier stage when the child progresses to the next. Let me illustrate the crucial theoretical point by reference to the best known demonstrations in this field, namely the conservation experiments (Piaget & Inhelder, 1962). Two basic approaches must be clearly defined before one tackles the less urgent task of finding out which psychologist believes exactly what.

One of these approaches has it that when the child is no longer fooled by the different shapes of the two containers into believing that they hold different amounts of liquid, he/she escapes from the appearance of things to the realm of pure reason, where he/she is no longer misled by perception. The other approach maintains that to judge the two columns of liquid by, say, their height is a legitimate first step toward the solution of the problem. To go beyond it, the child does not leave the domain of visual imagery — there is in fact no other place to go — but he/she proceeds to perceive the given situation in a more sophisticated fashion: instead of considering one spatial dimension only, he/she looks at the interplay between two, namely height and breadth. This is true progress on the scale of mental development, not achieved by getting out of the perceptual situation but, on the contrary, by going more deeply into it.

The fact that thinking of this kind must take place in the perceptual realm because there is no other place to go, is concealed by the belief that reasoning can be done through language. I can observe here only briefly what I have tried to show more explicitly elsewhere, namely, that although language is a valuable help in much human thinking, it is neither indispensable nor can it serve as the medium in which thinking takes place (Arnheim, 1969). It should be obvious that language consists of sounds or visual signs that possess none of the properties of the things to be manipulated in a problem situation. In order to think productively about the nature of, say, liberty, one needs a medium of thought in which the properties of liberty can be represented. Productive thinking is done by means of the things to which language refers — referents that in themselves are not verbal but perceptual.

As a further example, I would like to raise a question that is particularly relevant to psychologists: in what medium do we think about mental processes? Sigmund Freud (1933), in one of the few diagrams that accompany his theories, illustrated the relation between two triads of concepts: id, ego, and superego, and unconscious, preconscious, and conscious. His drawing presents these terms in a ver-

Figure 1.

tical section through a bulgy container, a kind of abstract architecture. The psychological relations are shown as spatial relations, from which we are asked to infer the places and directions of the mental forces that the model is intended to illustrate. These forces, although not represented in the picture, are as perceptual as the space in which they are shown to act. It is well known that Freud made them behave like hydraulic forces — an image that imposed certain constraints on his thinking.

Note here that Freud's drawing was not a mere teaching device, used in his lectures to facilitate the understanding of processes about which he himself thought in a different medium. No, he portrayed them precisely in the medium in which he himself was thinking, well aware undoubtedly that he was thinking in analogies. Whoever hesitates to believe this is invited to ask himself/herself in what other medium Freud — or for that matter any other psychologist — could have done his reasoning. If the hydraulic model was imperfect, it had to be replaced by a more suitable image, perhaps a more kinesthetic one. But perceptual it had to be, unless Freud, instead of engaging in productive thinking, had limited himself to trying out new combinations of properties his concepts already possessed, in which case an inexpensive computer would have done equally well.

In the beginning, I mentioned a basic objection that seemed to indicate that visual images could not serve as the medium of reasoning. Berkeley had pointed out that perception, and correspondingly mental images, could refer only to individual instances, not to general concepts, and was therefore unsuitable for abstract thinking. But if this is so, how can diagrams be used everywhere as vehicles for thinking at a highly abstract level? Take as an example the syllogism, that triumph of inferential logic. The device has been famous since antiquity because it permits the thinker to draw a valid conclusion from two valid premises. One obtains a new piece of reliable knowledge without any need to consult the facts of reality for confirmation. Now, when the formula of the syllogism is recited in words, the listener experiences a fine case of scampering in search of a thought model. He hears: "If all A are contained in B, and if C is contained in A, then C must also be contained in B." Is this proposition right or wrong? There is no way of finding out, unless one resorts to the kind of image which turns up in Janellen Huttenlocher's splendid experiments on strategy in reasoning (Huttenlocher, 1968). I want to refer here to the oldest syllogistic diagrams, introduced around 1770 by the

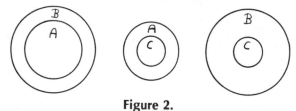

Figure 2.

mathematician Leonhard Euler in his book, *Letters to a German Princess*. Rather ungratefully the device is called "Venn circles" in the English-speaking countries. One glance at Figure 2 proves that the syllogistic proposition of the *modus barbara* is correct and must be correct not only in the present example but in all possible cases. In the drawing, the factual relations are shown as spatial relations, just as in Freud's diagram.

Evidently the syllogism uses concepts at a very high level of abstraction. They are despoiled of all particular characteristics, except the one of belonging under a superordinate category. The syllogism can serve to prove that Socrates is mortal or that cherry trees have roots, but neither Socrates nor cherry trees figure in the proposition. Visually, the circle is the most denuded shape we possess. But when we look at the drawing, we seem to find Berkeley's assertion confirmed: we see a particular instance of entangled circles and nothing else. How, then, do we reason so abstractly with particulars?

The answer comes from the psychological principle for which philosophers are searching when they discuss the problem of "seeing as" (Wittgenstein, 1953). I would formulate this principle by saying that all perception is the perceiving of qualities, and since all qualities are generic, perception always refers to generic properties. Seeing a fire is always seeing firiness, and seeing a circle is seeing roundness. Seeing the spatial relations between three circles lends itself quite directly to seeing the range of enclosure; and the topological aspects of enclosure are presented by Euler's images with the disciplined economy required by all good thinking.

By now it will be clear that the term "visual thinking" refers only to one facet of our subject. It fails to indicate that vision is only one of the senses that serve perception; kinesthesis is another important one. It also does not claim, as it should, that *all* productive thinking (as distinguished from the mechanical manipulation of data) must be perceptual. Furthermore, once we acknowledge that thinking has a perceptual base, we must also consider the mirror image of this claim, namely, that all perception involves aspects of thought.

These claims cannot but be profoundly relevant to education, and I propose to devote the remainder of this paper to a few more specific remarks on this subject. The teaching of the arts, an exclusively visual matter, seems to deserve a prominent place here. But this responsibility is not always clearly faced. We hear art educators say that the arts are needed to create a well-rounded person, although it is not obvious that being well-rounded is better than being slim. We hear that the arts give pleasure but are not told why and to what useful end. We hear of self-expression and emotional outlets and the liberation of individuality. But rarely is there an emphasis on the art room or studio as a training ground for visual thinking. Yet every art teacher knows from experience that drawing, painting, or sculpture properly conceived, pose cognitive problems worthy of a good brain and every bit as exacting as a mathematical or scientific puzzle.

How does one render in a picture the characteristic aspects of an object or event? How does one create space, depth, movement, balance, and unity? How do the arts help the young mind comprehend the confusing complexity of the world it is facing? These problems will be productively approached by the students only if the teacher encourages them to rely on their own intelligence and imagination rather than on mechanical tricks. One of the great educational advantages of art work is that a minimum of technical instruction suffices to supply students with the instruments needed for the independent development of their own mental resources.

Art work, intelligently pursued, lets the student take conscious possession of the various aspects of perceptual experience. For example, the three dimensions of space, which are available for practical use in daily life from infancy on, must be conquered step by step in sculpture. Such competent handling of spatial relations, acquired in the art room, is of direct professional benefit for activities such as surgery or engineering. The ability to visualize the complex properties of three-dimensional objects in space is needed for artistic, scientific, or technological tasks.

So directly and indirectly connected are the exploration of perceptual space and the categories of theoretical thinking that the former is the best training ground for the latter. We noted that Freud as well as Euler used spatial dimensions to comprehend the interplay of forces of the mind or the hierarchy of a system of logic. It stands to reason that a person familiar with the intricacies of perceptual relations will be equipped to deal more imaginatively with the properties of theoretical concepts such as inclusion, exclusion, dependence, interference, channels, barriers, sequence, random arrangement, etc.

What then are some of the desiderata of visual thinking for the various fields of teaching and learning? Let me mention the consequences for the use of language, an instrument needed by them all. If we look at language with some affectionate attention, we find that many so-called abstract terms still contain the perceivable practical qualities and activities from which they were originally derived. Words are monuments to the close kinship between perceptual experience and theoretical reasoning. They can promote the cross-fertilization between the two when, in the use of language, attention is paid to the perceptual matrices from which intellectual terminology is derived. This is the specialty of poets and other writers. They know how to revive the fossils buried in words and thereby to make verbal statements come alive. Their services are needed for the survival of productive thinking in the sciences. When we remark regretfully that psychologists today no longer write like William James or Sigmund Freud, we are not voicing a merely "aesthetic" complaint. We sense that the desiccation of our language is symptomatic of the pernicious split between the manipulation of intellectual schemata and the handling of live subject matter.

If I were asked to describe my dream university, I would have it organize itself around a central trunk of three disciplines: philosophy, the art studio, and the poetry workshop. Philosophy would be asked to return to the teaching of ontology, epistemology, ethics, and logic, to remedy the shameful deficiencies of the reasoning now common in the fields of academic specialization. Art education would provide the instruments by which to carry out such thinking. And poetry would make language, our principal medium for communicating thought, fit for thinking in images.

A glance at the practice of secondary and higher education today indicates that imagery has its representatives in the classroom. The blackboard is the venerable vehicle of visual education, and the diagrams drawn in chalk by teachers of social science, grammar, geometry, or chemistry indicate that theory must rely on vision. But a look at these diagrams also reveals that most of them are the products of unskilled labor. They fail to transmit their meaning as well as they should because they are badly drawn. In order to deliver their message safely, diagrams must rely on the rules of pictorial composition and visual order that have been perfected in the arts for some 20,000 years. Art teachers should be prepared to apply these skills not only to the exalted visions of painters whose work is fit for museums but to all those practical applications which the arts have served, to their own benefit, in all functioning cultures.

The same consideration holds for the more elaborate visual aids, the illustrations and maps, the slides and films, the video and television shows. Neither the technical skill of picture making alone nor the faithful realism of the images guarantees that the material explains what it is intended to explain. It seems to me essential to progress beyond the traditional notion that pictures provide the mere raw material and that thinking begins only after the information has been received — just as digestion must wait until one has eaten. Instead, the thinking is done by means of structural properties inherent in the image, and therefore the image must be shaped and organized intelligently in such a way as to make the salient properties visible. Decisive relations between components must show up; cause must aim at effect; correspondences, symmetries, hierarchies must be clearly presented — an eminently artistic task, even when it is used simply to explain the working of a piston engine or a shoulder joint (Arnheim, 1974).

I would like to conclude with a practical example. Some time ago I was asked for advice by a German graduate student of the Pedagogical Academy in Dortmund. Mr. Werner Korb was working on the visual aspects of classroom demonstrations in the high-school teaching of chemistry; and having discovered that gestalt psychology has worked out principles of visual organization, he asked for my permission to send me his material. From what I saw, I received the impression that, in the general school practice, a classroom demonstration is considered to be doing its duty when the chemical process to be understood by the students is made physically present. The shape and arrangement of the various bottles, burners, tubes, and their contents are determined by what is technically required and what is cheapest and most convenient for the manufacturer and the teacher. Little thought is given to the manner in which the visual shapes and arrangements reach the eyes of the students and to the relations between what is seen and what is understood (Korb & Arnheim, 1979).

Here is a small example. Figure 3 shows the arrangement suggested for demonstrating the synthesis of ammonia. The two component gases, nitrogen and hydrogen, each in its bottle, combine in a single straight tube, from which a short connection takes off with a sharp, right-angled break and leads the two gases to the container in which they form the ammonia. The single straight vertical tube is the simplest and cheapest way of making the connection, but it misleads the visual thinking of the students. It suggests a direct connection between the two components and bypasses their merging for the synthesis. A Y-shaped combination of two tubes, perhaps a trifle more troublesome for the teacher, leads the eye correctly.

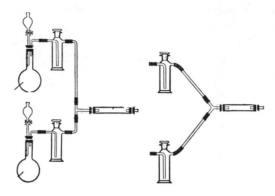

Figure 3.

My next illustration, also taken from Mr. Korb's material, shows first a typical classroom demonstration of the production of hydrochloride. The array of bottles

Figure 4.

on the shelf in the background has nothing to do with the experiment (Figure 4). It is the teacher's storage space, supposed to be ignored by the students. But the visual discrimination of figure and ground does not obey nonperceptual prohibitions. In perception, whatever is seen is supposed to belong; and since the crowded shelf is a part of the sight but not of the experiment, the contradiction threatens to sabotage the teaching.

There is no need to comment on the virtues of the counterproposal illustrated in Figure 5. A sense of well-being and order distinguishes the image. The eye is

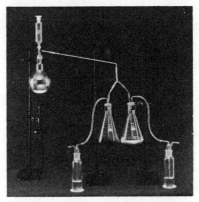

Figure 5

securely led, even before one has any conception of the particular nature of the chemical process.

As my modest examples will have indicated, visual thinking is inevitable. Even so, it will take time before it truly assumes its rightful place in our education. Visual thinking is indivisible: unless it is given its due in every field of teaching and learning it cannot truly work well in any field. The best intentions of the biology teacher will be hampered by half-ready student minds if the mathematics teacher is not applying the same principles. We need nothing less than a change of basic attitude in all teaching. Until then, those who happen to see the light will do their best to get the ball rolling. The seeing of the light and the rolling ball are good visual images.

REFERENCES

Arnheim, Rudolf. *Visual thinking.* Berkeley and Los Angeles: U. Cal. Press, 1969.

Arnheim, Rudolf. *Art and visual perception.* Berkeley and Los Angeles: U. Cal. Press, 1974. Pp. 156 ff.

Berkeley, George. *A treatise concerning the principles of human knowledge.* London: Dent, 1910.

Euler, Leonhard. *Lettres à une princesse d'Allemagne sur quelques sujets de physique et philosophie.* Leipzig: Steidel, 1770.

Freud, Sigmund. *New introductory lectures on psycho-analysis.* New York: Norton, 1933.

Huttenlocher, Janellen. Constructing spatial images: a strategy in reasoning. *Psych. Review,* 1968, *75,* 550-560.

Korb, Werner and Arnheim, Rudolf. Visuelle Wahrnehmungsprobleme beim Aufbau chemischer Demonstrationselemente. *Neue Unterrichtspraxis,* March 1979, *12,* 117-123.

Piaget, Jean and Inhelder, Barbel. *Le développement des quantités physiques chez l'enfant.* Neuchâtel: Delachaux and Niestlé:1962.

Shepard, Roger N. The mental image. *Amer. Psychologist,* 1978, *33,* 125-137.

Wittgenstein, Ludwig. *Philosophical investigations.* New York: Macmillan, 1953.

Author Index

Abbott, H. D., 51,64
Abelson, R. P., 32
Aguilar, I., 151, 166, 168
Ahsen, A., 2, 8, 11, 12, 13, 14, 15, 20, 21, 22, 24, 60, 61, 91, 102, 108, 111, 112, 113, 114, 115, 119, 120, 127, 129, 130, 131, 145, 146, 149, 153, 158, 167, 168, 171, 187, 192, 196
Ajaya, S., 126, 131
Ajmal, M., 165, 168
Allard, F., 52, 61
Allen, V. L., 212
Allison, J., 110, 115
Allport, G. W., 20, 24
Andersen, M. L., 70, 78
Angelergues, R., 45, 63.
Angyal, A., 89, 102
Antrobus, J. S., 4, 9, 102, 103
Ardhapurkar, I., 125, 126, 131
Ardis, J. A., 192, 193, 194, 196
Arieti, S., 3, 4, 8
Arneson, B. A., 49, 65
Arnheim, R., 215, 217, 221, 223
Arnold, M. B., 69, 78, 112, 115
As, A., 70, 78
Aserinsky, E., 53, 61, 196
Ashton, R., 77, 80
Assagioli, R., 91, 102, 122-123, 130, 131, 149, 168
Atkinson, G., 70, 73, 78, 80

Bagchi, B. K., 110, 115
Bailey, D. E., 133, 147
Bakan, P., 41, 47, 49, 53, 57, 61, 64
Ballentine, R., 126, 131
Bamber, D., 12, 24
Bandler, R., 60, 61

Bandura, A., 31, 37, 38
Bannister, D., 133, 146
Barber, T. X., 67, 68, 69, 70, 71, 72, 73, 76, 77, 78, 79, 80, 94, 102, 110, 111, 112, 115, 116.
Barrett, B., 200, 212
Barrett, W., 152, 168
Bartlett, F. C., 135, 146
Bateson, G., 59, 61
Beach, F. A., 25
Beck, A., 120, 131
Becker, R. E., 143, 144, 146
Beigel, H. G., 57, 61
Berdach, E., 57, 61
Berent, S., 48, 62
Berkeley, G., 215, 218, 223
Bevan, W., 200, 211
Beyn, E. S., 45, 61
Binet, A., 68, 78
Bloching, K., 152, 168
Bogen, J. E., 53, 61, 171, 181
Bosdell, B., 67, 78
Bowers, P. G., 2, 4, 8
Bowers, S., 2, 4, 8
Braff, D., 44, 62
Braga, J. L., 151, 168
Braga, L. D., 151, 168
Brainerd, C. J., 206, 211, 212
Brazier, M. A. B., 25
Brill, A. 62
Bromfield, E., 31, 39
Brooks, L. R., 200, 212
Brownfield, C., 57, 61
Bruner, J. S., 2, 8
Bryden, M. P., 41, 42, 43, 44, 45, 46, 52, 61, 64
Buckingham, V., 49, 65
Bugelski, B. R., 3, 8, 90, 102
Bugental, J., 4, 7, 8
Burnham, C. A., 12, 24

Burtle, V., 115, 168
Butler, M. C., 110, 118
Butler, R. N., 152, 168

Cairns, H., 166, 168
Calhoun, J. B., 54, 62
Camus, A., 152
Canale, J. A., 77, 78
Carmon, A., 46, 62
Cautela, J., 29, 38, 60, 62
Charron, P., 108, 115
Chase, W. G., 102
Chauncey, H. M., 110, 115
Chaves, J. F., 69, 72, 78, 112, 115
Chiappetta, W., 167, 168
Coe, W. C., 69, 70, 78, 79, 112, 117
Cohen, B., 48, 62
Cole, M., 45, 62
Cometa, M. S., 60, 64, 133, 140, 143, 147
Cooper, L. A., 90, 102
Cordner, G. M., 67, 78
Craig, K. D., 110, 115
Craik, F. I. M., 12 24
Crampton, M., 123, 131
Crawford, V. L., 77, 79
Cross, D., 98, 99, 103
Cumming, E., 152, 168
Curran, J. P., 37, 39
Curtis, Q. F., 12, 13, 14, 20, 24

Damashek, R., 68, 79
Davidson, R., 31, 39, 42, 48, 49, 62, 65
Davis, S., 70, 79
Dawson, J. G., 70, 79
Day, J. H., 47, 58, 62
Day, M. E., 41, 49, 62
De Alvarez, B. M., 77, 79
Deglin, V. L., 45, 62
Dember, W. N., 133, 146
Dement, W., 53, 64
Denenberg, V. H., 53, 54, 62
Den Heyer, K., 200, 212
Denny, N. W., 206, 212
Desoille, R., 109, 115, 120, 126-128, 129, 130, 131
De Stefano, R., 77, 79

Diamond, M. J., 70, 79
Diamond, R., 44, 62
Dilley, M. G., 200, 212
Dimond, S. J., 46, 62
Divine-Hawkins, P., 201, 212
Dolan, A. T., 15, 24, 109, 113, 115, 153, 168
Dolby, R. M., 95, 102, 103
Dollard, J., 33, 38
Don, N. S., 68, 79
Doob, L., 3, 8, 52, 62
Doongaji, D. R., 125, 126, 131
Dornic, S., 25
Dostoevski, F., 152
Dunn, R. F., 167, 168
Durio, H. F., 210, 212

Ehrlichman, H., 45, 49-50, 62
Ekehammar, B., 89, 102
Ekman, P., 30, 38
Elkind, D., 212
Ellis, R., 47, 50, 62
Endler, N. S., 89, 102
Engel, G., 167, 168
Erickson, M. H., 59, 62
Euler, L., 223
Evans-Wentz, W. Y., 165, 168
Even, R. L., 212

Farrington, L., 46, 62
Fenichel, O., 58, 62
Féré, C., 68, 78
Festinger, L., 12, 24
Fiske, D., 133, 134, 146
Flavell, J. H., 38, 51, 62, 212
Floyd, H. H., 167, 168
Forisha, B., 1, 8
Frank, J. D., 42, 59, 60, 62
Frankl, V. E., 59, 62
Franks, V., 115, 168
Fransella, F., 133, 146
Frankston, L., 207, 212
Frazier, P. B., 153, 169
Fretigny, R., 91, 102, 120, 129-130, 131
Freud, S., 32, 38, 55, 57, 58, 62, 123, 189, 190, 196, 217, 218, 220, 223

Freyhan, F. A., 106, 113, 115
Friesen, W. V., 30, 38
Frisch, V. M., 152, 168
Fromm, E., 8, 80, 118
Fusella, V., 90, 103, 109, 117

Gainotti, G., 43, 62
Galanter, E., 110, 117
Galin, D., 44, 45, 47, 50, 52, 58, 62
Gallwey, W. T., 42, 62
Galton, F., 2, 8
Gantt, E. H., 25
Garbanti, J., 53, 62
Gardocki, J., 53, 63
Garma, A., 107, 115
Garrity, T. F., 167, 168
Gazzaniga, M., 32, 38, 44, 62, 171, 187
Ghiselin, B., 4, 5, 8
Giannitrapani, D., 50, 62
Glass, L. B., 70, 76, 78, 112, 115
Glick, S., 53, 65
Goldberger, E., 109, 115
Goldstein, K., 43, 63
Goldstein, L., 53, 63
Goleman, D., 43, 63
Golinkoff, R. M., 201, 212
Gordon, R., 3, 4, 8
Gordon, W., 207, 213
Gorton, B. E., 112, 115
Gowan, J. C., 52, 63
Granit, R., 196, 197
Gray, C. R., 93, 102
Greenfield, B. M., 2, 8
Greinacher, N., 153, 168
Grinder, J., 60, 61
Grossman, M. J., 208, 212
Gummerman, K., 93, 102
Gur, R. C., 41, 63
Gur, R. E., 42, 63
Guttman, J., 201, 212

Haber, R. B., 51, 63
Haber, R. N., 51, 63
Hafez, E., 62
Haggard, M. P., 46, 63

Hall, E. T., 3, 8
Halliday, J., 44, 63
Hamilton, E., 166, 168
Haney, J., 23, 25, 153, 169
Harnad, S. R., 49, 63
Hebb, D. O., 25, 133, 146
Hecaen, H., 44, 45, 63
Heldmeyer, K. H., 209, 212
Henry, W. E., 152, 168
Hershey, M., 68, 79
Hilgard, E. R., 69, 70, 76, 79, 80, 95, 102, 112, 115, 118, 195, 197
Hilgard, J. R., 69, 70, 74, 79, 112, 116
Hiscock, M., 49, 63
Holden, C., 110, 115
Holt, R., 38, 89, 91, 102
Honiotes, G. J., 69, 79, 112, 116
Horowitz, M. J., 28, 38, 58, 63, 91, 102, 109, 116, 127, 131
Hudson, L., 4, 8
Hull, C. L., 15, 24
Humphrey, M. E., 53, 63
Hunt, J. M. V., 207, 212
Huttenlocher, J., 223

Ichazo, O. 149, 168
Ikemi, Y., 112, 116
Inglis, J., 45, 64
Inhelder, B., 201, 202, 212, 213, 216, 223
Izard, C., 30, 38

Jacobsen, E., 110, 116
Jaensch, E., 51, 63, 120
James, W., 50
Janis, I., 34, 38
Janov, A., 60, 63
Jaynes, J., 42, 50, 63
Jellinek, A., 108, 109, 116
Jerussi, T., 53, 65
Jeste, D. V., 125, 126, 131
John, E. R., 109, 116
Johnson, H., 110, 116
Johnson, R. F. Q., 112, 116
Jones, M. R., 39
Jordan, C. S., 119
Jung, C. G., 28, 58, 120, 121-122, 127, 130, 131

Kagan, J., 38
Kagan, N. I., 98, 103
Kahoe, R. D., 167, 168
Kaplan,.R., 53, 62
Kapoor, S. N., 125, 126, 131
Kastenbaum, R. J., 167, 168
Katz, N. W., 77, 79
Kearn, P., 68, 79
Keele, S. W., 12, 25, 200, 213
Kelly, G., 133, 134, 146
Keniston, K., 2, 8
Kenyon, F. E., 44, 63
Kepecs, J. G., 108, 116
Khatena, J., 52, 63
Kiddoo, K. P., 73, 77, 79
Kimura, D., 45, 63
King, F., 45, 63
Kinsbourne, M., 61
Klein, G. S., 57, 63
Kleitman, N., 53, 61, 196
Klinger, E., 33, 34, 37, 38
Klüver, H., 22, 24
Knyazeva, G. R., 45, 61
Koestenbaum, P., 152, 153, 154, 164, 166, 168
Koestler, S., 5, 8
Koppes, S., 105
Korb, W., 221, 223
Kroth, J. A., 57, 63
Kübler-Ross, E., 151, 153, 168, 169

Lachman, S. J., 106,107, 110, 116
Ladd, G. T., 196, 197
Lashley, K. S., 14, 25
Law, H. G., 73, 77, 79
Lazarus, A. A., 15, 24, 60, 63
Leaning, F. E., 190, 197
Lee-Teng, E., 70, 79
Lenneberg, E., 50, 52, 63
Lesgold, A. M., 201, 212
Leuba, C., 109, 116
Leuner, H. 29, 39, 60, 63, 91, 103, 109, 116,
    120, 127, 128-129, 130, 131
Leventhal, H., 46, 64
Levin, J. R., 201, 202, 212, 213
Levy, J., 42, 63
Lewin, K., 89, 103
Ley, R. G., 41, 42, 43, 44, 45, 46, 63, 64

Lim, D. T., 70, 80, 112, 117
Little, L. M., 37, 39
Lockhart, R. S., 12, 24
Loevinger, J., 2, 9
Logan, D. R., 69, 80
Long, J. B., 151, 165, 168
Luria, A. R., 51, 64
Luthe, W., 123, 124, 125, 128, 131

MacDonald H., 47, 64
MacKinnon, D. W., 2, 9
Maddi, S., 133, 134, 146
Maer, F., 31, 39, 42, 48, 49, 65
Magnusson, D., 89, 102
Mahl, G., 38
Malmo, R. B., 133, 146
Mancuso, J., 134, 146
Mandler, G., 11, 12, 13, 25
Marks, D. F., 77, 79
Maury, A., 189, 190, 197
May, D., 68, 79
May, J., 110, 116
May, R., 2, 4, 5, 9
McAdam, D., 47, 48, 64
McClelland, D. C., 56, 64
McConkey, K. M., 73, 77, 79, 98, 99 103
McCormick, C., 201, 212
McCullough, L., 29, 38
McDonald, P., 47, 64
McGuigan, F. J., 110, 116, 117, 131
McGuigan, P. J., 31, 39
McKeever, W., 46, 65
McKellar, P., 189, 190, 192, 193, 194, 196, 197
McLuhan, H. M., 42, 64
McMahon, C. E., 105, 106, 107, 108, 110, 114,
    116, 117
McPeake, J. D., 70, 80
McSeveney, R., 167, 168
Meeker, W. B., 76, 79
Meichenbaum, D., 29, 38, 39, 59, 60, 64, 120,
    128, 131
Meskin, B., 49, 64
Meyer, J. E., 151, 168
Miller, G. A., 11, 12, 25, 110, 116
Miller, N. E., 33, 38
Miller, P. H., 209, 212
Millikan, D. H., 64

Milner, P. M., 14, 15, 25
Moleski, L. M., 105
Moody, R. A., 164, 168
Morgan, A., 47, 64
Morgan, C. T., 25
Morgan, R. F., 57, 64
Morrison, J. K., 60, 64, 133, 134, 136, 139,
 140, 142, 143, 144, 145, 146, 147, 167, 168
Morsh, J. E., 51, 64
Morton, J. C., 54, 62
Mountcastle, V. B., 63
Mowrer, O. H., 12, 13, 14, 15, 18, 20, 25, 110,
 116
Müller, A., 153, 168
Munger, M. P., 70, 78
Musel, R., 154, 169
Mussen, P. H., 212
M'uzan, M. De., 110-111, 116
Muzio, J., 53, 64

Nachson, I., 46, 62
Nakagawa, S., 112, 116
Nebes, R., 3, 9, 42, 64
Neisser, U., 12, 25, 32, 36, 39, 100, 103, 134,
 135, 147
Nemiah, J. C., 110, 116, 117
Nichols, J., 166, 169
Nichols, R., 166, 169
Nisbett, R. E., 90, 103
Nissen, H. W., 25

O'Connell, D. N., 70, 80
O'Hara, J. W., 70, 78
Oliver, R. S., 2, 8
Ono, H., 12, 24
Orne, E. C., 74, 76, 80
Orne, M. T., 70, 80
Ornstein, R. E., 11, 25, 32, 39, 42, 47, 50, 52,
 62, 64, 110, 117, 171, 187

Paivio, A., 2, 3, 9, 32, 39, 73, 77, 79, 90, 91,
 103, 109, 110, 117, 118, 119, 131, 200, 201,
 210, 212

Panagiotou, N. C., 60, 65, 92, 100, 103, 108,
 109, 113, 117, 118, 119, 129, 131, 149, 153,
 169, 172, 188, 192, 197
Parkinson, A. M., 46, 63
Patanjali, 121, 125, 126, 131, 166, 169
Pavlov, I. P., 23, 25
Paz, O., 151, 169
Penfield, W., 109, 117, 192
Perard, A., 54, 64
Perez-Cruet, J., 45, 62
Perky, C. W., 109, 117, 153, 169
Perls, F., 149, 169
Perry, C. W., 70, 80
Perry, W. G., Jr., 2, 9
Piaget, J., 32, 39, 51-52, 133, 136, 147, 201,
 202, 209, 212, 213, 216, 223
Pickens, A., 199
Pines, M., 110, 117
Pope, K. S., 25, 28, 33, 34, 37, 38, 39, 57, 64,
 118, 131, 169, 188
Posner, M. I., 12, 25, 200, 213
Pressley, M. A., 202, 212
Pribram, K. H., 14, 25, 110, 117
Price-Williams, D., 207, 213
Prince, M., 190, 197
Progoff, I., 172, 188
Psotka, J., 51, 65

Rabbitt, P. M. A., 25
Radermecher, J., 115
Rahula, W., 165, 169
Rama, S., 126, 131
Ramirez, M., 207, 213
Rank, O., 2, 9
Rapaport, D., 31, 39
Ravindranath, S., 125, 126, 131
Reese, H. W., 201, 213
Reik, T., 61, 64
Reiser, M., 111, 118
Reyher, J., 28, 39, 108, 117
Richardson, A., 3, 9, 52, 64, 74, 77, 79, 109,
 117
Richardson, P., 105
Ripple, R. E., 212
Robbins, K., 47, 48, 64
Robertson, A. D., 45, 64
Robinson, R. H., 165, 169

Rockcastle, V. N., 212
Roffwarg, H., 53, 64
Rohwer, W. D., Jr., 201, 213
Rosadini, G. R., 43, 64
Rosen, J., 60, 64
Rosner, C., 68, 79
Ross, L. D., 38
Rossi, G. F., 43, 64
Roth, R. S., 49, 65
Ryder, B. L., 77, 79

Sackheim, H. S., 41, 63
Sacuzzo, D. P., 142, 147
Safer, M., 46, 64
Samples, B., 171, 188
Sapir, E., 2, 9
Sarbin, T. R., 69, 70, 71, 74, 78, 79, 110, 112, 117, 133, 147
Savage, C., 196, 197
Schachtel, E. G., 2, 9, 35, 39
Schachter, S., 133, 147
Schacter, D. L., 190, 197
Schank, R. R., 32, 39
Schlosberg, H., 12, 14, 25
Schneck, J. M., 116
Schofield, W., 142, 147
Schonbar, R. A., 111, 117, 118
Schoonover, R. A., 117, 131
Schultz, J. H., 123, 124, 125, 126, 128, 131
Schultz, W. D., 28, 39
Schwab, J. J., 106, 117
Schwartz, G., 30, 31, 39, 42, 48, 49, 62, 65
Scott, D. S., 77, 78
Seamon, J., 32, 39
Seay, B., 70, 79
Segal, S. J., 90, 100, 101, 102, 103, 109, 117, 153, 169
Seligman, M. E. P., 54, 65
Selzer, S. C., 206, 212
Semmes, J., 42, 65
Serrano, M., 121, 131
Shaffer, J. T., 171, 172, 188
Shallice, T., 12, 25
Shapiro, D., 30, 39, 109, 117
Shear, J., 166, 169
Sheehan, M. R., 120, 131
Sheehan, P. W., 8, 9, 22, 25, 63, 70, 73, 77, 79,
80, 89, 92, 94, 95, 98, 99, 101, 102, 103, 109, 112, 116, 117, 131, 190, 197
Sheikh, A. A., 25, 60, 65, 92, 100, 103, 105, 108, 109, 110, 111, 112, 113, 114, 116, 117, 119, 129, 131, 149, 153, 154, 163, 168, 169, 172, 192, 197
Shepard, R. N., 33, 35, 36, 39, 90, 102, 200, 213, 216, 223
Sherman, G., 53, 62
Shimron, J., 201, 212
Shontz, F. C., 39, 106, 117
Shor, R. E., 8, 69, 70, 74, 76, 80, 94, 103, 118
Siegel, R. K., 197
Sifneos, P. E., 110, 117
Silberger, H., 196, 197
Silverman, A. J., 48, 62
Simpson, H. M., 110, 118
Simpson, L., 190, 197
Singer, J. L., 4, 9, 25, 27, 28, 29, 30, 31, 32, 33, 34, 35, 36, 37 38, 39, 49, 57, 60, 64, 65, 102, 103, 110, 111, 118, 119, 120, 123, 126, 128, 129, 131, 133, 135, 138, 147, 169, 172, 188
Singer, M., 111, 118
Siuta, J., 77, 80
Smeltzer, W., 109, 117
Smythe, P. C., 201, 212
Sokolov, E. N., 12, 13, 19, 25
Solso, R., 25
Sommer, C., 68, 80
Spanos, N. P., 68, 69, 70, 72, 78, 80, 112, 115
Speidel, G. E., 199, 200, 213
Sperry, R. W., 41, 42, 63 65 171 188
Spielberger, C., 38
Staib, A. R., 69, 80
Steger, J. A., 200, 211
Stern, D., 44, 65
Stevens, R., 64
Stoltzfus, N., 53, 63
Strachey, J., 196
Straus, R. A., 77, 80
Stromeyer, C. F., 51, 65
Suberi, M., 46, 65
Sullivan, H. S., 89, 90, 103
Sutcliffe, J. P., 70, 80

Taft, R., 70, 79, 133, 147
Teasdale, H. H., 51, 65

Tellegen, A., 70, 73, 80
Terzian, H., 43, 44, 65
Teta, D. C., 143, 147
Tharp, R. G., 200
Tomkins, S. S., 30, 31, 32, 35, 36, 38, 39
Torrance, E. P., 52, 65, 207, 213
Trevarthen, C., 42, 63
Tucker, D. M., 45, 49, 65
Turner, D., 23, 25, 149, 153, 154, 169
Twente, G. E., 23, 25, 149, 153, 154, 169

Ullman, M., 92, 103
Underwood, G., 64
Upton, M., 12, 13, 25

Vahia, N. S., 125, 126, 131
Van Bogaert L., 115
Virel, A., 91, 102, 120, 129-130, 131

Wallace, R. K., 110, 118
Warren, H. C., 190, 197
Watson, J. B., 29, 89, 108, 118, 120, 210, 213
Watts, A., 3, 9, 149, 151, 169
Watzlawick, P., 59, 60, 65
Weinberger, A., 45, 49-50, 62
Weiner, H., 106, 111, 118
Weitzenhoffer, A. M., 69, 76, 80, 112, 118
Wenger, M. A., 110, 115

Werner, H., 2, 9
West, L. J., 197
Wever, E. G., 12, 13, 25
White, K., 77, 80
White, K. D., 73, 77, 79
Whittaker, C., 60, 65
Wigan, A. L., 41, 65
Willard, R. D., 69, 80, 112, 118
Williams, J. E., 69, 80, 112, 118
Wilson, S. C., 67, 71, 72, 73, 77, 78, 80
Wilson, T. D., 90, 103
Winer, R. A., 110, 115
Wittgenstein, L., 219, 223
Wittkower, E. D., 106, 118
Wolf-Dorlester, B., 49, 65
Wolff, P., 202, 213
Wolpe, J., 15, 16, 24, 60, 65
Wood, V. N., 151, 166, 168
Woodworth, R. S., 120, 131
Woody, R. H., 103

Yaremko, R. M., 110, 118
Yates, F. A., 107, 118
Yuille, J. C., 201, 212
Yutzey, D., 53, 62

Zangwill, O. L., 53, 63, 171, 188
Zeytinoglu, S., 206, 212
Zikmund, V., 109, 118
Zimmerberg, B., 53, 65

Subject Index

Active Imagination, 28-29, 121-122
Aesthetic experiences, 2, 199, 204
Affect system, 29, 30, 31, 35
Anosognosia, 44
Anticipation, 12-21
Art
    education, 208, 220
    relationship with mental imagery
        and cognition, 199-211
Autogenic Training, 28, 123-126

Barber Suggestibility Scale, 73, 76
Behavior modification, 27, 28, 29, 31
Betts Questionnaire, 49
Betts Test of Mental Imagery, 73, 77
Biofeedback, 30, 110

Centering, experience of, 183-184
Cerebral asymmetrics, 41-61
    emotional experience and imagery,
        41-61
Cognition, modes of
    concentrative-cooperative, 99
    cognitive-independent, 99
    cognitive-constructive, 100
Cognitive development, 199, 201-216
Cognitive shift, 52
Cognitive system, 30-31
Collective unconscious, 121-122
Compartmentalization of human life,
    1, 2, 8
Concept Assessment Kit, 205
Conditioning, 13, 14, 15, 16, 18, 19
Confronting death, 150-152
Consciousness, 11, 12, 13, 14, 21, 22, 42

relationship with anticipation
    and imagery, 11-24
Conservation, 201, 202, 206, 207, 209,
    216
Corpus Callosum, 178-179
Covert conditioning, 60
Covert sensitization, 37
Creative Imagination Scale, 67, 71-78,
    81-85
    correlation with other measures
        of imagery, 73-74
    usefulness of, 76-78
Creativity, 2, 4, 23, 52, 163, 199,
    207, 208, 210, 211, 217, 218, 219

Death
    confrontation of, 150-152
    meditation on, 164
    practicing, 165-166
    psychic, 167
Death imagery, 149-167
    benefits of, 163-164
    illustrative cases, 156-163
    origin, 153-154
    psychotherapy through, 155-156
    relaxation through, 154-155, 163
Death and Immortality Exercises, 166
Depression, 18, 22, 45, 176
Dissociation theory, 195
Dual coding system, 32

Eidetic
    image, 21, 22, 23, 51, 52, 53, 60, 93
    processes, 12, 91
    psychotherapy, 60, 113, 114, 115

130, 145, 153
Eidetic Parents Test (EPT), 158
Eidetic Psychotherapy, 60, 113-115
    145, 158
    and psychosomatic disorders,
        112-114, 158
Emergent Uncovering Method, 28
Emotion recognition, 45
Emotive Reconstructive Psycho-
    therapy, 60, 133-146
    advantages, 144-145
    case illustrations of, 140-141
    clients most suitable for, 144
    consumer-oriented approach,
        141-142
    operational approach, 137-140
    research evidence, 142-144
    special uses, 145
    theoretical approach of, 133-137

Freedom, 6, 17, 20, 22, 24, 29, 164
Frostig Developmental Test of Visual
    Perception, 204-205

Gordon Test of Imagery Control
    74, 77
Guided Affective Imagery Method, 29,
    60, 128
Guided Daydream Method, 126-128
Guided imagining and
    hypnosis, 67-78

Hallucinatory reaction, 13, 14, 18
Harvard Group Scale of Hypnotic
    Susceptibility, 74, 76
Hawthrone effect, 204
Hemispheres
    coding and storage of early child-
        hood experiences, 50-55
    difficulty in visiting, 175-176
    functions, 3, 32, 41-46, 49-53, 55-61,
        171, 175, 176, 183, 184
    health and illness in, 181-182
    and imagery, 47-50
    model for the exploration of,

172-175
    visit to, 172, 182-183
Hemispheric differences, 42
    in emotional behavior, 43-46
    experience of, 177-178
Hidden observer phenomenon, 95
High
    anticipation, 17
    event, 17
    futurism, 18
    images, 20, 21-24
Holism, 105, 115, 171-188
Homo Faber (Frisch), 152
Hydraulic model, 217
Hypnagogic fantasy, 189-196
    characteristics of, 193-195
    emotional response to, 191
    kinds of, 190
    perceptual origins, 191-193
Hypnagogic synaesthesia, 194
Hypnosis, 42, 58, 67-78, 94-95, 112,
    124, 154
    imagery, psychosomatic illness
        and, 111-112
    overlap between imagining and,
        68-78
    its relevance to the study of
        imagination, 94-95
Hysterical conversion, 44

Image buoyancy, 18
Imagery
    and affect, 109-110
    and affect in psychotherapy, 27-38
    early experimental studies of, 120
    and hypnosis, 89-102
    importance of, 2
    and learning, 200-211
    multiple determination of, 100-102
    and motivation, 91-92, 110
    and perception, 90, 109
    omnipresence of, 3
    and physiology, 110
    progression of, 22
    and psychosomatic personality,
        110-111
    and the reconstruction of content,
        36-38

a tool of liberation from the past, 6
  validity of, 2
Imagery, kinds of
  aversive, 29
  anticipatory, 202, 209
  buoyant, 16, 21, 24
  eidetic, 21, 22, 23, 51, 52, 53, 60, 93
  guided, 29, 60, 67-78, 128
  high consciousness, 20, 21-24
  hypnagogic, 189-196
  hypnopompic, 193
  imagination, 92
  memory, 21, 22, 92, 93
  nature, 21-22
  negative, 22
  positive, 21
  self, 38
  unbidden, 91
Imagery and psychotherapy
  early European approaches, 120-126
  current European approaches,
    126-130
Images and affective systems, 35-36
Imagic and lexical modes, 58
Imagination Inventory, 74-76, 86-88
Individual Differences Questionnaire,
  73, 77
Infantile amnesia, 55-56
Information processing, 12, 29, 30
  35, 46, 47
Integration of polarities, 2, 3, 4
  5, 7, 8
Interactionism, 89, 90
Interpersonal Process Recall Method,
  98

Leteralization by puberty hypothesis,
  52
Life After Life (Moody), 164
Lookers
  left, 49
  right, 49

Manhunt in the Desert (Ahsen),
  149, 168
Medical science
  history of, 105-106

Mega anticipatory kinetic response,
  13-20, 24
Metaphysical awakening, 163

Oedipus Complex, 33, 127
Ongoing thought, 33-35
Onirotherapy, 129-130
Outer and inner
  division of, 1-8

Parallel processing, 3, 119
Personality
  systems approach to, 29-31
Primal therapy, 60
Primary process thinking, 58, 94
Prosopagnosia, 45
Psychoanalysis, 28, 30, 32, 33, 54
  56, 57
Psychosomatic disorders
  contemporary views, 106-107
  and eidetic psychotherapy, 113-115,
    158
  and mental imagery, 105-115
Psychosomatic disorders, theories of
  constitutional - vulnerability,
    106
  emotional reaction pattern, 107
  organ response learning, 107
  personality profile, 107
  stimulus situation, 107
  symptom symbols, 107
Psychosynthesis, 122-123

Rapid eye movement (REM), 53
Reality replay, 18
Respondent process, 33, 37

Scripts, 31, 32, 33, 35
Secondary process thinking, 94
Self-reinforcement, 31, 37, 38
Self-system, 31, 38
Sensory deprivation, 57
Sequential processing, 3, 119
Signalling system

first, 23
second, 23
Singer-Antrobus Imaginal
    Processes Inventory, 49
Sokolov-signal, 19
Stanford Hypnotic Susceptibility
    Scale, 69, 74, 76
Stress, 134-135
Successful grieving, 166
Sufi contemplation upon death, 165
Systematic desensitization, 57, 60

Tantric psychology, 120-121
Tellegen Absorption Scale, 73, 74
The Idiot (Dostoevski), 52
Therapeutic
    words, 58
    setting, 57
    task, 59-61
Tibetan Book of the Dead, 165
Torrance Figural Test of Creative
    Thinking, 205, 207, 208
Transcendence
    experience of, 184-186
Transference situation, 27

Venn circles, 218
Verbal processes, 3
Visual thinking in education, 215-223
Vividness of Visual Imagery Question-
    naire, 77